ageless marketing

Strategies for Reaching the Hearts & Minds of the New Customer Majority

DAVID B. WOLFE with ROBERT E. SNYDER

Dearborn™
Trade Publishing
A **Kaplan Professional** Company

This publication is designed to provide accurate and authoritative information in regard to the subject matter covered. It is sold with the understanding that the publisher is not engaged in rendering legal, accounting, or other professional service. If legal advice or other expert assistance is required, the services of a competent professional should be sought.

Vice President and Publisher: Cynthia A. Zigmund
Acquisitions Editor: Michael Cunningham
Senior Project Editor: Trey Thoelcke
Interior Design: Lucy Jenkins
Cover Design: Jody Billert
Typesetting: the dotted i

Published by Dearborn Trade Publishing, a Kaplan Professional Company

Printed in the United States of America

05   10 9 8 7 6 5 4 3 2

Library of Congress Cataloging-in-Publication Data

Wolfe, David B.
    Ageless marketing : strategies for reaching the hearts and minds of the new customer majority / David B. Wolfe, with Robert E. Snyder.
        p.   cm.
    Includes index.
    ISBN 0-7931-7755-3
    1. Aged consumers.   2. Marketing.   I. Snyder, Robert E.   II. Title.
HF5415.32.W65 2003
658.8'348—dc21

                                                                2003011500

Dearborn Trade books are available at special quantity discounts to use for sales promotions, employee premiums, or educational purposes. Please contact our special sales department, to order or for more information, at trade@dearborn.com or 800-245-BOOK (2665), or write to Dearborn Financial Publishing, 30 South Wacker Drive, Suite 2500, Chicago, IL 60606-7481.

DEDICATION

To my wife, Linda, with love

Contents

We have been arguing for many years that "marketing as usual" is simply not working any more, and that fundamentally new thinking is needed to revive and rejuvenate this most vital and potentially noble of business functions—one that has, unfortunately, become the object of scorn and derision among most of its stakeholders. The book that you hold in your hands provides a large measure of such needed new thinking, and will complement very nicely our forthcoming book, *Share of Heart,* for which we are honored and delighted to have David Wolfe as a coauthor.

Marketing's problems are legion, and *Ageless Marketing* highlights many of them brilliantly. Our own observations over the past decade or so have led us to conclude that marketing has been losing efficiency as well as effectiveness over time. In other words, marketing has been and continues to be in the throes of a productivity crisis. Other business functions (most dramatically, operations/manufacturing, but also many management support functions) have made striking advances in both efficiency and effectiveness, and have been able to "do more with less" year after year. Marketing, on the other hand, has managed to *do less with more,* gluttonously demanding and receiving more resources year after year, while delivering worse results: declining customer satisfaction levels, shockingly low customer loyalty levels, increasing numbers of alienated customers, continued reliance on gimmicks and constant sales promotions.

There was a time when marketing's current *modus operandi* worked, and worked rather well. It was a time when most customers were young, the rate of household formation was high, national brands were few, national distribution was limited, national media were just emerging, television was in its infancy, latent demand in many product categories was high, and making things with reasonable quality and at low cost was a challenge. None of those conditions prevail any more. Yet, for marketers and their increasingly irritated customers, it seems, every day is *Ground-*

hog Day—recall the movie in which Bill Murray was condemned to relive the same day every day, without end.

We don't deny that marketing has added new things to its bag of tricks, such as pop-up ads on your computer screens (which make Web surfing akin to duck shooting as you attempt to close windows faster than they appear) and a tidal wave of increasingly over-the-top and offensive e-mail messages that fill your in-box to overflowing every morning, many disguised to seem as though they are from long-lost friends. The problem is that marketing remains fixated on its bag of tricks. Though many of those tricks were novel and even interesting at one time, they are anything but that today. Moreover, marketing's use of such tricks has increased geometrically as the Internet has greatly lowered the direct cost of dong so; more marketers than ever before can use these tricks with ever greater frequency.

The side effects of marketing today overwhelm its intended main effects. It seems that the more *marketed to* a customer is, the more frustrated and irritated he or she becomes, and the more manipulated and helpless he or she feels. This is clearly no way to win customers and influence buyers. Noise pollution, information overload, empty promises, outright exaggerations—marketing's negative effects on society have never been more pronounced. Sound marketing practices lead to low marketing costs coupled with highly satisfied customers, minimal spillover of marketing communication to groups outside the target market, long-term co-destiny relationships between companies and their customers, and a strong emotional bond between companies and customers. Unfortunately, these have become the rare exception rather than the rule.

The harsh reality facing marketers today is that their bag of tricks has become a useless, even dangerous relic of a bygone era. The power in the marketplace—economic, informational and psychological—has shifted to customers. Old-style marketers have themselves become sitting ducks now, and information-savvy customers can readily exploit them to their own advantage.

In order to succeed in this new environment (i.e., deliver a reasonable ROI on marketing spending), marketers have to radically change their mindsets. Not only must they accept the reality that customers today are far more empowered than ever before, they must embrace it to fashion a "new deal" with customers, one predicated on respect, integrity and a long-term vision.

Current demographic megatrends add to the urgency of the need to do so. Every market in the world is evolving rapidly. Emerging markets such as China and India are growing fast, but consumers there already have access to cutting-edge information tools that enable them to blunt the edge of traditional marketing weapons. Developed markets such as North America, Europe, and Japan are characterized by much slower growth and a simultaneous maturing of the population, blurring of gender distinctions, and the rise of feminine values in society and hence the marketplace. More and more consumers are in the more highly evolved, later stages of life, which is reflected in every aspect of how they lead their lives. Marketing must learn how to relate to such consumers.

The problem, of course, is that as people have matured and markets have evolved, marketing has not; it remains stuck in a juvenile time warp of gimmickry and shallow imagery. While people have become more preservation/conservation-minded, marketers have remained spend-thrifts and wasteful. While people have become more spiritual in outlook, marketing remains crassly materialistic. While people focus more on achieving their own potential, marketing remains obsessed with keeping up with the Joneses. While people are digging deeper to discover the substance of people and things, marketing remains fixated on outward appearances. While people are more concerned with authenticity in every aspect of their life, marketing is riddled with inaccuracy and insincerity.

Clearly, marketers have to change a great deal to adjust to this new world order. They will find many of the answers they need in *Ageless Marketing*. This book is a treasure trove of deep insights into consumer psyche, indeed into the human condition itself at the early stages of this still new millennium. David Wolfe weaves a rich tapestry of knowledge and wisdom, using threads from brain science, developmental psychology, sociology, demographics, and his own wealth of personal experience working with many of the leading companies and advertising agencies in the world. This book is a seminal contribution to the marketing discipline, and we are confident that it will impact the field for decades to come.

Jagdish N. Sheth
Atlanta, Georgia

Rajendra S. Sisodia
Boston, Massachusetts

Imagine yourself wandering through a bustling marketplace in a distant exotic land when a wise old man pops out from behind a streetside curtain holding a small bejeweled golden tube in his gnarled hands. He beckons you to take the tube and look through it. Hesitantly you pull it from ancient withered fingers and do as he asks. Raising it to your eye, with the old man straight in front of you, you look through the glistening tube and are astonished by what you see. You are peering *into* the old man's head, but instead of pulpy tissue in convoluted folds you see the most amazing landscape. You suddenly realize that you are seeing the thoughts of a human mind in pictures as they form. *It's like watching a movie.*

What company would not pay a king's ransom for a magical eyepiece that can look into customers' minds? This fable is not that far from reality and there is no need for you to barter away a kingly treasure.

Through the miracle of neuroimaging, brain researchers can now eavesdrop on the goings on between a person's ears as thoughts are being formed and decisions made. While they don't exactly see pictures, what they do see is radically changing our thinking about how motivations form, free will works, and information moves from our sensory receptors through the brain into the conscious mind.

Such new discoveries about the workings of the human brain and mind are driving a paradigm shift in how we see ourselves that may well equal in scope one set in motion over 400 years ago by Copernicus's revelation that the Earth was round and revolved around the sun, not flat with the sun revolving around it. That radical discovery did more than just change how people viewed the planet on which they lived. It led to revolutionary changes in how they viewed God, their rulers, themselves, and life itself.

What is being learned about human behavior in brain science, as well as in the hotly developing field of genetics, will inevitably change how companies view those who work for them and those to whom they market and sell things. However, it is not only genetics and brain science that will be changing how companies see workers and customers. Developmental psychology, which is a treasure trove of information about human behavior, though rarely drawn on in marketing, stands to assume an elevated role in business, especially in marketing.

Marketing revolves around predictions of consumer behavior. The primary purpose of consumer research is to get information that enables predictions of what consumers need, want, and do. However, developmental psychology, which delves deeper into the human psyche, offers crucial insights into consumer behavior that cannot be fathomed by traditional consumer surveys, interviews, and focus groups. In fact, developmental psychology may help resolve an ironic problem present in current marketing strategies: Despite information technology that provides us with more information on customers than ever before, marketing success rates have fallen over the past decade.

Part One of *Ageless Marketing* shows why marketing and consumer research have become increasingly less effective despite exponential increases in the amount of customer information. Chapter 1 is the attention-getting equivalent of hitting a mule upside its head with a two-by-four to get its attention, the answer to the classic question, "How do you get a Missouri mule to start plowing?" This "two-by-four" chapter, based on facts that stand beyond rational challenge, tells why continuing preoccupation with youth and young adult markets makes no logical sense in scores of product lines and for thousands of companies. The emergence of a new customer majority comprised of people 40 and older is the answer. This seasoned group of consumers is 45 percent larger than those between the ages of 18 and 39 (123 million versus 85 million), and will become even more numerous over the next decade and a half. A fact overlooked by the prevailing Madison Avenue mindset is that the majority rules in the marketplace as well as in politics. This New Customer Majority, not youth and pre-middle-aged adults, is the primary source of today's leading views, values, and behaviors in the marketplace. This historic change in consumer behavior has made much of what once worked in marketing obsolete. It has changed the rules of marketplace engagement.

Adapting successfully to these circumstances requires a different mindset than the one that has long governed marketing. As many thought leaders in business have already recognized, marketing success increasingly depends on abandoning the traditional *quantitatively* framed product-centric mind-set to adopt a *qualitatively* framed customer-centric mind-set. However, not many yet have figured out how to do this. Customer relationship management (CRM) was supposed to be the silver bullet to accomplish this, but has failed miserably. Part One provides a previously unrecognized explanation for CRM's widely chronicled failure—changes in the leading behaviors in the marketplace at the hands of the New Customer Majority. Its dominance has nullified many fundamental assumptions that underlie CRM as well as consumer research and marketing in general.

Part Two provides a behavioral foundation for viewing customers that transcends traditional statistical renderings represented by such terms as eyeballs, seats, lives, end users, and other dehumanized representations. In this new view, customers are seen from perspectives that are not accessible via traditional consumer research. With new information from brain science with which to work, this part of *Ageless Marketing* pulls back the veils of the conscious mind to reveal the very origins of customers' needs, motivations, and behavior, a feat that is simply not possible in conventional consumer research methodologies.

Part Two integrates new discoveries about human behavior gleaned from genetic and brain research with time-tested tenets of developmental psychology. In doing this, Part Two responds to a long-standing deficiency in marketing that costs companies tens of billions of dollars annually due to misleading research and marketing blunders. Unlike nearly all other major disciplines, marketing has no unified foundation to guide practitioners in their tasks. As a result, everyone with something to sell can claim without hesitancy to be an expert in marketing. There are no universally accepted benchmarks to challenge such claims. The lack of a common, empirically derived foundation unduly subjects marketing decisions to unfortified opinions much of the time.

Part Two concludes with Chapter 7 in which customer behavior is viewed through the prism of human development science. The spectrum of refracted images that results makes it crystal clear why consumer behavior has become less materialistic (less product-centered) and more metaphysical (more experience-centered). This has occurred because for the first time ever, most adults are in the years when the forces of self-actualization needs exert decisive influences on lifestyle aspirations, buying decisions, and overall consumer behavior. The marketer who gains an understanding of the dynamics of self-actualization will have a decided advantage in today's markets over the marketer who doesn't.

Ageless Marketing changes pace with an Interlude that questions the value of labels like "boomers," "Gen X," and "Gen Y," arguing that such labels inhibit critical thinking, are barren of significant meaning, and thus usually convey little of value when used. Interestingly, marketers put the term *boomers* in circulation in 1981, when the oldest boomers were 35 years old! Thus it seems that boomers lacked generational identity until the eldest were nearly halfway through their anticipated life spans.

Part Three features Value Portraits®, a summary of proprietary research developed by J. Walter Thompson and Market Strategies, Inc. Authored by Robert E. Snyder, a JWT senior partner who heads J. Walter Thompson's Mature Market Group, the two chapters of Part Three draw psychographic profiles of consumers in the second half of life. Seventeen Value Portraits have been drawn from surveys and interviews involving more than 7,000 respondents aged 45 and older. The first rounds of research involved people 62 and older while people 45 to 61 were studied in subsequent rounds. Members of each Value Portrait group are represented as sharing a mind-set that reinforces a predisposition to behave in certain ways and that this mind-set underlies specific attitudes, for example, towards purchasing certain products.

The central premise underlying Value Portrait research is that people generally have certain dispositions (values) that tend to remain the same throughout their lives, and that these values psychologically predispose a person's worldview and the general direction of his or her lifestyle behavior. One highly interesting dimension of the Values Portrait research is how a person's self-assessment of health is a strong indicator of consumer behavior even though, by objective reasoning, a person's current health picture should have no influence on his or her consumer behavior. Part Three reveals the self-perceptions that people in each of the two age groups studied have of their values, views, needs, and behavior. Of course, their self-perceptions may be flawed or even altogether false, but it is important for marketers to know about these perceptions and take them into account under the durable advice that people's perceptions are their reality.

Part Four opens with a discussion of a crucial missing focus in most marketing—customers' life satisfaction. Companies spend many millions of dollars annually researching customer satisfaction; that is, they research customer satisfaction or the lack thereof with companies and products. However, the stronger experiential foundations of consumer behavior in the New Customer Majority makes life satisfaction, which either can be set back or advanced by the customer experience, more salient to marketing success.

Part Four concludes with a discussion of three lifestyle stages of adult life, each of which is characterized by lifestyle aspirations that form the foundation of a person's buying behavior. Thus far, marketing remains rooted primarily in the materialistic values that generally hold the most sway over people in the pre-middle-age years of adulthood. Because of this, many members of the New Customer Majority feel marginalized by companies and their marketers. Perhaps no other single factor has done more to reduce the effectiveness of marketing.

Part Five offers fresh views on how to create receptiveness to marketing messages. Chapter 13 tells why, with due apologies to Gertrude Stein, a rose is not always a rose in the New Customer Majority. How a brand is perceived and what a marketing message means is more subjective in the older mind than is usually the case with younger minds. In fact, the older mind tends to be more resistant to marketers' attempts to fully define the meaning, benefits, and values of a brand. As Maslow put it, the older, more mature mind "resists enculturation." This disposition calls for subtler and more deferential approaches in addressing older markets. This is made more challenging by the fact that unlike the young who tend to perceive matters in more absolutist black-and-white perceptions, older people tend to perceive matters in shades of gray. Absolutist perceptions of reality are easier to play to because they are generally more closely tied to social consensus. Shades of gray perceptions are more subjective, thus pose a fuzzier target to hit among members of the New Customer Majority.

Chapter 14, the penultimate chapter, proposes that empathy—*identifying with and understanding another's circumstances, emotions, feelings, and motives*—is the very core of an authentic customer-centric mind-set. The final chapter, Chapter 15, positions the last season of life as a more fortuitous stage than many younger people believe is possible. The blessings that can be one's good fortune to experience in the winter of life at higher levels of psychological maturation include entry into a new dimension of human existence from which comes a steady flow of lofty experiences—what Maslow called *peak experiences*—and in which there arises enhanced coping abilities for dealing with any later life declines and losses that are inevitable. Of course, not everyone reaches such an advanced state of maturation. Nevertheless, because these aspects of self-actualization reflect perennial desires in life's second half, the marketer who understands them is more likely to connect most deeply with the more than 123 million people who make up the New Customer Majority.

The range, number, and depth of new thoughts that appear in *Ageless Marketing* due to the influence of genetic, brain, and behavioral sciences on the brain's development presented a major writing challenge—how to cope with the brain's bent for erecting defenses against new, possibly mind-changing information. A brain tends to shut down when its owner's threshold of tolerance for new ideas is reached. The positive side of this bent is that it helps us maintain stable, coherent pictures of the world. But on the down side, it slows adaptation to new challenges that cannot be grasped through old ways of thinking. The brain's first response to new mind-changing information is often to generate fight-or-flight responses because fight-or-flight responses are as readily triggered by threats to what we believe as by threats to life and limb.

In Tom Stoppard's play *Arcadia*, mathematician Valentine declares that "Everything is in disorder," as he observes that only a few times in history have we experienced changes on the scale we are experiencing today. As participants in business enterprise, we can catch the mountainous waves of change beating at the shorelines of old mind-sets and ride them to bountiful ends. Or we can stay ashore, safe for the moment, and refuse to participate. Individuals who don't participate will not experience the breathtaking wonder of it all, and that may not matter to them. But companies that chose not to participate will be putting their futures at grave risk.

These are the yeastiest of times. They challenge us as nothing has since the Age of Enlightment when the medieval metaphysical order was dissolved by the science-based order of modern times, an event that led to the radical transformation of human societies and paved the way for modern democracies, the Industrial Revolution, and free enterprise. Many in the first ranks of power resisted the coming of a new order—especially royalists and church leaders. But even the untutored common man got into the act, as memorialized by the apocryphal English worker Ned Ludd. He supposedly destroyed factory machines in the early years of the Industrial Revolution to preserve jobs. We now often refer to those who resist changes wrought by progress as Luddites. Luddites always wage a losing battle, for pursuit of change through progress is as inextricably developmental for the human species as it is for the individual, who from the moment of conception to the end of life is incessantly driven to be more today than he or she was yesterday and more tomorrow than he or she is today. The relentless urge to be ever more is a function of human DNA. It works on us as individuals and it works on us collectively to set the directions of our societies and cultures. We cannot escape this force of nature, we can only adapt to it.

So, once more we are being drawn inexorably toward a portal of epochal change. Beyond that portal lies a landscape wholly unlike the one we've been traveling through since the dawn of the Age of Enlightment. The signs of how this will change our lives swirl all about us amid frequent confusion over what the signs mean. *Ageless Marketing: Strategies for Reaching the Hearts and Minds of the New Customer Majority* is my attempt to illuminate and clarify the meaning of these signs to business enterprise, to highlight new opportunities they signal, and to propose ways and means for successfully navigating the most challenging times that companies and their marketers have experienced in a long, long time.

ACKNOWLEDGMENTS

Acknowledgments are the part of a book least likely read. However, it would be wonderful if every reader honored those I thank here by reading these acknowledgments, for they are part of who I am, and by virtue of that, are part of what this book is.

First, thanks to Robert Snyder, senior partner and head of the Mature Market Group, part of J. Walter Thompson Worldwide. Robert not only introduced me to the publisher of *Ageless Marketing*, Dearborn Trade Publishing, he contributed two chapters. He is a stalwart evangelist of ageless marketing and a militant against ageism in marketing, as recently evidenced in testimony before the Senate Sub-Committee on Aging on the economic and human costs of ageism in marketing. I also extend my gratitude to Jay Quinn, Creative Resources Manager of the JWT Mature Market Group who undertook the arduous task of securing of permissions for the use of quotations and figures used in *Ageless Marketing*.

To the extent *Ageless Marketing* seems coherent and well paced, Jon Sims of the Winston-Salem Interpublic Cos. agency Mullen LHC deserves much credit. In February 2003, feeling the need for a new headspace to facilitate the book's completion, I took the manuscript to Bottle Creek Lodge on the Caribbean island of North Caicos with my wife Linda as guests of Howard and Cheryl Gibbs. Before I left for North Caicos, Jon reviewed the manuscript and came up with many valuable suggestions—including *reorganizing the book*. I groaned, but took his advice, and *Ageless Marketing* is all the better for it. Special thanks, Jon.

Thanks also to you, Howard and Cheryl for your wonderful hospitality. Please remember us to Mac, the most gracious cabdriver and guide I've had the good fortune to engage.

Thanks also to Christian Cantrell who wrote the vignettes about John and Mary Erskine who are featured in *Ageless Marketing* as lifestyle exemplars for the later years. Christian, 22 when he wrote the Erskine's story eight years ago, astonished me with the insight he had into the minds of two 69-year-old people, proving that despite what some say, young marketing professionals can develop an empathetic connection with older people. Thanks for that, Christian, and also for being the father of my 13th grandchild, Hannah, and husband to my daughter, Michelle.

Writing a book that veers off the beaten tracks of the mainstream, as *Ageless Marketing* frequently does, is done not without trepidation, for new ideas will always draw disagreement from the mainstream, including from academe. It is the business of academicians to challenge, and I welcome their honest challenges. However I do so with the comfort of having a good friend, Raj Sisodia, Trustee Professor of Marketing at Bentley College, whose capacity for critical thinking is such that when he approves of an idea I have, I feel intellectually safer.

The support over the years given me by Ron Sugarman, Director of the Center for Customer Intelligence, a part of the Interpublic Cos. network, has often given me comfort that I'm on the right track in my takes on the ad business. Thanks, Ron, and also thanks for introducing Linda and me to Chin Chin's, home of the best Grand Marnier shrimp in Manhattan.

An article I wrote for the February 1998 *American Demographics,* which challenged the assumption in most consumer research that customers are the best sources of information about their motivations, drew the largest response in the magazine's history. Some readers became good friends and colleagues, including Gerry McDonough of Booth Morgan Consulting. We have worked on a number of projects together, along with his partner Rick Frazier who has become one of my most valued sounding boards. A number of ideas developed in *Ageless Marketing* are more mature as a result of our many conversations, Rick. Thanks.

No idea has intrinsic value. Ideas only have as much value as imparted to them by people who put them to practical use. Mike Baumayr, managing partner of Lavidge Baumayr for the Del Webb Sun City brand, has a number of my ideas to practical use. Because clients tend to be conservative about accepting ideas that take them away from familiar ground, Mike has more than once gone out on a limb with an idea I shared with him. Thanks Mike, for having the courage to pursue what you believe is best for your clients even when they fight you.

Ten years ago, 45 people met in Minneapolis and founded The Society, a family of friends working primarily in 40-plus markets. It is perhaps the first virtual trade organization in the nation. The most important virtue of The Society, which has neither bylaws nor dues, is that it allows its members to be vulnerable. Everyone has the freedom to *safely* bring issues of professional and personal importance to the table for discussion. My colleagues and friends in the Society have been my strongest source of moral as well as intellectual support.

Dick Ambrosious (Praxeis) is the closest the Society comes to having someone in charge. Without Dick, The Society might not have endured to enrich the lives of its members. Thanks, Dick, for that, and for many years of enduring friendship.

Several years ago, Society members pitched in to send Linda and me to North Carolina's Outer Banks to reinvigorate our spirits. Thanks, Vicki Thomas (Thomas & Partners) for organizing and surprising us with this marvelous gift of friendship from our Society friends—it worked! We came back with renewed vigor. And thank you to for many years of friendship.

Former NPR reporter Connie Goldman (Connie Goldman Productions), another Society member, has been a wonderful source of inspiration and guidance. Author a number of inspirational books, including her most recent book, *The Gifts of Caregiving*, Connie is affectionately known by Society members as Mother Wisdom, which these words from PBS *Newshour* host Jim Lehrer endorse:

Connie Goldman is on to something. It's called life. Life for all of us who used to be considered on the other side of the hill.

Other Society members to whom I am indebted include James Weil (Lifecare, Inc.) for his many years of encouragement to stay my course, and for being an exemplar of self-actualization whom I have drawn on in this book to describe the highest levels of human development; Mike Sullivan (50+ Communications) for all his moral support during difficult times and for new business opportunities he has created for me, and for helping to validate my work; Gary Solomonson (The Solomonson Company), whose stories told with great humanness have entertained as well as enriched us all; Rick Moody (Chairman, Elderhostel) whose intellectual depth enriches me in every conversation I have with him; Pat and Leyla Mason (Carolina Living) for years of support including several new business opportunities; Jim Gilmartin (Coming of Age) who truly honored me when he organized his company around my core ideas; and Tony Edwards (Bernstein-Rein) who is never hesitant to call me for advice but always gives me something back by way of new insights.

Other Society members who have contributed to who I am include Richard Adler (People & Technology) who is the nation's leading expert in the interface between seniors and technology; John Bowen (Bowen Consulting) who has helped me understand how the ad business works; and Harley Christensen (The Evergreen Project) whose steadfast dedication to establishing a new network of information resources for older audiences has been a source of great admiration.

Then there is Marvin Tolkin (founder of Jennifer Dale) and his wife Carol who are lively testaments as to why the later years can be the very the best years of life. Marvin told us at a Society meeting, "Retirement is not about *not* working; it's about redirecting your efforts toward other purposeful pursuits." Now that's a man who understands the new face of retirement!

Finally, I cannot adequately indicate in words my gratitude to everyone one in my family for how they have enriched my life. Aside from giving me the usual pleasures a family offers, each of my children have given me insight into some particular virtue: Sabrina, dedication to goal achievement; Laura, persistence in creative problem solving; Karen, authenticity in relationships; Brian, balance and equanimity; Michelle, social consciousness; Stephanie—through six years of single parenthood she taught me more about human development than any life experience I've had outside of book sources. And she has often made what I have read in books more real.

I end these acknowledgments by recognizing the person who has been my most creative sounding board, my best friend, and a continuously flowing source of renewal—my wife Linda. Five months ago, she gave me the freedom to take on a mistress—*Ageless Marketing*. Nothing has so commanded my attention in many years as the writing of *Ageless Marketing*. Without Linda's patience and understanding, I would not have been able to type the last period, on the last paragraph of the last chapter on March 24, 2003, a week ahead of the publisher's deadline. Thanks, Linda, for being such an understanding life partner.

David B. Wolfe

AN ERA OF NEW RULES

William Shakespeare's counsel from *The Tempest,* "Whereof what's past is prologue," is not absolute. There have been a few times in human history when what's past bore little influence on the unfolding future. We live in such a time. It is a time when waves of uncertainty deny the past and are plunging the present into churning disorder. Old rules do not explain new conditions. We suffer nettlesome frustration because solutions based on old rules fail us. Uncertainty reigns, but this much is certain: To regain a steady hand on the directions of our work, our society, and perhaps our own lives, we must unlearn a host of old rules and learn many new ones. There is no more daunting task we face than to adapt to the idea that much of what we thought we knew is wrong.

1

WHY MARKETING STOPPED WORKING

Doing Less with More

"**T**he Seniors are coming! The Seniors are coming!" So began *Serving the Ageless Market,* a book I finished nearly 14 years ago. This book extends many of the themes and ideas of *Serving the Ageless Market* (*SAM* 1990). While much of the earlier book was forward looking—The Seniors are coming! The Seniors are coming!—this book is more present-day-focused because *the seniors are here*. They are here in staggering numbers that are getting bigger by the year. This "pig in the python" demographic bulge called boomers will be entirely in midlife in 2004, when the youngest boomers will be 40 and the eldest 58.

We hear often that every seven seconds another boomer turns 50; however, for reasons that will soon be apparent, the "age floor" of this book is 40, the year marking the beginning of the second half of life and the first year of midlife by most reckonings.

UP MARKETING'S CREEK WITHOUT A PADDLE

After *SAM* 1990 hit bookstores, it seemed only a matter of time before Corporate America would awake to the demographics-driven transformation of the marketplace just getting underway as the last decade of the 20th century was beginning. Articles about the aging of America began showing up everywhere. Ken Dychtwald's *Age Wave* was published about the same time as *SAM* 1990 to sound yet another clarion summons to Corporate America to begin preparing for the largest wave of aging consumers in history. Who wouldn't take notice of this phenomenon, those of us tracking the event thought? We just needed to get a few facts and figures out there for everyone to see.

But Corporate America was preoccupied with other things, especially information technology from which it was wringing out costs and making historic productivity gains. But one sector of business did not participate in these productivity gains. Marketing, which revolves around information, ironically became *less* productive during the 1990s.

Television advertising lost much of its punch. The fact that Starbucks, New Balance, and other brands you will read about in this book became superbrands without advertising on television suggests that the tube is no longer the high-powered marketing tool it once was. A 1999 study found television advertising returning only 32 cents for every dollar invested.[1] Trackers of market trends report that consumers are paying less attention than ever to advertising. Growing numbers are using TiVo and ReplayTV to banish on-air advertising from their lives. More and more, consumers are tuning out and turning off.

Marketing's flagging effectiveness has strained relationships between marketing agencies and their clients. While agencies blame external conditions from media clutter to new wrinkles in customer behavior for falling productivity, clients blame their agencies because good marketers are supposed to know what to do when conditions change the requirements for marketing success. With growing dissatisfaction in ad agency performance, the number of years that clients retain the same agency has declined from 11 years to only 2½, according to an October 2001 survey by consulting firm Pile & Co.[2]

Other areas of marketing aren't doing any better. Recent research shows that 90 percent or more of sales promotions for packaged goods result in lowered profits. A 1995 study by Information Resources, Inc., found that 70 to 80 percent of new product introductions fail, with each failure resulting in a net loss of up to $25 million. Some observers claim that the failure rate runs as high as 94 percent.[3]

Direct marketing response rates were falling even before anthrax made headlines following 9/11. BAI Global reported that response rates for credit card marketers have steadily declined from 2.8 percent in 1992 to an all-time low of 0.6 percent in 2000.[4] And everyone knows that response rates to Internet-based marketing have sharply declined, driving a slew of Web sites that were dependent on advertising revenues out of business.

Despite this broad picture of decaying efficacy, marketing is consuming a bigger portion of corporate budgets than ever. In an analysis of 20 industries, half had selling, general, and administrative costs (SG&A) of more than 40 percent of every sales dollar, and all had SG&A of more than 30 percent. Between 1978 and 1996, SG&A expenses for the S&P 500 increased from 19 percent of sales to 24 percent—an increase of 25 percent. Spending on advertising increased from around 3 percent of revenues to over 4 percent during the same period—a 50 percent increase.

Thus, in an age when every other business function has had to do more with less, marketing has managed to achieve an unenviable track record of doing less with more.

The Costs (Not Savings) of Automating Marketing Functions

In golf, rule number one is keep your eye on the ball. In marketing, rule number one is keep your eye on the customer. Too many have lost sight of the first rule of marketing over the past several decades, especially during the 1990s when corporate bean counters became Johnnie one-note warriors battling for every dollar they could save. Automation became their weapon of mass destruction. Anything moving that could be automated was fair game. Researchers were replaced by data mining systems, telephone receptionists by automated phone systems, and salespeople by digital filtering systems that shoved product offerings before customers that were tailored to their "preferences" according to computer analysis.

CFOs, with their evangelistic fervor for cost cutting became the dominant force in business in the 1990s. Referring to one of the four largest ad agency conglomerates, I was told by one of its consultants, "The CEOs of the business units in [this conglomerate] are no longer in charge. Their CFOs, who have a direct line to headquarters, are in charge." With the tyranny of numbers that held unchallenged sway over so many companies in recent years, it is no wonder that accounting scandals have arisen on a scale never before seen. When even the once venerable Arthur Andersen gets caught up in such messes, we can sadly appreciate more than ever that when numbers dominate business decisions, morality becomes extraneous. Greed thrives and customers become irrelevant nuisances to the bean-counting priesthood.

Though the information revolution drove some of the largest productivity gains ever during the 1990s, many of the cost savings were illusory and few promises of improved marketing results materialized. As the 21st century began, marketing had fallen on hard times because everyone forgot rule number one: they took their eye off the customer.

Desperate for a "magic bullet" to cure mounting marketing woes, companies invested billions of dollars in customer relationship management (CRM) systems to automate customer analytic and transaction processes. Software vendors promised corporate clients a seamless integration of sales, marketing, and customer service around the needs of individual customers. CRM became big business overnight on the strength of such promises. The CRM software market, starting from scratch in the mid-1990s, had reached approximately $10 billion in annual sales by 2001, according to AMR Research. The global marketing research firm IDC estimated that the total worldwide CRM services business generated $40 billion in 1999, and will pass the $100 billion mark sometime in 2004.

Despite this flood of spending, however, the Gartner Group regularly reports that over half of all CRM initiatives fail to achieve their objectives. Many companies have given up on CRM. Wells Fargo pulled the plug on its CRM program in 2002 after spending $38 million trying to make it work. Research by Bain & Company found "an extremely low satisfaction rate and correspondingly high defection rate among those respondents who were already using CRM programs."[5]

Companies are learning the hard way that deploying expensive software "solutions" does nothing to address the fundamental philosophical, methodological, and organizational flaws that bedevil their marketing functions. Merely automating a business function that is deeply dysfunctional to begin with only makes matters worse. Companies must first learn to "do the right things before worrying about doing things right." They need to understand that the right things in today's more life-seasoned markets are often not the same as the things that were right when the consumer universe was dominated by 18-to-34-year-olds.

Reducing Human Contact May Reduce Payroll Costs but Increases Marketing Costs

Poor marketing doesn't simply move less product because it's less effective. It also moves less product because it angers and alienates customers. If the walk-around market research which I conduct on trains, in airports, on airplanes, and in other public places means anything, huge numbers of adults—perhaps even a majority—feel marginalized by most advertising. That's astounding. It indicates that media clutter, a surfeit of choices, product commoditization, and other commonly cited explanations for marketing's loss of productivity might not be the biggest problems after all. One of the biggest problems, and one not mentioned often enough in business media, is the dehumanization of customer experiences with a company.

Many gains in productivity over the past decade have been at the expense of the quality of the customer experience. When the only major airline making money these days is also the only one with live telephone receptionists, one wonders how long it will take Southwest's competitors to realize that automated telephone systems can drive business away.

Despite the ubiquitous "your call is important to us" recording, a company obsessed with automating interactions with customers shows its workers that it doesn't really give a damn about customers. Workers then adopt the same attitude, because as goes the top so goes the bottom. In any event, cutting their direct contact with customers puts workers out of touch with customers' hearts, minds, and issues.

CFOs don't think of themselves as revenue producers, but rather as cost controllers and money managers. As a result, they lack appropriate sensitivity to connections between their cost-cutting objectives and earned revenue production, especially with respect to specific staff relationships to earned revenue production. Think of how much experience, encoded in the memories of long-time employees, has been destroyed by aggressive early retirement programs. The human factor, be it with respect to workers or customers, appears to have become irrelevant in the theory and practice of organizational management.

The American Consumer Satisfaction Index reflects the extent to which a company's inattention to customers is marginalizing and alienating customers. Nearly 90 percent of the companies in the ASCI index had lower scores in 2001 than in 1995. Dissatisfied customers not only dissolve customer loyalty, they lead to higher customer maintenance and acquisition costs because what companies say in their advertising and other product messages becomes less credible when the human connection is weakened. With eroded credibility, companies have to spend more money to bring new customers aboard and keep them aboard.

The Seminal Cause of Marketing's Present-Day Woes

Consumer research—the customer knowledge industry—has played a big role in marketing's waning effectiveness. More companies are seeing this and taking actions that appear to presage the end of consumer research as we have known it. In the face of such high-profile failures as Procter & Gamble's ill-fated fat substitute Olestra (branded as Olean), on which it spent $800 million to bring to market, confidence in traditional consumer research is sagging. General Mills has abandoned focus groups altogether. It now conducts 60 percent of its consumer research online.[6] One Coca-Cola business unit reportedly is eying context-sensitive software to analyze research subjects' open-ended statements as an alternative to the restrictive close-end queries used in traditional quantitative research. Another Coca-Cola unit is experimenting with neuroimaging (brain scanning) to divine customer behavior. Research clients are desperate to try something, anything, that will work better than what is being used today.

Aside from contributions made by people-insensitive numbers people, what brought on these dark days in consumer research and marketing?

Mostly, it was the emergence of the *New Customer Majority*.

In 1989, adults 40 and older became the adult majority for the first time in history. No headlines proclaimed that event, but not since P. T. Barnum earned the title of "Father of Modern Advertising" has one event—not even television—led to so much change in leading consumer behaviors in such a short period of time. Television initially changed how people came to be informed about products, but did not initially generate big changes in leading marketplace behaviors. The New Customer Majority has done just that, and did it in well under a decade. Meanwhile, consumer research and marketing have failed to realize the relationship between changes in the leading values, views, and behaviors of the marketplace and the New Customer Majority.

MADISON AVENUE: STUCK IN THE 1960S

Customs often persist long after their usefulness. There is a story about a woman preparing for a dinner party with the help of a friend. Before shoving a beautiful slab of beef into the oven she cut a healthy slice off the end. "Why did you cut the end of the roast off?" her friend asked. "I dunno. I guess because my mother always did."

The next day the hostess called her mother to ask her why she always cut the end off her beef roasts. "I dunno. I guess because my mother always did." The hostess then called her grandmother and asked her why she always cut the end off her beef roasts.

"Well, when your grandfather and I were first married we just had this little teeny pan and a decent-sized roast wouldn't fit in it. So I cut the end off the roast to make it fit."

That story would resonate with CBS executive vice president Dave Poltrack, from whom I borrowed the title of this subsection. It was the title Poltrack gave a speech that he delivered in Fall 2002, in which he recalled the origins of age-based advertising. Poltrack observed that in television's early years, household television viewing patterns were not reported according to age. However, one network was instrumental in changing that. Third-place ABC sought to get out of last place (remember, there were only three networks and no cable in those days) in Nielsen's reports. ABC hit on the idea that because its audience was younger than those of either NBC or CBS, it could turn that distinction to its advantage in selling air-time. So it persuaded Nielsen to begin reporting viewing patterns according to the age of viewers.

So, there we have it. Age-based advertising, which as I will show is often counterproductive in the era of the New Customer Majority, was created to give a struggling network with a younger audience a perceived advantage over its competitors. ABC's pitch was "Get them young and before some other brand gets them." The problem is that this idea has become as outmoded as the dinner hostess's custom of slicing off the end of a slab of beef before putting it in the oven. The emergence of the New Customer Majority has left Madison Avenue up marketing's creek without a paddle to steer back into today's mainstream consumer population—people 40 and older. This is having a devastating effect on Corporate America, including equity markets depressed by anemic profits, and on the national economy.

This book presents a practical alternative to the age-based marketing that ABC and Nielsen collaborated to bring forth in the 1960s, the time period in which Madison Avenue is still stuck according to Dave Poltrack. This alternative is *ageless marketing*—marketing based on values and desires that appeal to people across generational divides. Age-based marketing *reduces* the reach of brands because of its *exclusionary* focus. Ageless marketing *extends* the reach of brands because of its *inclusionary* focus.

To avoid any misunderstanding, I need to say that targeting specific age groups remains a valid marketing gambit. One of the nation's most successful ageless marketers, New Balance, about whom I will say more later, does not ignore age. While the core values New Balance reflects in its general marketing are ageless, it targets specific age groups through media selection, the content of selected messaging, and how it manages its channel relationships. It stocks its retailers with a keen eye on the core age group served by each specific retailer. By practicing the art of ageless marketing with the skill of a neurosurgeon maneuvering probes through a patient's brain, New Balance has outpaced its competition—including powerful Nike—in annual sales growth since the mid-1990s. Its competitors continue to restrict the reach of their brands by sticking with age-based marketing.

Companies stuck in the age-based marketing mind-set of the 1960s lessen their chances of surviving to the end of this decade. The reason for this will become clear shortly, but first it would serve well to review an event that took place in 2002 that many of us who work primarily in middle age and older markets have been waiting for since the publication of *SAM* 1990. In 2002, Corporate America began awakening—still bleary-eyed, confused, and disoriented—to the fact that the young adult market had become a customer minority, spending significantly fewer consumer dollars than the New Customer Majority.

THE SHOT ON MADISON AVENUE HEARD 'ROUND THE BUSINESS WORLD

In late winter 2002, a shot was fired that was heard 'round the business world. It came in the form of a massive volley of criticism that ABC drew when it became public knowledge on March 1, 2002, that the network was negotiating with CBS's late night comic host David Letterman to replace Ted Koppel's venerable *Nightline*.

The motivation to dump Koppel was *Nightline's* older audience. The average age of its viewers was 52. Letterman's audience averaged 46. That six-year age difference translated into a 30-second ad rate of $40,000 on Letterman's show versus $30,000 on Koppel's show, despite Koppel's 10 percent larger audience.

Suddenly, not just ABC but Madison Avenue found itself under fire for its view that the value of marketing investment declines in inverse relationship to consumers' ages, starting at age 35, becoming virtually nil at age 50 in most product categories.

Numerous talk shows and a slew of news and trade magazine articles examined the issue in some depth, calling in marketing experts from big agencies and advertising companies to explain the reasoning behind why advertisers ignore much larger and far wealthier audiences in favor of smaller and decidedly less affluent ones. Interviewers and journalists often expressed their bewilderment over advertisers' willingness to spend as much or more for a 30-second spot on a show aimed at young audiences of five or six million as they might pay for the older and much more affluent audience of shows like *60 Minutes,* which attracts 15 or so million viewers. Clearly, traditional marketing ideas about the value of younger markets that emerged when the young ruled markets, were as embedded and as difficult to dislodge as impacted wisdom teeth.

Taunted by pundits who couldn't understand why the far wealthier New Customer Majority was being widely ignored, mavens of Madison Avenue defensively fired back ungrounded explanations of why companies should continue devoting most of their marketing dollars to younger adult markets with a population growth that is nearly nil in contrast to the explosive population growth of the New Customer Majority.

Consider the words a media buying company CEO uttered in defense of ABC's decision to fire Koppel and hire Letterman. The CEO, whose company spends over $4 billion annually in advertising buys, told Bob Garfield, host of National Public Radio's *On the Media,* "They [younger people] haven't made all their brand choices, particularly the younger side of that spectrum, and if you could reach them and get them to be users of your brand at an early age, you'll have them for a lifetime."[7]

In the vernacular, that's BS. No research supports that statement. Yet, it is one of the most commonly offered reasons to justify spending the lion's share of marketing dollars on youth and young adult markets. Not only is that the stuff of barnyard residue, new research buries it.

AARP, whose 35-million members obviously aren't very popular on Madison Avenue, engaged Roper ASW to assess brand loyalty by age. Roper found that product category correlates better with brand loyalty than age does. Within some product categories—for example, athletic footwear, leisure wear, car rentals, hotels, and airlines—people aged 65 and older were less tied to specific brands than 19-to-44-year-olds were.[8]

The idea that companies should spend money to get younger people into their brands so they will "have them for a lifetime" is specious. How many companies think and plan ahead two, three, or four decades? Corporate America is notoriously short-sighted. Most companies pay far more attention to Wall Street time frames than to long-term marketing time frames. Why risk betting on a future that is 20, 30, or 40 years away? How many of today's brands will even be around then? Most of us who are old enough to remember the JFK Camelot years can recall numerous late, great brands like Ipana, Woolworth's, DeSoto, Packard, Burma-Shave, Emerson, Philco, Nash, Old Gold, Life Buoy, Brill Cream, Teal, Collier's, and Pan American Airways.

It's time that marketing grows up, stops forcing ill-fitting answers like a cornered teenager with no rational defense for his actions, and becomes unstuck from 1960s thinking. The so-called aging of America (and all other developed nations) is dramatically, if not radically, changing the rules of marketplace engagement.

WHY CONSUMER RESEARCH STOPPED WORKING: KNOWING LESS WITH MORE

Astonishing gains in technology have placed at our fingertips more information about consumers than anyone had ever hoped for. Yet despite the wealth of information, there is a poverty of customer understanding judging by the rising tide of product and marketing campaign failures.

At a workshop on the New Customer Majority that I recently conducted for a Midwestern bank, I asked its marketing director, "How long have you been marketing director."

"About 12 years," he said.

I then asked, "With all the high-tech information systems at our disposal, do you think you have a better handle on customers today than when you first became marketing director?"

"No," he crisply replied, adding, "They are not acting like they used to and we don't really know why."

Can anyone who is aware of marketing's declining productivity during a time when the amount of customer information has never been greater conclude anything other than marketers don't understand customers now as well as they used to? It's easy to blame external factors such as weather, war jitters, weak economy, and so on, but marketing clients want solutions not excuses. Marketing is broken and needs fixing.

Kevin Clancy and Robert Shulman saw marketing's problems coming over a decade ago. They announced on the first page of their 1991 trailblazer *The Marketing Revolution,* "The marketing revolution is coming because failure is self-evident and everybody—stockholders, directors, CEOs, customers, the government—is angry because marketing, which should be driving business . . . doesn't work."[9]

Clancy and Shulman, the former chairman and CEO, respectively, of Yankelovich Clancy Shulman, went after consumer research in their no-holds-barred assault on marketing. They are hardly alone in criticizing their own field. A seasoned researcher at a global brand company recently told me, "The old ways of research are fraying. Poor guidance from research is costing companies bundles. We need new ways of looking at consumers because they've changed."

The head of consumer research for one of the world's largest pharmaceutical companies (who asked not to be named) called me after reading an article I had written for *American Demographics*[10] that drew the largest reader response in the magazine's history. The article described how contemporary brain research explains much about why consumers often mislead companies. "Even so," he said, "Something is wrong because results are getting less dependable even though we're doing research the way we've always done it."

I offered him the following thoughts:

Traditional research has become less dependable because methodologies are based on experiences in a marketplace dominated by younger minds. Traditional consumer research lacks sensitivity to the different mental processing styles of the older people who now form the adult majority. It is structured around how minds operate in the "much coveted 18-to-34 demo." The younger mind is more linear, literal, and categorical. This makes it easier to render what they say into statistical statements. Also, younger minds are less sensitive to context when inferring the meaning of things because their thinking style is more absolutist. Things either *are* or *are not*. There are few grays, few in-betweens, because perceptions are more sharply defined—more broadly etched in unambiguous black and white. Thus, what they tell researchers is more clear-cut, less context-sensitive, and less conditional than what older people may tell researchers. So, the gaps between truth and error are narrower between young research subjects than between older subjects.

Older subjects' mental processes tend to be less absolutist and their perceptions tend to be more subjective. They generally feel less compelled to align what they think with what others think. An older person's greater sensitivity to contextual influences when inferring meanings of things can yield research testimony laced with ambiguity and murky results. The older person often wants to answer a question with "it depends" but is frustrated by research instruments that prevent him or her from doing so. The result? Subjects mislead researchers by doing the only thing they can do in response to black-and-white questions: They provide black-and-white answers that distort reality. This is not arcane theory. A large body of research literature describes how mental processing styles evolve from a more objective, absolutist bent in adolescence and early adulthood to a more subjective, conditional bent in the second half of life, where most adults are today. By the time a person nears the half-century mark, this developmental change in mental processing only can increase the tentativeness of research results if it is not taken into account in designing the research.

"Of course!" the pharmaceutical consumer researcher said, almost shouting over the phone. "I should have known! I also do research on physician markets. I've seen what you just described. When I interview young doctors I often know what their answers will be before I ask a question, but it's harder for me to predict how the older guy will answer the same question."

THE PERSISTENCE OF RESISTANCE TO THE NEW CUSTOMER MAJORITY

When attendees at my workshops first see the eye-opening numbers you will shortly see, this question often arises: Why have the brightest minds in business ignored the New Customer Majority? Call it the cognitive equivalent of Newton's law of inertia, replacing the words *at rest* with the words *in place:* a belief in place tends to stay in place. The human brain evolved to resist change in the interest of keeping things predictable and stable for its owner. Just as Newton taught that objects tend to keep doing what they are doing, people tend to keep believing what they believe, and do so with a natural sense of defensiveness. The first response we all have to an idea that contradicts what we believe is to deny that idea a landing site in our minds.

The idea that an aging customer universe changes the rules of marketing can be unsettling. It means giving up beliefs that undergirded successful marketing in a time when younger people defined the rules of marketplace engagement. However, it is now time that companies and their researchers and marketers break away from the inertia against changing their beliefs and form new mind-sets that are more appropriate in a marketplace dominated by people in the second half of life—*second-half markets.*

Because people in second-half markets see and hear product messages differently than people in first-half markets, companies and their marketers need to learn about these differences in order to put marketing more in sync with customers 40 and older.

Significant differences exist in the deeper, subtler *core* needs and desires between people in first-half and second-half markets. A 45-year-old is likely to have very different reasons for buying the same product a 25-year-old buys. Both may give a researcher the same reason for buying a product, but deeper, subtler core needs of which neither has awareness may drive the final decision.

University of Virginia psychologist Timothy Wilson addresses in his book *Strangers to Ourselves* our inborn resistance to change—the cognitive inertia that often keeps us from changing beliefs when objective reason says we should. Wilson examines what goes on outside of consciousness in our brains to shape our perceptions and beliefs: "When an event is not easily explained by what we know, we alter what we know to accommodate the new event."[11]

I first read those words around the time I listened to Bob Garfield's interview with the media buying company CEO who argued that youth markets are more attractive because of their influence on markets in general. Sounding something like a teen, he told Garfield, "Let's talk about, you know, the rap culture's influence on, on really suburban youth, or let's talk about Nike and its belief that the basketball court on West 4th Street is the epicenter of the Nike brand. I, I think it's a pretty well-accepted proposition that you have, you know, circles of influence that emanate from a central point."

Timothy Wilson might conclude that the CEO was altering what he knows to fit a new event that he doesn't understand. The CEO knows from experience that market segments with the most consumers spending the most money are where marketing dollars should be concentrated. But according to that old knowledge, his company should now be making bigger media buys in second-half markets. These markets are 45 percent larger than young adult markets and spend considerably more money. Yet, rather than adapt to that new reality, the CEO alters what he knows from past experience to accommodate the new event.

There's a saying that *people won't change until the pain of staying the same becomes greater than the pain of changing*. That could help explain the resistance of marketers to shift attention and marketing dollars toward the New Customer Majority.

The pain of staying the same in marketing must be getting close to exceeding marketers' pain tolerance. The advertising industry has been in its biggest slump since the Great Depression. Ad agency revenues fell in both 2001 and 2002, the first back-to-back negative growth years since the 1930s. Interestingly, consumer sales remained remarkably strong during the same period. In the past, strong consumer spending meant the advertising business was doing well, but not recently.

The CEO of the media buying company was indeed correct in saying that marketplace behavior is subject to "circles of influence that emanate from a central point." However, that central point is now smack dab in the middle of the New Customer Majority. "Now hear this," I wanted to shout back into the radio, *"The majority rules—in the marketplace, as well as in politics."* Adults under 40 once were the majority, and they ruled the marketplace. Adults 40 and older are now the majority, and they now rule the marketplace—in numbers, in spending, and in determining the rules for successful marketplace engagement.

Today's Leading Customer Behavior Attributes Were Predictable Decades Ago

The Yankelovich Monitor, a consumer trends information service, provides subscribers intelligence on what customers are thinking and doing. It recently described the leading views, values, needs, and behavior in the marketplace in ways that would not have surprised a prominent American psychologist who dedicated his professional life to studying human development, especially in the second half of life. But for his death in 1971, Abraham Maslow might review a 2002 Yankelovich Monitor report and say, "Of course." In fact, he could have predicted more than two decades ago much of what the Yankelovich Monitor and other consumer behavior tracking reports are saying today about the leading values, views, needs, and behavior in the marketplace.

How is that possible? And why is that significant today?

First, as to its significance: Obviously, being able to predict changes in marketplace behavior years in advance would have great value to companies. Fourteen years ago, when I was immersed in writing *SAM* 1990, it was being widely predicted that boomers would enter old age, still self-centered, still chasing hedonistic pleasure, still playing more the grasshopper than the ant, and running out of money. *SAM* 1990 drew a different picture. It described how aging boomers (not all, but many) would increasingly turn their attention to altruistic pursuits and begin pursuing simpler pleasures, with many going into old age in financially better shape than their parents. This would happen because a substantial number of boomers, upon reaching midlife, would change their worldviews and begin moving—in Abraham Maslow's words—"toward the higher levels of humanness," toward the maturational state of *self-actualization.*

About 3.7 million boomers turned 40 in 1986, the first to do so. Throughout the 1990s, around 4 million more turned 40 each year to begin their ascent to higher levels of humanness that would make them less self-centered and more concerned with matters beyond their own skins. With more than 60 million boomers entering midlife between 1986 and 2000, it is more than coincidence that philanthropy and volunteerism has experienced unprecedented gains.

The American Association for Fundraising Counsel <www.aafrc.com> reports that annual growth in philanthropy exceeded 10 percent during much of the 1990s, far faster than growth in incomes and family wealth. According to Larry Wheeler, director of the North Carolina Museum of Art, "In several recent years, the growth in philanthropy has been recorded at above 20 percent."[12]

Many companies could have saved great sums over the past few years had consumer researchers been savvier about characteristic behavioral changes in midlife. Procter & Gamble's Olestra fiasco is just one high-profile example that could have been avoided.

Companies have widely misread aging boomers. Bent on catching the "age wave" of these boomers, they had researchers survey and interview boomers about their lifestyle patterns and needs five to ten years into the future, as leading-edge boomers were entering their 40s. A few years later, a car company wanting to learn what boomers would want as they entered retirement called me about participating in such a study. At the time, the oldest boomers were 53. I was unsuccessful in persuading the person who called me that it would be futile to ask preretirement boomers about their retirement lifestyles because many would have different attitudes influencing vehicle purchase decisions after retiring. I know this from 20 years of experience working in midlife and older markets. Still, that experience counted for nothing to the researcher who desperately needed something to statistically analyze because his company insisted on having numbers on which to base its decisions.

"Big Breasts and a Soft Fatty Little Tummy"

Movie actress Jamie Lee Curtis, a 43-year-old boomer, recently demonstrated quite dramatically how lifestyle attitudes often dramatically change in midlife. In doing so, she became something of a pinup girl for many aging boomers who wistfully wish that they might once again have the body of a svelte and fit 21-year-old, but not so seriously that it has much influence on their lifestyles.

Curtis stunned readers of the September 2002 issue of *More* by appearing in a full-page photo, sporting a two-piece black sweat outfit that revealed recently acquired love handles connected to a thickening waist. Jamie confessed, "I don't have great thighs. I have very big breasts and a soft fatty little tummy. Glam Jamie, the perfect Jamie . . . it's such a fraud." She added with great dignity and self-respect, "The more I like me, the less I want to be other people."[13]

Jamie Lee, who talked about her earlier obsession with physical appearance, had undergone a change of attitude in ways quite normal for people in midlife. Yet, her self-appraisal is at odds with what many have predicted about aging boomers, tempting companies into making costly ill-founded decisions. The makers of fat-free ice cream lost a bundle betting on boomers retaining their narcissistic values in midlife and beyond. More on that later.

At age 23, Jamie Lee Curtis could not have imagined showing off her love handles in a popular magazine. But a 43-year-old Jamie is not just a 20-years-older version of her 23-year-old self. She is in many ways a different person. However, the person she is today evolved along a somewhat predictable path—*the seminal idea that is the foundation of this book.*

About 4.4 million people in the United States share Jamie's birth year. Many have no doubt come to terms with themselves in much the way that Jamie has. Ahead of Jamie are 50 million other boomers who have already passed 43, many of whom are quite far ahead on the road to the higher levels of humanness that lead to dramatic changes in buying behavior.

The general predictability of personal development in midlife would have enabled Maslow 25 years ago to predict that by 2002, "The characteristic behavior of developmentally advanced adults that I wrote about in *Toward a Psychology of Being* will have a strong presence in marketplace behavior." The certainty of that prediction was secured by the fact that a downward trend in fertility rates presaged middle-age dominance of the marketplace by the 1990s. Fewer births in the late 1960s and early 1970s and, finally, the dropping of the fertility rate below population replacement levels meant that the percentage of older people would steadily rise until people 40 and older would become the New Customer Majority.

Maslow would have reminded a doubting Thomas that personal development does not end with adulthood. Rather, it continues for all of life in somewhat predictable ways. He would surmise that a marketplace dominated by people in the second half of their lives would inevitably make the values, views, needs, and behavior characteristic of that time of life the leading behavioral attributes of such a marketplace. Maslow might then have noted that marketers would have to change much of their thinking and the way they do things to be successful in a market-place so configured.

Yankelovich CEO J. Walker Smith said in a 2001 speech that Monitor research reported that consumers were acting more paradoxical, wanting less "stuff," reprioritizing their lives, showing greater self-reliance, and seeking more balance in their lives.[14] Maslow would not have been surprised to find that people in the second half of life were now the adult majority. For instance, he said in *Toward a Psychology of Being* (1968) that at higher stages of maturation people reflect "polarities and oppositions" in their behavior ("paradoxical behavior"); strive to simplify their lives (less "stuff"); experience changes in values ("reprioritizing"); become more autonomous ("self-reliant"), and avoid extremes ("more balance").[15]

So, in the end, consumers are not acting all that strangely, as many have claimed. Rather, most have simply outgrown the old youth-based marketing paradigm. Members of the New Consumer Majority think and act the way people in midlife and older have always thought and acted. It's more accurate to say that the supply side of the equation has been acting strangely—sticking with old ways of doing things as though the worldviews, values, needs and behavior of young minds still ruled the marketplace.

THE TRILLION DOLLAR TRUTH NO ONE CAN AFFORD TO IGNORE

Companies have nothing to lose and everything to gain by becoming more ageless in their marketing. In *SAM* 1990, I saw a long-term anemic economy on the horizon as a result of population shrinkage in younger age groups, and suggested that the well-being of the entire economy could depend on companies giving more attention to older markets:

Creative action taken today in penetrating older markets will allow for a smoother transition after the heady growth we have enjoyed for nearly a half-century. I firmly believe that older people, within the limits of financial prudence dictated by their individual circumstances, can generally be induced to spend more than past history indicates. To the degree that increased spending occurs, however, it will be brought about by a much better understanding of the psyches of older consumers than currently exists. It is their behavior patterns, not their number or their affluence, that will influence their future contributions to the consumer economy.[16]

It's a good bet that many older people don't spend as much as they might because they feel marginalized by Madison Avenue. Try something. Start asking people you run into who are over 40 if they think that the people who make ads think their age group is important enough to be targeted in advertising. Then ask them if they think ad makers understand them. Keep score by age of respondent. It won't be scientific, but the results might be revealing. Remember as you do this walk-around consumer survey that you will be talking to consumers in an age group that is 45 percent larger than the much-coveted 18-to-34 age group.

Corporate America, as well as society at-large, cannot afford the persistent, pernicious ageism that prevails in marketing. Advertisers, marketing agencies, consumers, and, not the least of all, governments who depend on a healthy consumer economy to generate tax revenues are all suffering, and stand to suffer even more as this decade rolls on. Here is the chilling reason why:

> The New Customer Majority is the *only* adult market with realistic prospects for significant sales growth in dozens of product lines for thousands of companies.

Overall, the population growth among young adults is barely moving the needle. The traditionally all-important 25-to-44-year-old age group, which in the past contributed more to the gross domestic product than any other 20-year age group, is *shrinking*. It will be smaller by 4.3 million people in 2010 than it was in 2001. This follows population shrinkage in the 18-34-year-old age group that took place during the 1990s, when the number of 18-to-34-year-olds fell by more than 8 million. That triggered the end of sales growth in many youth-oriented industries including music CDs, youth apparel, and athletic footwear. Now, even though the population of the younger half of this much coveted 18-to-34 demo is starting to grow again, it is not enough to offset population shrinkage among 25-to-44-year-olds.

People in the 25-to-44-year-old age group have been crucial to a healthy consumer economy because they tend to highly leverage the purchasing power of their incomes through loans and revolving charge accounts to buy "stuff"—lots of "stuff." People in the 25-to-34-year-old age group lead in vehicle spending, while 35-to-44-year-olds lead in housing and housing-related spending. All told, spending in this age group is projected to decline by $115 billion between 2001 and 2010.

In sharp contrast, the 20-year cohort of 45-to-64-year-olds will grow by 16 million people during this decade. Sales are projected to grow by $329 billion. Taking into account the full range of New Customer Majority spending, by 2010, *spending by people 45 and older will be a trillion dollars greater than spending by people between the ages of 18 and 39*—$2.6 trillion to $1.6 trillion. (See Figure 1.1.)

The population count for all adults under age 40 is now about 85 million in contrast to the 45 percent larger New Customer Majority, which numbered a little over 123 million in 2000. By 2010, the number of adults under 40 will have increased only by about 2 million people, while the New Customer Majority market will become 60 percent larger than the younger adult age group by adding more than 13 million new members. (See Figure 1.2.) In light of these figures, what argument can convincingly demonstrate that Madison Avenue and Corporate America are on sound footing in putting the lion's share of marketing dollars into young adult markets?

"When an event is not easily explained by what we know, we alter what we know to accommodate the new event." These words from University of Virginia's Timothy Wilson offer a new perspective on why a turnabout in thinking on middle-age and older markets is moving so slowly. Those who defend their continuing preoccupation with first-half consumers do not understand the event of dramatic changes in customer behavior, so they alter what they already know to accommodate it. The welfare of the consumer economy, indeed of the entire national economy and thousands of companies, is being compromised by an unwillingness to change mind-sets to accommodate the new event of the New

FIGURE 1.1 *Spending Trends by Ten-Year Cohort*

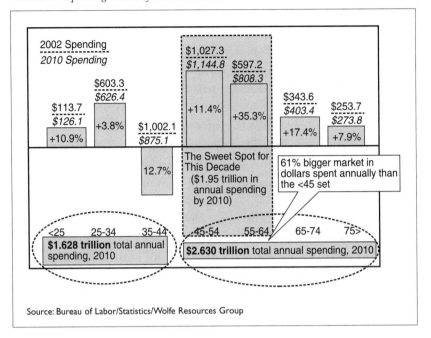

Source: Bureau of Labor/Statistics/Wolfe Resources Group

FIGURE 1.2 *The Biggest Source of Sales Growth*

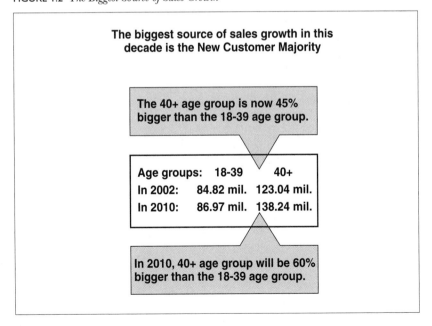

Customer Majority's emergence as the most powerful force in the consumer marketplace today.

This book explains why research and marketing have lost their way from a fresh perspective, from a new *consciousness,* as it were. Albert Einstein's famous words "a problem cannot be solved from the same consciousness that created it" describe what is necessary to begin repairing marketing, as well as consumer research. Marketing's present-day problems have not been generated by customers, or by 9/11, or by war jitters, or by any other externality. They have been generated internally by the persistent existence of a consciousness that occludes the vision necessary to figure out why things are not working so as to be able to move on to problem solving.

No thoughtful reader will agree with everything I say in this book. Some readers may be caustically critical of some things I say. But this I promise to every reader: No one who reads this entire book is likely to ever see customers and the art of marketing quite the same. By the end of this book, I hope every reader who needs to do so will become unstuck from the 1960s, as CBS's Dave Poltrack would put it. Beyond that, it is my intention to give every reader a sizeable array of new thought tools to better navigate the era of the New Customer Majority.

2

STATISTICS DON'T BUY

As far as the laws of mathematics refer to reality, they are not certain, and as far as they are certain, they do not refer to reality.

Albert Einstein

What in the world was Einstein on when he, the greatest scientist of the 20th century, made that statement? Imagine him telling a corporate CFO, after reading a company financial statement, or a typical senior marketing VP, after looking over a numbers-studded proposal for a new marketing campaign, "Your numbers do not refer to reality."

What Einstein was pointing out, of course, is that numbers are only symbols and the picture they add up to is a made-up picture, not a real picture. Judiciously speaking, a numbers-rendered picture is at best an approximation that inevitably omits important details.

In *The Loyalty Effect*, Frederick Reichheld issues a scathing rebuke of management by numbers, at least by the numbers that many MBAs in finance love with near superstitious aplomb. He observes in a discussion of State Farm—whose worker, agent, and customer loyalty is probably without surpass in the insurance industry, and which in Reichheld's view is why State Farm insures over 20 percent of American households—that its competitors can't fathom how State Farm has become such a power-house. Reichheld explains why: "We all use mental models to sort out relevant information from noise and then organize that information into useful patterns. When these models are accounting paradigms, managers quite simply cannot grasp the economics of learning and loyalty that sustains State Farm's success. *They may listen to* [State Farm founder] *Mecherle's words, but they fail to hear his message."* [1] (Italics added.) Pure and simple, State Farm operates from a different consciousness than nearly all of its competition does. Operating from an accounting-defined consciousness, it is impossible for competitors to see what State Farm's management sees with great clarity.

This chapter begins with the objective of doing no less than plotting the path toward a new consciousness that will clear away a numbers-saturated fog that obscures a clear-eyed view of why marketing has been grossly underperforming and defining what is necessary to identify and implement solutions of the problem in the era of the New Customer Majority.

GETTING BEYOND THE NUMBERS

The consciousness of traditional marketing is unquestionably numbers-dominated, starting with consumer research in which rules of statistical math are given greater weight than principles of behavior. A poverty of influence by behavioral science on research and marketing is why this is so. It speaks volumes that a person can earn an MBA in marketing without taking a single course in behavior. If marketing is not about attracting and holding the interest of minds and persuading them to a course of action, then what is it about? Most marketers feel marketing is about moving as much product as feasible, at the lowest cost, with the highest possible margins. Marketing's current woes are not solvable from that numbers-defined, product-centric consciousness. The salvation of marketing and consumer research depends on a better understanding of human behavior than is generally the case.

Better grounding in behavior will not only improve research quality and marketing productivity, it will give companies a better picture of upstream markets. The last chapter told how the Yankelovich Monitor informed its subscribers that consumers are acting more paradoxical, wanting less "stuff," reprioritizing their lives, behaving with greater self-reliance, and seeking more balance in their lives. Proof that these changes in behavior were predictable years ago is suggested by the fact that *SAM* 1990 foresaw these changes. Those predictions were based on the certainty that middle-age and older people would soon dominate in numbers and spending, as well as in determining that the New Customer Majority would shape the leading behavioral attributes in the marketplace.

More sophisticated surveys, more sophisticated statistical analyses, better data mining, or more of anything other than getting a handle on the basics—not opinions—of human behavior will not change things for the better in research and marketing. Statistical mathematics obviously has a valuable role to play in analyzing customer behavior and plotting marketing directions, but it hardly is qualified to be the cornerstone of research and marketing that custom has made it. Another bit of Einsteinian wisdom indicates why that is true:

> "Not all that can be counted counts and not all that counts can be counted."

Those words emphasize the core truth in the epigram to this chapter: *The laws of mathematics do not refer to reality.* Yet, in every sector of business most decision makers believe that "what the numbers say" refers to reality.

Customer relationship management (CRM) has taken the idea of marketing as a numbers game to new heights. Lusting after great fortunes in the CRM space, software vendors and consultants proposed that virtually everything worth knowing about customers could be captured in databases. However, they have been tripped up by the fact that not everything that counts can be reduced to numbers. Over half of all CRM initiatives fail. They fail mostly because the core drivers of human behavior are left out of the CRM equation. CRM installations do not account for the fact that *customers' decisions are based in nonrational processes that resist reduction to bits and bytes.* How does one reduce motivations, dreams, emotions, and feelings to Boolean logic?

Mr. Spock's Problem

Antonio Damasio, who heads up the neurology department at the University of Iowa, studies patients with brain traumas that have robbed them of their emotional functions in the cortical layers of their brains, what Damasio calls *secondary emotions.* His patients still experience primitive emotions deep in the midbrain, but those emotions at that level resist rational constraint. They are reflexive responses to basic urges including the urge to fight or take flight in the face of threat.

Damasio's patients are rather like *Star Trek's* Mr. Spock. They have fully functioning memory, comprehension, and reasoning abilities. Their biggest problem, aside from missing the rich joys of emotional life, is that they find it virtually impossible to determine when something has personal importance to them.

Poor Mr. Spock. He would have a hard time deciding what car to buy or what toothpaste or deodorant he should put in his shopping basket. Thankfully, Star Fleet uniforms relieve him of the need to make clothing decisions, for if he wore civvies, he'd have a problem, similar to problems Damasio's patients have, figuring out what to wear to his next power meeting with Captain Kirk. Despite being much like you and me in reasoning abilities, likely Mr. Spock and certainly Damasio's patients, cannot determine the importance of something to them through reasoning processes. The bottom line of Damasio's research is:

Emotions are the touchstones of personal relevance.

To give emotions the scant attention they get in CRM applications is to ignore the most influential force in buying behavior. As a result, rather than being the silver bullet many thought it would be, CRM has been a poison apple for many companies. It has proven counterproductive in important respects, including contributing to lowering customer satisfaction and loyalty. When companies go overboard replacing human beings with technology, the quality of the customer experience falls.

Despite billions spent automating marketing and sales functions via CRM platforms, it is becoming clear that the company-customer relationship cannot be automated to the degree once hoped. What a company might save in manpower costs it often stands to lose in customer attrition and in the costs of replacing customers who abandon a brand because a company offers them no emotional incentives for remaining loyal. Moreover, as Reichheld details (with numbers, by the way), when corporate consciousness is numbers-driven, the subtler behavioral aspects of workers and customers simply don't get on the corporate radar screen. As a result, much of what it would take to retard worker turnover (which is cost saving) and to attract and retain customers (which is cost saving, too) never gets done.

CRM grew out of a product-centric consciousness as a high-tech means for getting more products into customers' hands by matching company product to customer profile. This is neither customer-centric nor a new idea. Marketers have been doing that for decades. CRM is simply a *theoretically* more effective way of matching products to customers. Change CRM to read CDM—customer *data* management—and you have a more accurately descriptive name for what CRM is really about: *moving more product less costly.* It is less about serving customers than many claim—a lot less!

HOW TECHNOLOGY CAN BE A LOSE-LOSE DEAL FOR COMPANIES *AND* CUSTOMERS

Confidence in what numbers can do, when processed at near light speed by computers, has put product and process at center stage and customers in the wings. Much of the human touch has been drained from the customer experience, making customers feel increasingly marginalized as human beings.

Take automated telephone systems, for example. Their ubiquity is a product of the numbers mind-set that rules Corporate America: replacing live telephone receptionists with automated systems saves payroll dollars. So, today's customers phoning in to anything other than mom-and-pop companies are usually greeted by a recorded litany of buttons to push. Often, the button the customer pushes drags her into another frustrating round of menu listings. When connection is finally made to a line that the caller thinks *may* be the right one, her human dignity is often further assaulted by a shameless recorded voice: "We apologize for the wait. Your call is important to us. Thank you for your patience."

People programming automated telephone systems fail to realize how hollow those words are and how they discourage customer loyalty. A recording telling customers how much the company values them while they have to wait to talk to a live human being is disingenuous.

Authenticity is not optional if you want to build strong relationships with customers who belong to the New Customer Majority. A recorded voice saying "your call is important to us" is not authentic. If my call is important to you, why make me listen to a recording telling me what buttons to push, then after I push one, make me sit through another recording after which maybe, *just maybe*, I'll end up on the right line where I wait minute after minute for a live human voice to say "My name is Jill. How may I help you?" Jill doesn't give a damn about me because you, her employer, don't.

Too many bean counters view the telephone as a necessary evil rather than as a moneymaking communications tool that can be used to serve customers, save customers, build brand loyalty, and grow sales. Keepers of the corporate coin compare the costs of staff time on the phone with customers against the costs of an automated telephone answering system and, voilà, it's cheaper to buy and operate a machine that answers phones automatically. Apparently, these numbers-driven folk would like nothing better than a marketplace where all human contact with customers could be eliminated.

Give yourself a treat. Call 800-435-9792. You will be greeted in a friendly though businesslike manner by another human being. The person who answers the phone works for Southwest Airlines, the famously cost-conscious budget airline. It is the only major airline where actual people answer customers' incoming calls. Notably, Southwest is also the only major airline currently making a profit. Further, over its 30-year history investors never stopped loving it. In fact, Southwest's stock symbol appropriately is LUV. Tough-talking, bourbon-swilling, chain-smoking Southwest cofounder Herb Kelleher chose LUV as his company's stock symbol. Doesn't that say something important? Doesn't it suggest that Kelleher is having a ball and, like Virgin Atlantic Airlines cut-up CEO Richard Branson, wants his workers and customers to be part of the ball?

Ranking seventh in size in the United States, Southwest's market cap is bigger than the six larger airlines combined. At the time of this writing, the market cap of the world's largest airline, American, was $576 million. Southwest's market cap on the same day was $10.7 billion. Several months before it filed bankruptcy, the market cap of the second largest U.S. airline, United, flying over 900 planes, was $90 million—less than the price of a single Boeing 747.

CUSTOMERS AS ATHLETES AND COFFEE DRINKERS, NOT DATA SETS

The biggest winners in the era of the New Customer Majority will be companies that can break away from the mind-set that there is a technology-associated solution for every customer-related challenge. One CEO of a global company with a balanced perspective of customers and technology said, "We don't want to let IT take over this company. We are not a systems company. We use technology to create better products so we can serve our customers better; we do not let technology lead us. We use technology as a tool, not as a strategic target. We want people talking about people and products and how we can develop and achieve strategies to serve our customers best." That was Nestlé CEO Peter Brabeck in a *Harvard Business Review* interview.[2]

The big winners in today's marketplace see their customers as people first, numbers second. This is not novel. Some great brands have come about by companies treating their customers as people, not as data sets. Nike CEO and cofounder Phil Knight had a nonstatistical view of customers from the founding days of his vast sportswear enterprise. That may seem a bit ironic, given his BBA in accounting from the University of Oregon and MBA from Stanford. However, Knight was a serious runner (a 4:10 miler) who understands the mind of the athlete. Athletes were Knight's core customers from the time he hawked shoes at games and meets from the trunk of his car. His intuitive grasp of human nature enabled Nike to spawn a revolution in sports apparel. Many credit Knight with doing more than any one else to bring the exercise and fitness movement in the United States to life.

The lion's share of Nike's research dollars goes into product design and development rather than into consumer research. In fact, before he interviewed for the top marketing job at Nike in 1987, brandmeister Scott Bedbury was advised to not use the word *research* when speaking to Knight.[3] Nike's founding father has undisguised disdain for statistically driven marketing. In its then 16-year-old history, Nike had become a powerhouse with annual sales of $800 million without relying on traditional consumer research.

While holding Nike out as a successful example of a company that eschews a numbers-defined consciousness, I am aware that the company has struggled in achieving annual growth rates in recent years strong enough to keep Wall Street happy. However, a big problem Nike has is that the younger markets it uncannily connected with in the past have slowed in growth. Nike has been unable to transfer its magic to the New Customer Majority. Perhaps by the time this book is out, Nike will have learned that it must make changes in its brand husbandry, as The Gap finally learned after two years of dismal sales growth resulting from overemphasis on teen fashions. Within several months of launching its "Gap: For every generation" campaign, the retailer reversed its long downhill slide that was marked by 23 months of consecutive losses.

Starbucks, which Bedbury later joined, followed much the same route to global stardom. Starbucks founder Howard Schultz has the same intuitive understanding of coffee drinkers that Phil Knight had of athletes. He didn't feel it necessary to endlessly grill coffee drinkers in large-scale research projects.

Bedbury says, "The greatest problem with relying on traditional methodologies used by most outside market-research firms, I've found, is that they provide management with reams of statistical data, which may tempt those lacking in confidence to go against their common sense and gut intuition."[4] What an indictment from one of the best minds in brand husbandry today!

Southwest's Herb Kelleher says, "I'm always willing to look at [market research], but I never want to get bogged down in it." He adds, "We get a lot of employee feedback on what they hear as to our customers' likes and dislikes. I'd rather we be out there doing things for the customers and gauging their responses on the front line."[5] No slave of numbers, he built one of the most cost-control-minded airlines around.

A Parenthetical Note

We don't usually warm to others who attack us. With that in mind, perhaps it's timely to say that despite criticisms leveled at customer research at various points in this book, it is not done without an appreciation for the fact that consumer research can be a valuable decision-making tool. However, traditional research is broken and it needs fixing. Consider the following three statements made by two highly respected researchers, Kevin Clancy and Robert Shulman, formerly chairman and CEO, respectively, of Yankelovich Clancy Shuman:

1. "Because consumers don't choose rationally, any research that forces rational answers has to be flawed."
2. "[Brand] positioning cannot be developed from what people say they want."

3. "While it is possible to divide the American public into different segments psychographically, it's often of no practical use."[6]

What could be a stronger indictment against traditional, numbers-obsessed consumer research than that made by these two highly regarded pros in consumer research?

Phil Knight, Howard Shultz, and Herb Kelleher are keenly aware that much of what they want to know about customers cannot be reduced to numbers. They realize that numbers often distort rather than clarify pictures of customers, or, in line with Einstein's cautionary words, often don't refer to reality. Jon Steele, the advertising account planner who played a lead role in developing the "Got Milk?" campaign, comically addressed obsessions with statistics when he said in *Truth, Lies and Advertising,* "Statistically speaking, Americans have one testicle and one breast."

Why Customer Research Often Points Companies Down the Wrong Path

Statistics can prove the false as persuasively as they can prove the truth. In survey research, people often tell researchers things that are untrue without either respondent or researcher realizing it. These falsehoods are then statistically analyzed and presented in a final report as truth revealed. One area particularly prone to such falsity is motivations. Read what renowned neurologist Richard Restak, whose work was the basis for PBS's award-winning series *The Brain* and *The Mind,* says about our awareness of our motivations:

> "We have reason to doubt that full awareness of our motives and other mental activities may be possible."[7]

Bernard J. Baars, a leading researcher in the study of what goes on behind the curtains of consciousness to shape our behavior, makes the same point more directly:

> "Our inability to accurately report intentions and expectations may simply reflect the fact that they are qualitatively not conscious."[8]

The views on motivations held by Restak and Baars represent consensus in contemporary brain science. Marketing researchers and practitioners need to join that consensus. Brain researchers have made it quite clear that to understand people's needs, motivations, and behavior, it is necessary to go behind the curtains of consciousness. The roots of needs and motivations lie deep in the brain, beyond the direct reach of research subjects' conscious minds. How to get to those roots is a major focus of this book, but to give you a peek into the topic in personal terms, let's look at how a particular need and motivation might arise below the levels of your conscious mind.

It's midafternoon and your energy level is sagging. Suddenly, a craving for chocolate sweeps over you. The craving sprouted outside your conscious mind in a tiny organ above your kidneys when it sensed a sugar shortage. The sugar supply sentinel responded by setting off a gush of neuropeptide Y to carry a message your brain. "Send in some carbs—and hurry!" Your brain takes notice and alerts your conscious mind by generating the craving. You now know that you desire chocolate, but you don't really know where the desire came from.

The conscious mind plays the chief executive officer to the brain's subordinate role as data gatherer, researcher, analyst, and communications center for all points in the body that need to get information to the CEO for a decision. The brain gets the conscious mind's attention by whipping up cravings or desires. That's how motivations (or temptations!) are born.

Beside the fact that the origins of motivations lie outside consciousness there is another reason why research subjects often mislead researchers by telling them things that later events in the marketplace contradict. Damasio discovered that when people think about something that is hypothetical, they use different brain sites and processes than they use in a real-life scenario. Thus, the person in the focus group or one who is being surveyed is not quite the same person that goes shopping later that day.

Influence by such new insights into the workings of the brain is changing how a growing number of companies get information about customers. More research is moving into cyberspace all the time. Mark Schar, Procter & Gamble's vice president for iVentures and consumer knowledge, says, "I would say it's pretty clear to all folks involved that the Internet is going to be the future backbone of our consumer-research activity."[9] P&G along with an expanding list of other companies are using the Internet as a testing ground for new products. Shoppers go to specific sites to get product samples, which they try out before coming back to the site to give feedback to the company. The company then reviews the feedback before it invests large sums in a major launch. In other words, more and more companies are evaluating customers in real-life shopping scenarios as opposed to surveying, interviewing, and focus group testing—grilling them in artificial environments.

Some researchers are getting even more personal with customers by employing ethnographic research methods. In ethnographic research, the researcher becomes part of the scene studied. This is a radical change from consumer research of the past because in classical science, whose protocols have strongly influenced consumer research, the researcher must stand apart from what is being studied.

Anthony Edwards, an account planner at Bernstein-Rein in Kansas City, makes extensive use of ethnographic research. He recruits people to organize barbeques and dinner parties that he attends as one of the guests. He gives his hosts guidelines for invitees to ensure that participants represent the market being studied. Edwards will stand around a barbeque grill, beer in one hand, hamburger in the other, not only questioning guests directly, but also encouraging them to examine each other's ideas and attitudes. According to Edwards, the nice thing about these informal groups, is that "unlike in focus groups, you don't have to wonder whether what someone says is true or just making an effort to position himself."[10] Edwards says he gets truths from such gatherings that would not be revealed in focus groups and that cannot be uncovered in survey research because of the subtle nature of many crucial truths about customer behavior.

An ethnographer visiting a research subject in her home may ask the subject for documentary evidence like grocery receipts, notes on refrigerators, magazines she gets, or other sources of information that might shed light on her views and behavior. Ethnographic research does not follow a tightly structured preconceived plan. There is no moderator's guide like the ones used in focus groups. Instead, the ethnographer lets the research follow a trail determined by incremental results of the research process. Rather than trying to control the direction of the research, the ethnographer takes a *heuristic* approach. Each new revealing insight lays the groundwork for the segment of the research project.

The final ethnographic report is not the usual sterile treatise. The research client gets a narrative—a story extracted from a real-life setting in which people act out their lives in a natural daily manner. An ethnographic report even can be fun to read!

AN AGING CUSTOMER UNIVERSE CHALLENGES TRADITIONAL IDEAS ABOUT SEGMENTATION

Notwithstanding limitations on how much people can tell researchers about their motivations, needs, and other dimensions of their behavior, what young people tell a researcher tends to be more useable than testimonies by older adults. That is because the worldviews, values, and behavior of young people tend to be more closely aligned with those of their peers. This makes it easier to segment younger people and target them according to the characteristics by which they have been classified.

Meaningful segmentation of older people is more challenging because they are more *individuated*. In one shopping context, an older person may fall into one segment, while falling into another segment in another shopping context.

Take 58-year-old Janet Greene. Yesterday she checked out her weekly groceries at a total cost of $137.46 less $12.78 in meat selections marked down because of expiring buy dates, $17.71 in Safeway Club card savings, and $4.75 in manufacturers' coupons. Her total savings were a bit over 25 percent of her total cost, or $35.24, making her final bill $102.22. She walked away from her neighborhood Safeway that day feeling quite proud of herself. Last week her savings came to only 19 percent.

Janet and her retired 65-year-old husband George watch their spending closely. Janet's product selections and buying behavior put her in a category of like-minded, like-behaving retirees who are highly price sensitive. Or does it?

Driving away from her neighborhood Safeway that day, in a 10-month-old Lexus, Janet stopped at Sutton Place Gourmet to get two prime porterhouse steaks for dinner. They cost her $12.99 a pound. (Safeway had porterhouses on sale at $5.99 a pound, $3.00 less than its regular price for porterhouse.) She then made one more stop before going home. She needed to pick up tickets from her travel agent. She and George are planning to spend a month with her family in Taipei, where she was born and where she and George met in 1978 while he was there working for IBM.

Into what market segment does Janet, nee Jiang Li, best fit? What about George, who grew up in Columbus, Ohio? In what segment does he belong? Perhaps Janet belongs in one segment and George in another. But that makes marketing to the household complicated. Many purchases are jointly decided. Should the household be categorized in yet a third segment? How can the shopping and buying behavior of this household, and of George and Janet as individuals, be reduced to numbers? Whose "numbers" should prevail in a predictive modeling program? Perhaps we should just forget George as an individual customer because as salespeople who work with retirees know, all things being equal, women more often prevail. So, maybe things are not quite all that equal.

Gerontologists have a saying: The older you are, the more you become you. As you become more your own person, you become less classifiable as being of one type of customer or another. What or who you are depends on context. The challenging truth facing researchers and others trying to figure out people in the New Customer Majority is that with each passing year in the second half of life, a person becomes a more complex customer. This means that as the adult median age continues to rise, the challenges of researchers—as well as those of marketers—become more complex. Asking customers about themselves will not help greatly in meeting those challenges because they generally have limited awareness of some of the more crucial dimensions of their buying behavior and lifestyle choices.

Having surveyed various problems besetting researchers and marketers in an aging and explosively growing middle-aged and older customer universe, and having argued for shifting from a numbers-based consciousness to one that is more balanced between numbers and behavioral science, it is time to enter the new consciousness. In the next chapter we pass through a portal to view second-half customers through a new consciousness. That new consciousness arises from seeing customers through the lens of *developmental psychology*, a field that is almost completely ignored in consumer research and marketing even though it offers astonishing insights into customer behavior that cannot be gained through traditional consumer research.

3

SECOND-HALF CUSTOMERS SEEN THROUGH A NEW CONSCIOUSNESS

A friend who works in the senior care housing industry once told me about a conversation he had with an 80-year-old man about how old people deal differently with aging. My friend was getting a bit aggressive in pursuing his points when the elderly gentleman summarily declared the discussion over by saying, "I think I know a bit more about this than you do because you've never been 80, but I've been 40. You're talking like a 40-year-old, not like an 80-year-old."

You can just as appropriately imagine such a conversation between a 50-year-old and a 30-year-old ending the same way. The point is, anyone working in markets whose members are a generation or more older than he or she is should know that it takes more than focus groups and statistically processed surveys to get the understanding of older customers that leads to a *knowledge advantage* over competitors. Giving readers a knowledge advantage is another way of stating this book's chosen purpose.

This chapter introduces insights that *generally* define the foundation of second-half customer behavior. Please note the words *generally* define. You already may have noticed that I often qualify statements with conditional terms such as *generally, tends to, likely, likelier, probably, usually,* and *perhaps.* Little in this book is presented as hard-and-fast universal truth that applies to all people or even all people in a given category. When I ascribe a behavioral trait to a particular group of customers, I do so know-ing that exceptions exist.

THE SEMANTIC PUZZLE: WHAT DO YOU CALL *THEM*

As the 1960s began, a third of the people 65 and older lived below poverty levels. By the late 1980s, that figure had dropped to around 12 percent, and with in-kind benefits accounted for, less than four percent of America's elderly lived below the poverty level. That truly remarkable achievement was accomplished in less than 25 years. Nevertheless, the rush of U.S. companies toward these more affluent elder markets never got underway as some of us thought would happen after the 1980 cen-sus revealed a population boom in older age brackets with historically high levels of financial security and independence.

The 1980 census did stir new and expanded interest in older markets in three industries: financial services, retirement housing, and health care. However, most companies in other industries stuck with their tradi-tional markets, seemingly unaware of the unprecedented population growth in older age groups.

The senior care housing industry was one industry that took off in re-sponse to the 1980 census. Generally serving people over 75, senior care housing offers domiciliary services, social programs, and limited care. The field attracted the interest of hoteliers Marriott and Hyatt, both of whom established senior care housing divisions. Even Avon, the cosmetics com-pany, jumped into the business, though it was quickly abandoned after learning that it was a more complex business than Avon had anticipated.

Commonly called *retirement communities,* senior care housing presented a challenge to traditional retirement communities that offered amenity-rich recreational packages, often including golf. Because retirement com-munities are commonly seen as gussied-up nursing homes without smells and uniforms, the amenities-rich havens for swinging retirees needed another name so they began calling themselves *active adult communities.*

Calling 55-to-75-year-olds *active adults* always seemed confusing be-cause younger adults are also independently active, as are many adults over 75. The term betrays a pervasive awkwardness in the language used to refer to people who are age-qualified for AARP membership. I'm often asked, if *senior, retiree,* and *elderly* are turn-off terms, what should we call older people? "Call 'em people," I say.

We have a long-standing resistance in our society to dealing forth-rightly with the inescapable fact that, barring mishap, everyone gets old. Encouraged by the culture of Madison Avenue, many pretend that aging is mostly an illusion. I asked one woman, "When do you think middle age starts?" she crisply answered, "It won't if you don't let it." The idea of get-ting older bothered her. Centenarians usually say one of their secrets for long life is gracefully taking it as it comes, bumps and all, with aging never a matter of great concern. Those who deny their aging could be acceler-ating age-related problems because denial of age gives credence to nega-tive stereotypes of aging, turning them into self-fulfilling prophecies. The idea of beliefs about aging being self-fulfilling prophecies is not specula-tion. Some studies have found that people who expect memory problems in later life are likelier to experience them when later life arrives.

NEGATIVE STEREOTYPES OF AGING ARE FORTIFIED BY LANGUAGE

Discomfort with aging plays a large role in Corporate America's re-luctance to move aggressively into second-half markets, despite the fact that this reluctance cannot be rationally defended. How does one intel-ligently, objectively, and rationally defend gross inattention to a second-half market that is by far the largest adult age group spending the largest number of dollars?

There is a strong consensus among people who work in older mar-kets that views the widespread resistance to the aggressive pursuit of these markets as owing much to the negative stereotypes of aging that pervade our society. Entertainment and advertising exuberantly project the idea that youth is the ideal state of humanness. After 40, forget it—you're on a downhill slide in your desirability as a worker, as a woman, as a human being. By age 50, you are over the hill. Never mind that you have more technical competence in what you do, more wisdom in how you sort things out, more patience to see things through, and are better able to clearly make judgments because your ego is likely in recession.

Ageism in marketing is cruel. It is cruel in the workplace. It is cruel in retail outlets. For example, how would you feel if a clerk at a department store cosmetics counter told you, "Be with you in a minute," then turned her attention to a twentysomething just walking in? This happened to a 57-year-old friend who said she got a stare from the clerk that would melt an ice cube when she insisted that she should be served first. "I thought you were still looking," the clerk feebly responded.

That ageism can be unmercifully cruel has been borne out in a slew of studies. For example, Yale epidemiologist Becca Levy conducted research in which she sought to gauge somatic influences of negative and positive images of aging on subjects. The research found that when older people were exposed to negative images of aging, they experienced significant increases in blood pressure and heart rate. However, when the same individuals were presented with positive images of aging, signs of cardiovascular stress fell significantly.[1] Who says sticks and stones can hurt my bones but names can never hurt me?

Ageism has the power to kill, and I'm not talking just about people. In this decade, it will kill a number of companies whose ageism-laced consciousness prevents them from seeing salvation in second-half markets amid anemic or slipping sales.

Levy's work lends substance to the bon mot "Age is a thing of mind over matter—if you don't mind it, it don't matter" (variously attributed to Mark Twain, Jack Benny, Satchel Paige, among others). People who mind their aging quite a lot might not only be working against their mental well-being; they could indeed be setting in motion future declines in memory abilities. Older people who are shown words negatively associated with aging before taking a memory test, don't do as well as subjects shown positive words about aging before taking the same test.

More than you might realize, the quality of life in your later years may be tied to what you think about old age today. If at age 30 you think memory loss is a natural consequence of age, you are likelier at age 60 to think your memory is declining just because you're 60. This is borne out in a study by Levy and Harvard psychologist Ellen Langer. Expecting native Chinese and deaf Americans to have less exposure to negative stereotypes of aging, Levy and Langer tested both young and old people in each group. They found memory abilities among elderly deaf to generally be superior to those of elderly Americans who could hear. They also found that the memory abilities of Chinese elderly were similar to those of young people.[2] So, perhaps the next time you want to send a friend a birthday card that jokingly invokes negative stereotypes of aging you'll remember that you may be helping to set in motion the future decay of your friend's memory and perhaps even help shorten his or her life.

Maybe We Should Redefine the Word *Senior*

When Buckminster Fuller, the great engineer and inventor of the geodesic dome, was in his late 20s, he stood pensively one dark night at the edge of Lake Michigan planning to end his life. He was jobless, penniless, spiritless, and seized by unbearable grief over the recent death of his four-year-old daughter Alexandria from pneumonia. As he edged toward the icy waters, suddenly a wave of scintillating thought, bright with newly defined life purpose, swept over him. He would reorient his life and dedicate it to the betterment of humankind. In pursuit of that mission, he might reclaim vitality, peace, and fulfillment.

As he contemplated his spiritual rebirth, he reflected on how language pulls one in the direction of conformity. He wanted a mind liberated from such a limitation. Bucky Fuller wanted to transcend the cognitive limits of language to discover new meanings about life. So it was that he returned from the edge of Lake Michigan that wintry night with a pledge to speak to no one, including his wife, during the first year of his new, born-again consciousness. He wanted to be as fully purged of preconceptions imposed on him by his culture as possible.

Were he alive today, Bucky Fuller might advise us to abandon the term *senior,* for it has contributed much to help embed stereotypes of aging people into the national psyche. Who now wants to be a *senior?* Just ask anyone who has just received his or her first welcome letter from AARP.

What better explains the widespread disregard of the New Customer Majority despite its great size and affluence than buy-ins to aging stereotypes? Why is it that most companies would rather duke it out with like-minded competitors in younger markets, despite anemic or even falling prospects of sales growth? Keep in mind as you ponder the answers that by 2010, adults 40 and older, spending $2.6 trillion annually, will be outspending adults under 40 by $1 trillion. That surely is an eye-popping, mind-catching difference that makes it worthwhile to get beyond pernicious ageism in corporate decision making.

To help people in business begin seeing older customers more benignly, I have a Bucky Fuller solution. Why not change what *senior* means by including younger people—everyone 40 and older—in the group that defines the term? Wait . . . don't slam this book shut book if you are about to turn 40 and can't bear the thought of being a senior before your time. Hear me out, please.

Senior is not an inherently negative term. High schoolers like being seniors, having senior privileges, and going to senior proms. Being a senior in college is a good thing, too. People eagerly break open the champagne when they achieve senior partner status in a law firm. Business professionals proudly wear the title senior vice president. Bruce Fleisher is happy he qualifies for the PGA seniors tour, having racked up $2 million–plus in winnings in 2001.

Being a senior connotes superior standing in virtually every context but aging. So let's change that by making 40 the threshold of senior status. The age at which you become a senior is not set in stone. AARP first sees you as a senior on your 50th birthday. The U.S. Department of Housing and Urban Development calls you a senior at age 55. Movie theaters have chosen 60, while many airlines give you a seniors' discount when you reach 62.

One reason many older people resent being called seniors is that the term carries a lot of unwanted baggage. It symbolizes the socially reinforced idea that after 50 you move to the sidelines of life where you begin a downhill path of progressive decline and loss. No one wants to be associated with such negative images of aging.

So let's simply declare age 40, the midpoint of life, as the time when people enter the senior class with all its privileges. Aside from the likelihood of resistance to this idea that people achieve senior status at age 40, there is a good reason for making 40 the magic number. Around 40, it is quite common for people to experience a *personal paradigm shift* in which they begin viewing their lives differently than they did earlier in adulthood.

THE CHANGE OF LIFE DECADE

The fifth decade of life is the *change of life decade,* and not just in the sense of physical changes. The mind also goes through a change of life experience. The hot flushes of the mental change of life are stabbing feelings of emptiness, desperate hopes that there must be more to life. All go through some form of mental change of life, though some are more aware of it than others. Many suffer a searing realization that they have done less in life than they thought they would when they were 25. Others are confused that having accomplished everything they thought they would and more, they feel something vital is missing in their lives. Things that once thrilled no longer do. Things that mattered have suddenly become unimportant. Pursuit of ambitions is being moderated by pursuit of balance. Life *was* about winning, getting, having, controlling; now it's more about getting a better fix on who one is and where one is going. It is a time that is eerily reminiscent of an adolescent going through identity crisis. Questions like *What is my life about, anyway?* and *At the end of the day, what matters most in life?* pop into consciousness. Many new midlifers think: I only get one go at life, so maybe I should try for the brass ring one more time. I need something—perhaps *someone*—to restore meaning and completeness to my life. In this mental milieu, wives may kick husbands out of their lives and enroll in self-help programs or return to college, and husbands may leave wives and head for a car dealership to buy a sporty new convertible.

Around the onset of midlife, people often amaze themselves by having the courage to make dramatic changes in their lives that earlier in life they couldn't have imagined making. This is often seen in midlife marital breakups. "My God, she and George did what? . . . They split? . . . Pat just walked out? . . . No, she'd never do that." But it is not newfound courage that let Pat do something in midlife that shocked her family and friends. It is more likely the weakening of peer influences and of urges to impress others that freed her to make life-changing decisions. Her *persona*—her social mask—is dissolving. People begin a search for the *real self* after years of catering to the needs of the *social self.*

Pat's journey toward self-actualization has begun.

Self-actualization, which is about developing and experiencing the *real self,* is the most autonomous state of humanness. Its sculpting impact on behavior makes people in second-half markets more than just older versions of their younger selves. They are different people with different values, views, needs, and motivations. You cannot connect deeply with the hearts and minds of customers who are on a self-actualizing track by projecting values that are more appropriate to the lifestyles of the young.

WHY THE CUSTOMER EXPERIENCE HAS BECOME MORE IMPORTANT

People in second-half markets are defined more by their core values and lifestyle profiles than by their ages. In other words, age conveys less about a person in the second half of life than it does in the first half of life. What is more telling is a person's position in his or her lifelong journey toward the pinnacles of psychological maturation.

The idea that a strong connection exists between human development and customer behavior draws no attention in discussions of why marketing is hurting, yet this connection is at the root of what has gone wrong in marketing. Specifically, though the motivational forces of self-actualization needs are among the most powerful influences on customer behavior in the second half of life, they get almost no attention from marketers. Even former Nike and Starbucks brandmeister Scott Bedbury bows out on that one. While enthusiastically telling marketers to connect with the first four needs levels in Maslow's hierarchy—basic physical, safety, love, and esteem needs—he says, "Speaking as one who has seen firsthand the power of a brand unleashed, there is no brand on earth that can deliver the top of Maslow's pyramid. The best that marketers can do is to respectfully acknowledge that the need exists."[3]

But marketers can do more than simply acknowledge that the need exists. They can reinforce values and lifestyles that promote self-actualization (as Nike competitor New Balance does, as you will see). They can also play a catalytic role, helping people move toward self-actualization. Frequent flier programs that let customers donate mileage points to Make a Wish and other charities are catalytic agents of self-actualization because an increase in altruistic behavior is part and parcel of discovering and actualizing the real self. Bedbury reminds us of this when he calls to mind in *A New Brand World* Maslow's assertion that self-actualizing people long to be involved in "a cause outside their skin." Bedbury describes this as a "critical and extremely powerful need," so why not help second-half customers process that critical and extremely powerful need as they wind their way through the complexities of life's second half?

Producers of organic foods serve as catalytic agents of self-actualization, and make good money doing it. Eggs from free-range hens raised on foods without additives sell for three times the amount of regular eggs. Free-range eggs don't taste any different, but many people feel better buying them because they are contributing to a cause beyond their skin—a healthier earth and a morally better society. While not everyone buying free-range eggs is in a self-actualizing state, the behavior is typical of self-actualizing personalities. Some people buy free-range eggs to make social statements. Others buy them as part of defining their identities along certain moral lines. Those are not self-actualizing behaviors. We'll find out more about what constitutes self-actualizing behavior a bit later.

Abraham Maslow summed up the course of human life by saying every infant enters the world with one overriding task: to become ever more human. He didn't mean that infants are not biologically fully human, but rather that they are far from the beingness state that distinguishes us most from other animals: self-actualization, the most complete expression of humanness. Like gravity, the forces of self-actualization exert a constant tug on each of us, pulling us along the path of personal development until we become "fully human," even though people differ in how far along that path they progress.

In marketing to the New Customer Majority, it is crucial to understand how the forces of self-actualization drive changes in people's life purposes, core needs, and buying behavior. This is a life stage development that has yet to be adequately appreciated in marketing. The term *life stage* is commonly used in marketing, but it usually refers to *social* life stages that are triggered by some event, such as school graduation, marriage, new baby, kids reaching teen age, empty nester status, and retirement. Though these obviously are important factors in customer behavior, they are superficial influences. Parents may welcome the last child's departure for college, but how they take advantage of their new empty nester status is more defined by their stage of psychological development than by the superficial fact of becoming empty nesters.

Companies that will do best in the New Customer Majority will be those that have an understanding of the role of self-actualization in shaping customer behavior in the second half of life. On that score, one fact that is of no mean significance is:

> For the first time in history, the majority of adults are in the years
> of life when self-actualization needs play an ever-expanding role
> in customer behavior.

General ignorance of that fact in marketing is playing a big role in the declining productivity of marketing. This fact is, behind the falling effectiveness of selling product features, functional benefits, and economic value, and the rising importance of the customer. The narcissistic and materialistic values that undergird the behavior of first-half customers make product features, functional benefits, and economic value more salient to them. The real self, headed for the summits of full maturity, looks beyond product features, functional benefits, and economic value in making purchase decisions. People on a self-actualizing track become more keenly interested in the qualitative aspects of the customer experience, especially when buying big ticket items like a car—a fact that Lexus has a better handle on than other luxury car brands, including Infiniti.

Infiniti, which first came to market at around the same time as Lexus, went after younger drivers, believing this would be more profitable than going after older customers already committed to a brand.

Lexus saw things differently. It went after older car owners who were the most loyal customers in the luxury car business: namely, Cadillac and Mercedes owners. The average age of Cadillac and Mercedes owners is 53 and 45, respectively[4]—too old by conventional marketing wisdom to be worth the cost to get them to switch to Lexus. Yet Lexus separated car owners from their Cadillacs and Mercedes by giving them a higher-quality customer experience.

Lexus's counterintuitive strategy paid off. Many former loyal Mercedes and Cadillac owners will now be Lexus owners for life, provided Lexus continues delivering on the customer experience. Lexus has the highest repurchase rate of any car—21 points higher than Infiniti.

The Lexus success story demonstrates a key fact about members of the New Customer Majority. They will resist entreaties to abandon a brand to which they are deeply attached, but they will abandon a brand in a New York minute when it fails their expectations of the customer experience and another brand seems likely to do better.

It can cost next to nothing to provide loyalty-building customer experiences that give a brand a powerful competitive edge. In a July 1999 release, J. D. Powers said, "Lexus *and* Saturn have become customer service benchmarks and shaken up the automotive industry by offering automotive service programs that effectively address customer expectations."[5]

Product-centric corporate cultures make product features, functional benefits, and economic value the core focus of their marketing.

But these core values are grounded in the narcissistic and materialist worlds of the young. The emergence of the New Customer Majority calls for product-centric cultures to turn themselves into customer-centric cultures. Customer-centric companies acknowledge the role of customers in determining the value of a product, as C. K. Prahalad and Venkatram Ramaswamy observe in a richly insightful paper entitled *The Value Creation Dilemma: New Building Blocks for the Experience Revolution:*

> The Holy Grail for the consumer is *fulfilling experiences* . . . As a consumer view of value takes hold, *experiences become the basis of value creation.* (Their italics.)

The Internet has obviously played a big role in changing the rules of marketplace engagement by shifting the balance of information power toward customers. Customers now often enter a buying transaction with more knowledge about a product line than salespeople. But nothing has done more to change the character of customer behavior than the fact that most adults are in the years when self-actualization needs emerge with greater force. Even those who aren't making much headway toward self-actualization are strongly influenced by it. Take George Parker.

Friends of 48-year-old George Parker say he's never matured beyond the skirt-watching, beer-drinking, fun-loving days of his college years. A bit of exaggeration, perhaps, because George is not a heavy imbiber and for all his talk, ranks low on the philanderer's scale of sexual excess. He has been materially successful, but less so emotionally and spiritually. Married, divorced, and remarried, George is once again wondering what it takes to find life satisfaction. Across the street from George and his wife Sandy live Jack and Margo Erskine. To George, Jack and Margo are nearly the perfect couple living nearly the perfect life. For whatever reason, Jack seems closer to becoming "fully human" than George even though they are the same age. In fact, the prospects of George reaching a self-actualizing state are not promising. A person stuck trying to meet lower-level needs cannot move as far ahead in his or her maturation as a person who has been more successful in meeting lower-level needs.

George Parker's lifestyle reflects narcissistic and materialistic values that are more often associated with the young. He is good for the consumer economy because he continues putting much effort and money into trying to impress others, which means he spends a lot on appearance items. He is driven by the needs of his social self at an age when many other men have moved onto a more inner-directed path of growth. Thus, while George Parker and Jack Erskine are the same age, and by general appearances approximately equal in social and economic standing, their lifestyles are quite different.

Differences in the lifestyles of George and Jack reflect differences in levels of personal development, and differences in consumer behavior. For instance, still feeling a need to make social statements in what he buys, George buys a new car more often than Jack does. The classic marketing strategy of design obsolescence does not carry with Jack, but it does with George because he still feels the need to make social statements in what he buys, consumes, and otherwise does. George has a young adult's ambition to be *in* or be ahead of others.

Jack and others like him are proving to be a boon to the auto parts industry because people in the New Customer Majority tend to buy new cars less frequently. Instead, they spend more money on parts to keep their cars in good running condition.

While some of his friends may see him as a bit immature, George is a likeable guy—life of the party, great joke teller, and generous. But beneath George's social veneer lies a suffering soul seeking daily approval from others. He lives "the unexamined life" and feels the emptiness of a midlife inner self that he ignores. In that way, self-actualization processes influence him, but he is unable to respond appropriately because he is not maturationally advanced enough to turn away from the social self toward the inner self. He remains bound to a lifestyle dominated by the temporal and materialistic values of a more youthful life. He does sense that many others in his age range have deeper feelings of purpose and completeness than he does. But this only increases his midlife angst and feeds his mounting fear of growing old. His lifestyle is that of a seeker still looking beyond the self to others for the life satisfaction that eludes him.

Aging Boomers Are Not Turning Out Like Many Said They Would

George Parker is an aging boomer. He's much like the picture painted of aging boomers back in the 1980s, when the first boomers turned 40 and nearly everyone seemed to be saying that boomers would hang onto the narcissistic, materialistic values of their youth, remain self-indulgent, and

enter the twilight of their lives more self-centered than previous generations of older people. They will fight against their aging tooth and nail, it
was said. Now, however, it is becoming clear that aging boomers are generally following the same path into later life that their parents did. Notwithstanding the fact that out of 78 million boomers some are George Parkers,
most face better prospects for a more fulfilling second half of life.

A San Francisco–based research company, American LIVES, has
dubbed a large group of people made up mostly of middle-age boomers
as *Cultural Creatives*. According to America LIVES, Cultural Creatives are
exerting strong influence on the cultural ethos both here and abroad in
other developed nations. Cultural Creatives represent a quarter of all
adults in the United States.

Cultural Creatives are projecting the transcendent values of advanced states of psychological maturation as described by Maslow, Jung,
Erikson, and others who have studied adult development in the second
half of life. Cultural Creatives do not reflect the "I am me" ethic that many
predicted aging boomers would carry with them into old age.

As this book first arrives in bookstores, the oldest boomers are 57. Despite many predictions to the contrary, the core needs of 57-year-old
boomers are generally not materially different from the core needs of
their parents at the same age. For instance, boomers core need to achieve
self-actualization is no different from their parent's need to achieve self-
actualization. Aging boomers' differences from previous generations are
a matter of style rather than of substance. They might differ in how they
meet their core needs, but not in what their core needs are. Core needs,
which are at the heart of what defines us as human beings, do not change
from one generation to the next. Without a firm grounding in the core
needs of midlife and beyond, the behavior of people in second-half markets often seems puzzling, or as the Yankelovich Monitor said in describing present day customer behavior, "more paradoxical."

THE PUZZLING BEHAVIOR OF
SECOND-HALF CUSTOMERS

Customer behavior psychologist Ralph L. Day wrote:

"Marketing professionals have learned that the mechanical use
of standard demographic variables may result in simplistic and

counter-productive segmentation strategies. As difficult as it is to do, marketers must learn to depend more heavily on the non-observable variables such as attitudes, emotions, and behavioral intentions . . . marketing professionals should [not] become better technicians, but better social and behavioral scientists"[6]

What Day calls *nonobservable variables* are the big bugaboo in consumer research, which tends to dismiss what can't be sliced, diced, and measured. Take the issue of customers' exercise of choice. Most research settles that matter by getting customers to say what they like and why they would buy it. However, for reasons pointed out in the last chapter, consumers are not highly reliable experts when it comes to reporting on their motivations because motivations are undergirded by non-observable variables.

The brand choices of first-half customers are made simpler by the fact that peers determine what is acceptable, what is *in*. This restricts their range of choice. Matters are more complicated in second-half markets. Because peers have less influence, second-half customers have the emotional liberty to select a brand from a wider range of choices. This makes predictions of their behavior a bit dicier.

Another source of puzzling behavior in the second half of life is the tendency of men to start acting more like women and women to start acting more like men. Northwestern University psychologist David Gutmann who has examined this midlife phenomenon says, "We find that, by contrast to younger men, older men are more interested in giving and receiving love than in conquering or acquiring power. We also find, across a wide range of cultures, that women age in the reverse direction, psychologically. Even in normal patriarchal societies, women become more aggressive in later life, less affiliated, and more managerial or political."[7]

Describing this as part of the maturation process, Jung saw it as men getting in touch with and integrating their *anima* (feminine side) into their later life self, and women doing the same with respect to their *animus* (masculine side). This marks the emergence of a fuller and more expressive human being. Yet, how many ads directed to middle-age and older men reflect the emergence of a more nurturing self? How many ads intended for older women are likewise appropriate? Few indeed, because most creative work in marketing is done by people well under 40 who understand manhood and womanhood from the perspective of young adulthood.

EXPERIENTIAL SEGMENTATION: A KEY TOOL IN AGELESS MARKETING

In *Market Segmentation,* Art Weinstein maintained that the greater the diversity of lifestyles of a given market, the more difficult it is to segment.[8] He wrote that in 1987. Market history since then bears out his view. Greater individuation within the customer universe—meaning greater diversity—resulting from the emergence of the New Customer Majority makes it more challenging to sort its members into neat little boxes. Making matters even more complex, second-half customers have fewer socially imposed encumbrances on their choices; thus their buying behavior reflects greater diversity.

Many argue that CRM makes customer segmentation meaningless because it enables companies to target *segments of one.* Customer segmentation is a tool for mass marketing, which Don Peppers and Martha Rogers declared dead in a 1995 *Marketing Tools* article: The mass marketing game [is] over.[9] Believing this makes brands largely irrelevant, they said: Once any marketer takes over the customer relationship, the consumer will have very little need for a mass-marketed brand name. It's that simple.[10] Peppers and Rogers' bias against branding reflects a background in direct marketing, the most numbers-driven branch of marketing and one often indifferent to brand husbandry.

But thus far, numbers-driven CRM doesn't seem to have made mass marketing obsolete. Yes, mass marketing may not be working as effectively as it once did, but that is because it is more often out of sync with today's more developmentally advanced consumer population.

Interestingly, Peppers and Rogers unwittingly explained why CRM hasn't proven to be the panacea many thought it would be when they said in the *Marketing Tools* article: The fallacy is in thinking of a "relationship" as emotional. In the 1:1 future, "relationship" will be increasingly synonymous with "convenience."

That statement contradicts findings in brain research over the past two decades indicating that emotions are the glue that holds together all voluntary relationships, whether they are relationships with other people or with companies and brands. Customer loyalty simply *cannot* exist in the absence of emotional connections with a company or brand.

In dealing with the emotional dimensions of customer behavior, which is more crucial in second-half markets than in first-half markets, basing marketing on *experiential segmentation* can be more effective than basing it on market segmentation. In experiential segmentation, brands are positioned according to the experiences they might lead to, rather than by features and functional benefits according to market segments. For example, a car can be positioned in terms of well-engineered performance attributes (product-centric positioning) that appeal to given market segments, or it can be positioned as a source of engaging experiences (customer-centric positioning), including experiences with a car dealer.

Positioning a car by its features and functional benefits limits the points of customer connection with the brand and also limits the range of customers that might be drawn toward the brand because there are only so many product features and functional benefits that will be worthy of customers' attentions. However, the range of experiential possibilities is virtually infinite because customers define them in subjective terms according to their unique worldviews, values, and aspirations. When companies position brands by product features, functional benefits, and economic values, they are working in a product-centric consciousness. Companies that position brands by experiential possibilities work from a customer-centric consciousness.

Experiential segmentation is a cornerstone of ageless marketing, which you will recall extends a brand's reach by appealing to multiple age groups. Experiential segmentation prompts customers to insert themselves into a company's customer portfolio by enticing their imaginations to flow toward its brands like a cartoon character led toward a tasty treat by a visible stream of aroma. In other words, *they self-segment.*

The main premise of experiential segmentation is that people buy experience opportunities more than they buy products. Experiential desires fall into two broad categories:

1. *Positive experiential desires.* Desires to feel comfort and pleasure.
2. *Negative experiential desires.* Desires to avoid feeling discomfort and pain.

Hence, customers' choices are based on their perceptions about how much a brand will help them enjoy feelings they want to experience or avoid feelings they don't want to experience.

Experiential segmentation makes it easier for customers to emotionally connect with a brand by enabling them to define the brand in terms of *their* perceptions, not those of a copywriter. In product-centric marketing, copywriters and artists define a brand. At a meeting that included a prominent consumer researcher, I mentioned that *authentic* customer-centric marketing lets customers define a brand. The researcher was appalled. Reflecting a product-centric mind-set, he shouted, "That's the dumbest thing I ever heard of. You can't let consumers define your brand."

The truth is, consumers have always provided the final definition of brands, and when they cannot define a brand in their favor, they reject it. Experiential segmentation only recognizes what has been true all along. A major difference in marketing in the past and the present is that when the young dominated the marketplace, brand definition was a group exercise. Today, the more individuated New Customer Majority makes brand definition more personal and idiosyncratic.

Consider what can happen when a company tries to take a brand in a new direction, as the Coca-Cola Company did with New Coke. It got burned. Once a brand has been released into the marketplace, its sponsoring company becomes a trustee of the brand on behalf of its ultimate owners—customers. A company may be the *de jure* owner, but customers are the *de facto* owners of the brand. In the end, brands only survive through collaborations between companies and customers.

A Retailer That Understands the Role of Customer Imagination in Brand Affinity

Anthropologie is the unlikely name of a company that knows how to collaborate with customers in creating and growing a brand. Launched in 1992, this outside-the-box purveyor of women's fashions and home accessories has had net sales growth of an enviable 40 percent compounded annual rate over the past five years—years of great struggle for many retailers, during which a number have disappeared into the dustbins of retailing history. A remarkable thing about Anthropologie, which had $200 million in sales in 2002, is that it has never advertised.

Anthropologie has thrown away the numbers playbook. Its approach is grounded in a customer-centric behaviorally based consciousness. It understands the experiential aspirations of women in its target category. It styles its stores and inventory in ways that prompt imaginative interchanges between customers and the brand's retail environment. Anthropologie is a concrete expression of the principle of experiential segmentation in a retail context.

In describing why Anthropologie has been so successful, architect Ron Pompei, who sets the creative direction for each Anthropologie space (no two stores are alike!) puts it this way: "We developed Anthropologie as a place for [customers] *to be*. The way people evaluate themselves and others boils down to three main things: what they have, what they do, and who they are. The mainstream focuses on what you have. Recently, what you do has become more important. *We wanted to respond to the shift toward 'who you are.*"[11] (Italics added) Bingo! Anthropologie has positioned itself to be in sync with a very major midlife issue—who am I—which is about pulling aside the mask of the social self to reveal the real self.

The *Fast Company* article in which Pompei made those remarks described Anthropologie as a retailer "selling a sense of adventure and originality—and the promise of self-discovery." Self-discovery is another prominent midlife issue. It is about discovering the *real* meaning of one's life and of all life.

Pompei says, "We wanted to create an experience that would set up the possibility of change and transformation, where the visitor's imagination was just as important as that of the designer." Another bingo! Change and transformation form the third and, perhaps, the overarching driver of behavior in the first half of the second half of life. It is a testament to the fact that personal development is a lifelong task.

Anthropologie is definitively a right brain-oriented brand. You will be hearing quite a lot throughout the rest of this book about *lateralization,* the term brain researchers use in discussing the discrete specialties of the right and left hemispheres of the human brain. Lateralization is a topic of crucial importance in understanding customers and in creating successful marketing executions. Because of its importance, this is a good place to explain more about the "right brain" and the "left brain."

The Right Way of Winning Customers Over to Your Brand

Three decades of research into the two hemispheres of the brain have yielded a number of hard facts about how we process information, be it an ad or whatever. Most readers probably already know that the left brain is associated with reasoning functions and the right brain with creative functions. But there are numerous other specialties that everyone in marketing should know about. For example, while the left brain plays the primary role in processing words, the right brain plays the primary role in processing visual images. In fact, because the right brain has no independent word processing abilities, it processes information in the language of the senses—visual, acoustical, olfactory, tactile, and taste. An ad "speaks" to the right brain when it stirs neurons in the *somatosensory* system in the cortex, or deeper down in the limbic system, which olfactory neurons call home.

The right brain is also the primary zone of emotional functions in the brain's cortex—the thin convoluted covering that gives the brain something of an English walnut look, and is sometimes called "the thinking cap." We think with our left brains and feel with our right brains. That is a bit of an oversimplification, but close enough to the truth that, outside of a lecture hall presentation on neuroscience, it works quite adequately.

Marketers stand to gain in very large ways by knowing something about how the brain works. Brain research, especially in the last decade, has revealed an astonishing amount of information on motivations, perceptions, emotions, and reasoning that can lead the way to curing the sagging productivity in marketing and reverse the declining efficacy of consumer research.

Anyone tempted to think that brain science has little of critical importance to offer marketers and researchers is dismissing a source of knowledge tools that in the deft hands of others will transform the face of consumer research and marketing sooner rather than later. Already, brain imaging experts are bringing their technology into marketing research as they look for income sources other than clinical applications. While brain scientists using neuroimaging equipment are gaining astonishing insights into brains while thinking is going on, there remains the task for marketers to put these insights to work. Knowing something about the wondrous and often mysterious workings of customers' brains will be of inestimable value in accomplishing this.

I do not know how much the folks at Anthropologie know about the brain, but I suspect someone has a pretty good idea. All the signs of that were evident to me while making my first tour of an Anthropologie store. It was an engaging sensuous experience clearly directed toward the right brain where relationships are formed and maintained.

Each store is designed to stimulate imaginative intercourse between customers and the retail environment. Imagination is a specialty of the right brain. The left brain is not so inclined. Rather than seeking new ways and new experiences, the left brain is more comfortable following a path already traveled. It has less appetite for adventure than the more playful right brain does.

Anthropologie connects with what are called *Being Experience* aspirations in Chapter 14. Being Experiences are ineffable, transcendent experiences that stimulate the pleasure centers of the brain. They turn on the spigots through which endorphins flow to give us those feelings of highs. Being Experiences challenge fully rational explanation because they are sensuously experienced as feelings. Feelings always extend beyond the capacity of words to capture their full impact. They are more heartfelt than mindfelt.

Anthropologie disavows direct selling. Its salespeople are not trained to qualify prospects and close sales. Instead, they seek to jump start shoppers' creative juices to define what they see in an Anthropologie store in highly personal and creative terms. When they do so, *customers sell themselves*.

Anthropologie is not afraid to go against retail tradition. For example, most retailers spend considerable effort finding ways to control and manipulate customers. They place displays in key spots, hoping to increase spontaneous purchases. They plot the pathways they want customers to take through their spaces.

Anthropologie thinks differently about its customers. There are no aisles to control their passage through a store. It employs a somewhat chaotic right brain approach in laying out each store. Floor plans randomly provide customers with sensuous, scintillating, evocative experiences through which the customer ultimately defines her experiences. There is customer relationship management thinking at Anthropologie. The customer manages the relationship. Anthropologie is just a catalyst of delightful experiences.

Experiential Segmentation Calls for Rethinking the Idea of Brand Positioning

Al Ries and Jack Trout introduced the concept of *product positioning* in 1972 with a series of articles in *Advertising Age* entitled "The Positioning Era," and in so doing, quite possibly introduced the last big original marketing idea in the pre-Internet era.

Ries and Trout said positioning, which is about getting a brand fixed in customers' minds on a mass market basis, is most effective when it travels into the cerebral folds of the brain on wings of simplicity and without equivocation—for example, Avis: "We try harder." Miller Lite: "Everything you want in a beer. And less." Coca-Cola: "The real thing." But, with due respect to Al Ries and Jack Trout—and they deserve much—the New Customer Majority has changed the rules of positioning.

The more autonomous bent of the older mind tends to make it less receptive to copywriters telling them what a brand means. Among members of the New Customer Majority, marketers will often find it more productive to employ *conditional positioning* in lieu of *absolute positioning*, which worked better in younger markets of the past. Conditional positioning encourages customers to *subjectively* define a brand in ways that resonate with their unique blend of values, views, needs, and behavior.

Reis and Trout's landmark book *Positioning: The Battle for Your Mind* speaks to the product-centric objective of controlling customers and what they think. Absolute positioning is about the product, not about the customer. Taglines usually reflect whether a brand is positioned from a product-centric perspective or from a customer-centric perspective. BMW's "The Ultimate Driving Machine" and Xerox's "The Document Company" are examples of product-centric absolute positioning.

The aim of absolute positioning is to project a brand's image in such a way that everyone sees the brand the same way. Absolute positioning is left brain–oriented because the left brain prefers certainty over ambiguity. This is why Reis and Trout's ideas on positioning were spot on when younger age groups dominated the marketplace. To borrow a certain president's word, the young are not very much into "nuancing." They want things straight, clean, and clear. No ambiguities. No nuances. Brain scans of adolescents show weaker responses to subtle changes in facial expressions than adults experience. Younger minds, for example, find it harder to tell disgust from fear in photographs presented to them while being studied in a neuroimaging device.

As worthy as absolute positioning was when first-half customers ruled the marketplace, it is often too hard-edged, too controlling, and too determinative in today's more individuated and autonomous customer universe.

While absolute positioning tends to be left brain–biased, conditional positioning has a right brain bias. The right brain is more comfortable with the ambiguities of conditional positioning. Ambiguity invites more creative interpretation of product messages, including positioning statements, than unambiguous absolute positioning does. Ambiguity makes room for customers to attribute to a brand the traits they like best in people. Apple Computer's "Think different" is an example of a conditionally positioned tagline. It is customer-centric, not product-centric. It invites customers' creative participation in the brand definition process. What constitutes thinking "different" is completely an individual matter— *different from what?*

Conditionally positioned brands can reach across generational divides because they make it easier for each person, regardless of age, to emotionally connect with a brand. Harley-Davidson is a perfect example of a brand that does just that. Its advertising recognizes that there is a bit of Harley in each of us whatever our age—a dash of the rebel, as it were. To make it possible for both 20-year-old studs (and adventuresome young ladies) and 50-year-old granddads (and grandmas!) to connect with a Harley, Carmichael Lynch never shows a person on a Harley clearly enough that anyone can tell the person's age, and often, not even a person's gender.

A couple of now-retired but still widely remembered taglines of two competing beer brands illustrate the sometimes-subtle differences between conditional positioning and absolute positioning of products. Miller Lite's tagline "Everything you always wanted in a beer. And less." may at first seem conditional because it's about what customers may want, but it is more aptly viewed as an example of absolute conditioning because it implicitly promises that Miller Lite will please the palate while doing so with fewer calories. It is product performance-oriented.

In contrast, Michelob's "The night is for Michelob" exemplified conditional positioning. It invited people to use their imaginations to define the experiential possibilities that can be associated with the brand. The tagline is not about the product but about a gateway to enjoyable experiences. This makes it a customer-centric tagline.

Conditional Positioning Increases a Brand's Sales Potential

Conditional positioning is not just another clever idea that might draw temporary interest until another clever idea comes along. It is a powerful marketing tool based on research about how people respond to absolute statements versus conditional statements. Harvard psychologist Ellen Langer has done some of this research. Langer found in multiple experiments that the more absolutely someone defines an object for others, the less creatively the others will perceive it. For example, people in one group in one of her experiments were told that certain objects were just what everyone would agree they were: a hair dryer *was* a hair dryer; an extension cord *was* an extension cord; a dog's chew toy *was* a dog's chew toy. Subjects in the second group were told, "This *could be* a hair dryer, this *could be* an extension cord, this *could be* a dog's chew toy."[12]

Subjects in both groups were then given forms to fill out, with researchers purposely giving them erroneous instructions. Then the researchers, with mock embarrassment, announced the error and told people in each group that the project had to be cancelled because there were no more blank forms. Subjects in the first group accepted the researchers' decision without further question. However, those in the second group came up with a creative solution to the problem. They reasoned that because the dog's chew toy was made of rubber, it could be used as an eraser to restore the blanks in the forms.

Subjects in both groups felt a vested interest in seeing the research project through, but only those to whom the objects used in the experiment were conditionally defined put their imaginations to work so that they could see the research through. To get customers to do the equivalent, a brand's positioning should be more about the customer than the product. That gives the customers a vested interest in imaginatively inferring meanings of the brand according to his or her terms, not those of a copywriter.

TRANSCENDING THE AGE OF EXPLICITNESS

We live in an age of explicitness. Hollywood movies leave little to the imagination. Reality TV as well as television action programs leave little to the imagination. Absolute positioning leaves little to the imagination. From a neurological perspective, explicitness feeds both stimulus *and* response to the brain, thereby dulling imaginative responses. They aren't necessary because everything is spelled out. Thus, explicitness preempts imaginative interpretation of the stimulus. Brain scans of children watching a story on television show much lower levels of neuronal activity than brain scans of children who listen to the same story without the visuals.

When she was 15, my daughter Stephanie, who has seen more than her share of Stephen King and *Friday the 13th* movies, said after seeing *The Blair Witch Project* that it was the scariest movie she had ever seen. *The Blair Witch Project* was intensely scary to her because of what it *didn't* show, the same cinematic technique so famously and effectively used by Alfred Hitchcock. *Blair Witch* left room for Stephanie's imagination to go to work and, like millions of young people who grew up in the age of explicitness, she found the movie almost unbelievably terrifying.

One reason why response rates in advertising have plummeted is a poverty of storytelling skills combined with a surfeit of explicitness that forecloses involvement of viewers and listeners' imaginations. The culture of Madison Avenue reflects obsession with technical novelty, while giving little attention to involving customers' imaginations, as *Blair Witch* did for millions of young moviegoers.

Going through the processes of experiential segmentation to identify engaging experiences with which a brand can be associated and *implicitly* representing those experiences through the art of conditional positioning can yield powerful product messages. The question is, will clients buy into an ad that leaves out details so customers' imaginations can fill in the missing pieces? Or will they be bound by the classic insistence that you have to tell consumers about the product, why it's better than any other product, and why they should buy it now?

A perennial problem that marketing agencies endure is negotiating the clients' opinions of what will work and what won't. Time and again, the account executive who tries to keep the client happy is caught in the middle. He battles with the client and returns to his agency to battle with the creative director. Of course, when the client prevails in a decision that turns out wrong, it's usually the agency's fault.

There is a way to reduce the undue role that opinions play in marketing decisions, whether they be on the client side or the agency side, and in the process improve marketing productivity. It involves curing the largest defect in the edifice of marketing: the total absence of an empirically grounded foundation that is subscribed to by everyone on both the agency side and client side, which is the platform from which everyone works in carrying out their marketing-related tasks. The next section of this book describes such a foundation that is soundly rooted in empirical science. Companies chart their futures by drawing on empirical science in technology to produce new and better products. It's now time that they and their marketers and consumer researchers begin following directions set by empirically grounded behavioral science in carrying out marketing tasks.

THE NATURE
OF CUSTOMERS

Believing that by querying customers we can learn almost everything necessary to understand them, the foundations of human behavior nestled in the breast of Nature get ignored. A profound understanding of customers depends on understanding the role of Nature in the origins of their behavior.

Consider this: A new infant begins life with a schedule of developmental events that marks her movement toward adulthood. That schedule is laid out by Nature in DNA code. But development does not end with adulthood. All our lives we experience Nature's constant nudging to continue developing into ever more complex and higher functioning beings. This is not so much for individual benefit, as ultimately for the benefit of all. Nature does not leave the fate of our kind to individual will. Taking the long view, she protects the future of our species against individual folly by setting the general course of each life with a bias toward preserving humanity. Pleasure is the seductive elixir she uses to entice us to follow her will.

As the Roman philosopher Seneca said, "All we must do to live, Nature compels us through pleasure to do it." But sometimes we get detoured as Pinocchio did on the day he abandoned his path to school to join a band of toughs headed for Pleasure Island. Still, as with Pinocchio, something stitched into our makeup time and again pulls most of us back from self-destructive paths. It is the nurturing tug of Nature bent on restoring us to a pathway toward what Abraham Maslow called *full humanness*.

Part Two is an examination of powerful forces that influence customer (human) behavior, forces of which they have no direct awareness. To not know of these forces and the dynamics of their operation is to have only a few fragments of the total picture of customer (human) behavior.

4

NATURE VERSUS NURTURE
A Marketer's Perspective

A friend who is a computer science engineer at Sun Microsystems called me one day to complain about having had to spend most of the previous week with "marketers." He uttered the term as though it were an expletive.

"*God,* they're an insecure bunch!"

"What do you mean, George?" I asked.

"Marketers are too defensive, too close to the chest. They're not open. They get pissed off when you challenge them. Engineers are much more open to challenge. Sometimes we'll do a white paper on an idea we have, and then ask colleagues to tear it apart. That's how we learn."

"But George," I said, "engineers have something marketers don't have."

Eager to have this puzzle solved, George snapped, "What's that?"

"A common foundation. It's called mathematics. Marketers don't have a common foundation."

"Why does not having a common foundation make marketers defensive?" George asked.

"It's simple. Without a common foundation to work from, everyone determines his own starting point and assumptions. With no basic rules that everyone follows, opinions often play a bigger role in marketing than facts. Engineering is not a matter of opinion. It's about facts. It's easier to defend facts than opinions, so what you experienced last week was marketers' insecurity about how well their opinions could stand up to your engineer's left brain scrutiny."

I added, "To have an interesting experience, go to a marketing seminar. It's like the Tower of Babel. Marketers are all over the place about what works and what doesn't. Speakers may follow common themes, but the paths they take often run in different directions. Aside from some clichés, nothing is tied to a fundamental set of propositions that everyone agrees with."

"That's crazy. How can you get any efficiency when everyone thinks differently?"

Engineers think in terms of efficiency. George didn't know that marketing is a grossly inefficient discipline. Sooner or later everyone in marketing hears about department store magnate John Wanamaker's lament that half of his advertising was wasted, but he couldn't determine which half. Any engineer would find that level of efficiency intolerable.

It is no secret that opinions play an indefensibly undue role in marketing, whether they emanate from the agency side or the client side. Gerald Zaltman, a marketing professor at Harvard, wrote in his book *How Customers Think* that Peter Barbeck-Letmathe, vice chairman and CEO of Nestlé, told a group of agribusiness leaders at the Harvard Business School that marketers "treat personal common sense as superior to science-based knowledge and to what the humanities have to tell us." *Personal common sense* is another term for opinion.

Zaltman then went on to quote another CEO of a global consumer products firm:

> "If [marketers] read popular business magazines, they feel on top of things. They disdain anything else. People with these attitudes would not last in any other profession."[1]

Not only do customers increasingly have problems with marketers' credibility; denizens of the executive suite are having similar problems. So, as marketers (and researchers) do, do we simply defensively say "they don't get it" or blame external conditions over which we have no control, or do we start looking to ourselves for reasons why we are not looking as good as we used to as a profession?

This and the next three chapters take on the challenge of making it possible for marketers to get beyond marketing based on anecdotal articles in popular business magazines, opinion exchanges that ignore science-based knowledge, and, indeed, the statistical caricatures of customers that too often guide marketers into dead ends. This chapter starts by introducing the first two planks in a *wholly* new framework for customer research and marketing practice. This new framework takes into account two seminal facts about the sources of human behavior that have been long ignored in consumer research, marketing practice, and, indeed, academe:

1. The roots of behavior lie in our biological makeup, beyond the direct reach of the conscious mind, thus undiscoverable by traditional consumer research.
2. The conscious mind acts as the executive officer who senses, perceives, thinks about, and acts on urges that originate outside of consciousness.

Research and marketing have been too preoccupied with what's in customers' conscious minds, giving scant attention to forces in the brain outside of consciousness that predispose much of what's in customers' minds. This chapter describes two seminal principles of human behavior that offer a way for researchers and marketers to become less dependent on customers to learn about their needs, motivations, and other dimensions of their behavior.

A NEW MARKETING PARADIGM: *DEVELOPMENTAL RELATIONSHIP MARKETING*

No branch of behavioral science offers richer practical insight into customers' needs and motivations—nor is more ignored—than *developmental psychology*. What I learned from developmental psychology enabled me 14 years ago to correctly predict the leading values, attitudes, needs, and behavior in today's marketplace. Let me reveal that I am not a psychologist. I simply have been fascinated with human behavior since the days many years ago when I was a landscape architect who read books on psychology to learn how to design better playgrounds, parks, and community master plans.

In 1979, I read my first book on the brain, Richard Restak's *The Brain: The Last Frontier.* I got hooked. Since then I have read dozens of "brain books," tracking with a never-ending sense of awe the rising tide of new developments in brain science. On July 17, 1990, President George H. W. Bush issued a proclamation designating the 1990s as the decade of the brain. It called for a sharpened focus on exploring Restak's last frontier. New developments in brain research mushroomed during the 1990s, presaging dramatic, even radical, changes in how we see and think about ourselves. Many of the new insights into human nature as seen through brain studies have yet to deeply penetrate mainstream thought although articles and television shows about the brain for popular audiences are on the rise. By now, many people have heard of the Mozart Effect, the influence of classical music on childhood mental development. Former Governor Zell Miller of Georgia became aware of the Mozart Effect and issued an executive order calling for every mother of a newborn infant to be given a CD of classical music.

Growing awareness of new insights into human behavior arising from contemporary brain research is just beginning to take place in some sectors of consumer research and marketing. It can only be a matter of time before a tipping point is reached and how customers are researched and marketed to will be radically changed. This book is intended to make a contribution to expanding the awareness of forces in the brain, behind the curtains of consciousness, that help to catalyze and mold customer behavior.

This book integrates key findings from brain science with empirically derived tenets of developmental psychology to formulate a new paradigm for consumer research and marketing called *developmental relationship marketing* (DRM). DRM is a heuristic or nonalgorithmic framework for discovering salient information about customers and for guiding the development and implementation of marketing programs.

DRM facilitates an authentic 360-degree view of customers. The term *360-degree view of customers* originated in the CRM space, but CRM actually precludes a 360-degree view of customers. With its dependence on reducing customers and their attributes to algorithms, CRM programs bypass crucial nonquantifiable dimensions of customers' subjective selves. Dreams and nightmares, hopes and fears, and a universe of other subjectively experienced factors exert strong influences on shopping and buying motivations and decisions. Yet all this goes unrecognized in CRM initiatives. You can track what people do, and CRM systems do this well; however, you cannot track with certainty *why* people do what they do. Nor can you predict with great certainty what they will do in the future. Just think about how wrong many of the generalized predictions about aging boomers are proving to be.

The only way to obtain anything approaching a 360-degree view of customers is by integrating the biological and psychological generators of their behavior to obtain a *bicameral* view of the *whole* customer. What follows is the outline of a foundation for all marketing and consumer research activity that I hope would give my friend George better respect for marketers.

THE ULTIMATE SOURCES OF CUSTOMER BEHAVIOR

A bicameral view of customer behavior that integrates biology with psychology creates a far more complete picture of customers than researchers and marketers have traditionally had to work with. The two-part view of customer behavior described in this chapter begins to pave the way for reducing research costs and increasing marketing productivity. Throughout later chapters case histories will demonstrate the effectiveness of this truer-to-life view of customers.

Everyone knows that visual depth perception results from a convergence of the lines of sight from two eyes. Similarly, an in-depth understanding of customer (human) behavior depends on the convergence of multiple perspectives. Too often, people promote a single perspective as *the truth,* such as in the classical nature versus nurture argument. The truth is that nature and nurture work together to shape behavior. A bicameral view of customer (human) behavior reflects a sighting taken from the vantage point of nature—the *biological realm*—and a sighting taken from the vantage point of nurture—the *psychological realm.* At the point of convergence of those two lines of sight is seen the authentic 360-degree picture of customers. (See Figure 4.1.) More specifically:

- The *biological realm* is the seat of what defines us as humans, hence the realm in which we are most like each other. DNA, the biochemical encoder of physical development and the behavioral dis-

FIGURE 4.1 *A Bicameral View of Behavior*

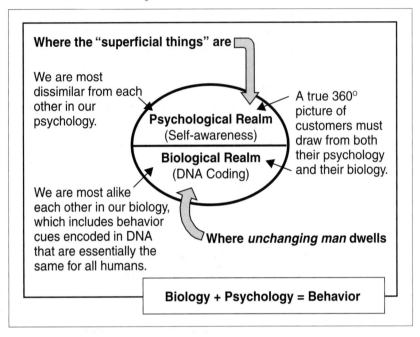

Where the "superficial things" are

We are most dissimilar from each other in our psychology.

Psychological Realm
(Self-awareness)

Biological Realm
(DNA Coding)

A true 360° picture of customers must draw from both their psychology and their biology.

We are most alike each other in our biology, which includes behavior cues encoded in DNA that are essentially the same for all humans.

Where *unchanging man* dwells

Biology + Psychology = Behavior

positions that are essential to continuation of the human species, rules in this realm with a bias toward Nature's plan for perpetuation of the human species. This is the foundation of *unchanging* human behavior.

- The *psychological realm* is the seat of the conscious mind, the theater in which our values, views, and feelings project onto the screens of awareness to activate rational processing and from which we project ourselves into the outside world. This realm contains recallable memories of the past, awareness of the present, and sense of the future. Here, we mentally conjure up and creatively manipulate options from which we choose courses of action and anticipate outcomes of actions before they are taken.

Most of us adhere to the traditional idea in Western cultures that conscious behavior originates in the mind, be it a whole or misshapen mind, a brilliant or dim-witted mind, a conscientious or sociopathic mind. But the roots of temporal behavior are biological. What we do in our minds is mediate responses to urges that arise biologically.

Assuming all behavior is driven by some purpose, however benign or malevolent, I define behavior as *goal-oriented activity arising from the inter-*

action of biological and psychological functions. Biology initiates; psychology disposes.

CUSTOMERS ARE MORE ALIKE UNDER THE SKIN THAN WE THINK

Scientists who mapped the human genome made a discovery that astonished even them: Humans are genetically 99.99 percent the same—the most alike of all mammals. Our closest cousins, chimpanzees, are only 94 percent genetically alike. As remote from marketing as the subject of the human genome may seem, the discovery of human genetic sameness has major significance for consumer research and marketing. Were he still with us, Bill Bernbach, one of marketing's greatest minds, would immediately see the significance.

Not long after World War II, Bill Bernbach turned a car conceived by Hitler that was unsafe, unheated, cramped, and propelled by little more than an estate-sized lawn mower engine into an American icon. The car did not even have a fuel gauge. When you ran out of gas, you turned an auxiliary tank lever and had one gallon to get you to the nearest gas station. Members of Bernbach's staff thought the Volkswagen was such a loser brand that they vigorously argued against taking the account. Bernbach took it on anyway and wrote into marketing history one of the greatest brand stories of all time. The foundation of Bernbach's thinking was this belief:

> "Human nature hasn't changed for a billion years. It won't even change in the next billion years. Only the superficial things have changed. It is fashionable to talk about the *changing* man. A communicator must be concerned with the *unchanging* man—what compulsions drive him, what instincts dominate his every action, even though his language too often camouflages what *really* motivates him."[2]

Bernbach turned the ugly duckling VW into a rousing success by presenting it to the marketplace with disarming self-deprecation (e.g., "Think small"), an affect that charms *unchanging man*. He gave the VW a personality that symbolized the anti-status-symbol mood of the 1960s. The VW was latched onto by young people in the 1960s in reflection of one of the strongest influences on unchanging man in adolescence and the earliest years of adulthood: the urge to challenge the previous generation. This imperative is present in every generation; only the way in which it is acted upon changes.

Had Bernbach based his strategy for VW on the superficial things of changing man, the campaign would have failed. Customers would have compared VW's features and functional benefits with those of other cars. It would have drawn thumbs down on nearly all points. Bernbach positioned the "Bug" in the public's mind not as a product, but as a unique experience in self-expression. Some people bought and drove it as an anti–status symbol even though they could afford a Rolls Royce. I knew a wealthy young lawyer in the early 1960s who had a robin's egg blue VW convertible, and an equally well-off young physician who also had the convertible model, one he had custom-colored in deep forest green. The wealthy lawyer openly called it his anti–status symbol, which I found interesting given that he left his office each day in his robin's egg blue VW to return home to a multimillion-dollar estate for which I had been commissioned to design a comprehensive landscape plan. (I wonder to what consumer segment he would be assigned.)

The marketing plan for the first VWs in the United States was not based on the superficial things of segmented consumers, but on values that influence behavior across a wide range of ages and socioeconomic strata, values that persist from one generation to the next.

When the New Beetle was released four decades after Bernbach's first VW campaign, it remained true to the personality of the first model. Sales drew from a broad spectrum of customer types. The success of the New Beetle's re-release has shown, as Bernbach knew, that when a brand taps the soul of unchanging man it will likely never have to change its core personality. As Polonius advised Laertes in *Hamlet*, "above all else, to thine self be true," be you person or brand. Brands usually die when they betray themselves.

The Dog That Inspired a Car's Personality

Jungian psychiatrist Clotaire Rapaille helped Chrysler design perhaps the first car purposely intended to connect with unchanging man. Bernbach's Volkswagen marketing was Chrysler's inspiration. Chrysler wanted a car that would generate a cult-like following as Bernbach succeeded in doing for the VW decades earlier. Cult-like behavior draws from the visceral realm of biology, not from the rational realm of psychology.

Rapaille created an archetypal profile to guide the design of the PT Cruiser. Archetypes are unformed images in the biological realm that predispose people across the planet to infer similar meanings from given images and symbols, such as God, devil, angel, hero, mother, baby, lover, circle, pyramid, etc. Because archetypes appear to be ever-present in every generation, we might view them as inchoate images in an undeveloped film that become visible upon interaction with an external catalyst. We don't acquire these undeveloped images from culture. They are fully present in the formed *in utero* brain.

Rapaille faced a challenge similar to one that Bernbach faced 40 years earlier. The original VW for the United States was to be marketed at a time when big fast cars with flashy cutting-edge styling were favored. As Rapaille began his work, Americans were buying "big" in the form of SUVs, minivans, luxury sedans, and plush trucks. Subcompacts, like PT Cruiser was planned to be, tend to be bought more for economic reasons than for their designs. That hardly seems a good foundation for generating a cult-like following.

Chrysler also wanted to sell PT Cruisers overseas. However, car owners abroad generally prefer subcompacts made in their own land. PT Cruiser's design team had to simultaneously compete with American's love for "big" and the preferences of car owners abroad for made-at-home subcompacts. No small challenge, that.

Bryan Nesbitt, who led PT Cruiser's exterior design team, tells how he and his team settled on a brand persona that could appeal across diverse cultures and customer segments. One day Nesbitt chanced upon a book on dogs. As though guided by a divine hand, he opened the book and suddenly before his eyes was the inspiration for PT Cruiser's personality.

"It showed a picture of a flat-faced pug. It was described as small, but able to hold its ground. Street smart. Confident. Affectionate. The ultimate companion. And rewarding to be with. That is what I wanted the PT Cruiser to be."[3] Nesbitt made these remarks in an interview after PT Cruiser was on the street. It makes a nice story, but do people really see PT Cruiser as having the same attributes as a flat-faced pug with round popping eyes?

I sat down with my wife for evening cocktails on the day I read the Nesbitt interview and asked her to describe PT Cruiser if it were a living personality. She answered, "Small, but it can hold its own. Smart in a practical way. Affectionate. Fun to be with." Bingo! She identified four of the six traits that Nesbitt wanted PT Cruiser to project. Each of those traits are perennial values of unchanging man. PT Cruiser's design team successfully connected with my wife, Linda, in the biological realm, where PT Cruisers and pugs are archetypal kin.

PT Cruiser's retro look helped solved the challenge in U.S. markets of small versus big. Subtly reminiscent of a 1930s gangster car, PT Cruiser has the affect of the archetypal outlaw—one of a dozen or so of the top archetypal images projected by successful brands, according to Margaret Mark and Carol Pearson, authors of the *Hero and the Outlaw,* a landmark work on brands and archetypes. The outlaw in PT Cruiser's persona does not celebrate mobsters' values. Rather, it reflects universal attitudes about laws against fun, which the Volstead Act that established Prohibition in 1919 was widely seen to be. Many otherwise rules-abiding people went against Prohibition by imbibing mobsters' booze. Unchanging man resists restrictions placed on his modest pleasures by others. Self-control is one thing, but control by others is another.

PT Cruiser proved, as Bernbach did four decades earlier, that a brand's market potential can be greater if it is not tightly identified with one customer segment or another. By connecting with unchanging man, PT Cruiser became a segment-busting brand.

Unfortunately, PT Cruiser may not be able to retain its panache according to a friend who has been in the vehicle marketing game at the manufacturer's level for years. He says that in recent times PT has fallen into the"incentives trap." This, he believes, tends to trivialize the archetypal affects that originally brought it enviable success as a new car brand.

CONCLUSION

As already observed several times, most of what companies would like to know about customers—their deeper needs, archetypal hot buttons, root motivations, unrecognized but powerful emotions, etc.—is not accessible to the conscious minds of subjects in consumer research. The most that subjects can do for researchers, to be admittedly arbitrary, is to give researchers maybe 5 percent of the total information companies would like to have—perhaps less. People are fond of saying we only use 5 percent of our brains. Well, what goes on in the other 95 percent? By ignoring the biological roots of needs, motivations, and behavior, and how their presence comes to be known by the conscious mind, researchers can't hope to capture more than 5 percent of *available* information about customers

This question now arises: Because behavior draws from both our biological and psychological makeup, how do our brains and minds bridge the material biological realms of nature and the immaterial psychological realms of nurture to yield coherent and fruitful behavior?" Answering that question is the task of the next three chapters.

5

THE NEW *S* WORD
IN MARKETING

Sex, invoked to sell everything
from cars to you name it, has long been the big *S* word in marketing. But
the new big *S* word in marketing is *self-actualization*. As noted earlier, for
the first time in marketing history—in *all* history for that matter—the
majority of adults are living in the years of life when self-actualization
needs exert a major influence on customer behavior. To ignore this seminal fact in marketing is to ignore one of the biggest influences on New
Customer Majority behavior.

A PRIMAL DESIRE THAT IS AS STRONG
AS THE SEX DESIRE

Melinda Davis, founder and CEO of the Next Group, a New York–
based consumer research firm, obliquely but forcefully speaks to the motivating forces of self-actualization needs when she says:

Human behavior is now being ruled by a new pleasure imperative
—a new primal desire—that is at least as powerful as the one that
brought each of us into the world.[1]

How many twentysomethings or even thirtysomethings believe that nothing is more powerful than the sex drive? Yet, Melinda Davis proposes that some new motivating force has at least equal status with the sex desire. How can that be?

First, a minor quibble: Davis prefaced *primal desire* with the adjective *new*, but it is not the desire itself that is new, for then it would not be primal. What is new is the elevated importance of that primal desire in contemporary life, and certainly in the consumer economy.

Seeing how sex might have gained a new competitor for people's attention, as Davis suggests, is made easier by viewing the issue in terms of the most powerful primal desire of all: to preserve and perpetuate self and the species. Sex is the device by which we satisfy that desire *physically*. Offspring allow us to preserve something of ourselves generations ahead while helping to perpetuate the species. What Davis calls the new primal desire is about the *metaphysical* preservation and perpetuation of self and the species. In more familiar terms, it is about self-actualization as Maslow defined it.

For sure, people of reproductive age in the first half of life spend more than a little amount of time thinking about and pursuing sex. And though only an infinitesimal amount of that time is actually spent with purposeful intention of producing a baby—if ever—sex serves other self-preservation needs such as promoting companionship, getting support from others, and even contributing to one's vocational success even though physical innocence may prevail. Sexy people are attractive people and that helps quite a lot in getting one's way, even without anything happening physically.

What happens when men grow older and stop thinking about sex once every 27 minutes—*Is that really true?*—and women start thinking more about other things? The answer is, they seek to preserve and perpetuate self and species in nonphysical or *metaphysical* ways. College campuses around the country are studded with evidence of this in buildings named after people who had enough money to buy naming rights. Thousands of foundations organized to support everything from shelters for homeless cats to cures for human scourges offer further evidence.

The new *S* word in marketing—self-actualization—is changing what it takes to be successful with today's more life-seasoned customers. So let's find out what self-actualization is all about.

The Origin of the Term *Self-Actualization*

Abraham Maslow may have never used Bill Bernbach's term *unchanging man* but he was fully aware that the foundations of human behavior lay not in the ephemeral traces of the mind but in the enduring biology of homo sapiens where unchanging man dwells. Otherwise, what defines us as human would not have survived over the millennia in essentially the same form. We would be something else today. Maslow's famous hierarchy reflects the 99.99 percent human sameness that repeats generation after generation to preserve unchanging man's behavioral foundations.

Most everyone in marketing has heard of Maslow's pyramidal structure of basic human needs (see Figure 5.1). It has endured as one of the most influential models of human motivation. It is often cited in organizational management literature and was woven throughout the work of Douglas McGregor who formulated the x-y theory of business management, which sought balance between authority-driven management and participation management.

As nearly everyone knows, self-actualization tops out Maslow's list of basic needs. He proposed that people generally enter a self-actualization track only in the second half of life and that it usually takes five to six decades of living to reach a continuing state of self-actualization.

I'm sometimes asked, How will you know when you are self-actualizing? It won't be something that happens all at once, no more than arrival in adolescence is a sudden, cohesive event. Hallmark doesn't make cards saying, "Congratulations on achieving self-actualization," as though it were an adult equivalent of bar mitzvah. In the first place, one does not achieve self-actualization; *one lives in a state of self-actualization*. It is the developmental target toward which a newborn infant is pointed by instructions in her DNA for developmental sequencing and timing.

In psychological terms, self-actualization is the end game of life, which absent untoward events, we all move toward from infancy on. However, the *teleological* pull of self-actualization rarely becomes self-apparent before the cusp of midlife when the journey toward the summits of full maturity reaches the final grand stage. A person might become aware of first entering a final self-actualizing track when he or she begins to more deeply examine the meaning of life, personally and in general. Sometimes one experiences regrets for what they have not accomplished.

FIGURE 5.1   *Maslow's Hierarchy of Basic Human Needs*

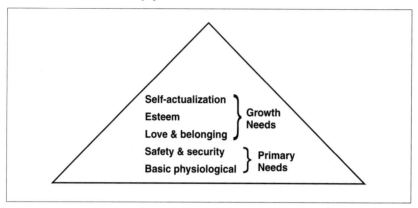

Sometimes one experiences feelings of emptiness despite what one has accomplished. In either case, the guiding hands of Nature indicate that it is time to begin taking stock of the meaning of one's life, a necessary precursor to reaching a state of self-actualization.

Self-actualization is not a term coined by Abraham Maslow, as many believe. Kurt Goldstein, a psychologist who studied brain-damaged soldiers, coined the term. Many of his patients, generally young men in their late teens and 20s, appeared to have catapulted ahead in maturation. Their worldviews were more like those of 60-year-olds than like those of people just beginning adult life. Goldstein described these patients as maturing or self-actualizing decades ahead of most people. A good guess is that a review of Goldstein's patient records would reveal that those who attained a state of self-actualization had suffered left hemisphere brain injuries, resulting in a shunting of certain mental activities over to the right brain. This is not academic.

WHY SOME MENTAL FUNCTIONS MIGRATE TOWARD THE RIGHT BRAIN IN THE SECOND HALF OF LIFE

In what at the time was somewhat intuitive, *SAM* 1990 explained:

As people grow older, they tend to move from a left brain orientation to a right brain orientation, which among other things, sharpens their sense of reality, increases their emotional capacities, and enhances their sense of connectedness to others and life in general.

Since that statement was made, discoveries have been made that support it. That statement continued (in edited form):

As people age, the central nervous system slows down. This leads to a slower processing of visual and acoustical information, which reduces the capacity for distinguishing between colors and light intensities as well as between acoustical tones, pitches, and volume. In an attempt to compensate for these growing deficits, a person's processing of externally derived information may at times lead to excessive and uncoordinated neuronal firings. By shifting to more right-hemisphere-oriented information processing, a person may be reducing some of the neuronal overloading. Robert Ornstein observes in *The Psychology of Consciousness* that the right hemisphere processes information with greater simplicity of operation. Jacqueline Wonder and Priscilla Donovan report in *Whole Brain Thinking* that an overload of words, arguments, or demands for concentration exhaust the left hemisphere which then allows the right to take over.

Evidence of increased dependency upon right brain information processing also lies in the fact that while older people tend to suffer declines in the ability to recognize and recall nonsense syllables (analysis of verbal information is generally processed on the left), they retain without decrement their ability to recall visual images.

Susan Whitbourne adds further evidence of a psychobiological shift to greater right brain dependence in her research which has led her to suggest that older people may compensate for decrements in short-term memory by using life experiences and repetition of stimulus trace (the "etching" of stimuli into memory). Reminiscing and repetitive mental activity tend to invoke right brain activity or at least cooperation between both hemispheres.

Providing there is significant validity to the foregoing discussion of hemispheric shift in later life, the conclusion emerges that this shift can occur without respect to levels of maturity, notwithstanding Maslow's characterizations of how highly matured people change in their cognitive patterns. It may simply be that the more mature a person is, the more pronounced the shift. In any event, it would seem to be a good bet that heavier employment in marketing programs of stimuli designed to invoke right brain responses would generally lead to greater response from older consumers.[2]

This migration of mental functions toward the right hemisphere strongly correlates with many of the changes that have taken place in the leading worldviews, values, views, and behavior in the marketplace since the emergence of the New Customer Majority. This migration of mental functions also helps to explain weaker responses to marketing communications because they still reflect the more left brain bias of marketing in the past. Marketing responsiveness will not materially improve unless marketing communications begin reflecting more of a right brain bias.

HOW THE DEVELOPMENTAL CHANGES IN WORLDVIEWS ALTER CUSTOMERS' PERSPECTIVES

Every product message that a customer's senses detect is screened through the lens of his or her worldview. In her quite remarkable book *The Quantum Self,* a landmark treatise in my estimation on the subject of consciousness, Danah Zohar defines worldview as:

"A theme which integrates the sense of self, the sense of self and others, and the sense of how these relate to the wider world—to Nature and other creatures, to the environment as a whole, to the planet, the universe, and ultimately to God—to some overall purpose and direction. . . . A successful worldview must, in the end, draw all these levels—the person, the social, and the spiritual—into one coherent whole. If it does so, the individual has access to some sense of who he is, why he is here, how he relates to others, and how it is valuable to behave."

Note that worldview *is not about what people believe*. It is about how a person connects to all that lies beyond his or her skin. People's worldviews predispose many of their needs and much of their behavior. The person who sees the world opportunistically, as young people are prone to doing, interacts with the external world differently than a person who connects with it in more detached experiential terms, as commonly is the case in the second half of life, and generally more so the older people are.

The worldviews of older people tend to be more cohesive and stable than those of people in the first half of life. The worldviews of young people tend to be somewhat fragmented and out of balance because of a strong bias toward immediate needs and desires, especially in the context of the social self and one's vocational interests. Balance is not a major concern of the adventuresome, ambitious, acquisitive young mind. Extreme attention to matters is a virtue that often serves the young person well. Brute force of effort and will rather than the subtler approaches of prudence and wisdom rule their lifestyles.

However, in the second half of life the pulling forces of self-actualization draw a person in the direction of balance. These forces foster seamless connectivity between all parts of a person—in Zohar's words, into "one coherent whole." Thus, second-half customers present marketers with more complete and more complex worldviews that translate into more complete and more complex behaviors, from how they assess value to how they choose brands they want to *experience*—not simply *have* or *use*.

Self-actualization involves processes of becoming or actualizing the real self—the *authentic self*, as Jamie Lee Curtis might say. It is the self that is not concealed by the persona—Latin for *mask*—that Jung used in referring to the social self.

The persona is crucial in adolescence and early adulthood, but the mask is worn at the cost of concealing the real self which must be submerged to make it easier to be successful in seeking intimate relationships and getting ahead vocationally. However, as midlife approaches or soon after its arrival, innate forces incline people to begin changing from a social and vocational developmental track to a self-actualizing developmental track. This promotes processes of self-discovery that lead toward self-actualization. These processes do not mean squelching the social self, but rather integrating the social self with the real self.

The real self is more introspective (self-informed), more individuated (less subject to peer and other social influences), and more autonomous (more self-reliant). People who are able to connect strongly with their real selves are often more comfortable following their gut feelings than following what others say. The real self is a less imitative self. It is more authentic by definition (again, recall the story of Jamie Lee Curtis from Chapter 1). This is why product endorsements by famous people usually don't carry as much weight with older people as they do with younger people.

Think of self-actualization as the opposite of *social actualization,* the primary developmental focus during the first half of life. To have the best chances for a satisfying life, a person must first become socially developed, that is, socially actualized. However, as midlife approaches, the real self begins clamoring for more attention. Some people answer the midlife call of the real self while others ignore it, as Steve Martin's character in the movie *Grand Canyon* did. In contrast, Kevin Kline's character affirmatively answered the summons of Nature's call to tend to the needs of the real self. Moviegoers are left with the clear impression that Steve Martin's character will age unhappily while Kevin Kline's character will experience the best years of his life as he grows older.

Thus it is that in the first half of life our worldviews point outward on behalf of the social self while in the second half of life our worldviews point inward on behalf of the inner *real* self. This might seem to indicate that the traditional idea along Madison Avenue that marketing to older people runs a high risk of turning off younger people is fundamentally correct. However, that is not necessarily so. Companies can transcend age in their marketing through the practice of *ageless marketing.* In fact, by restricting marketing efforts to younger age groups, as is most often done in many categories, companies increase the risk of not being around when this decade ends.

HOW SELF-ACTUALIZATION NEEDS CHANGE SHOPPING AND BUYING BEHAVIOR

While interest in what the other *S* word stands for does not dissolve after 40, midlifers and older people do tend to have different attitudes toward sex than they had in their youthful prime. They also have different attitudes about other subjects that challenge common views of what being "older" is like. Their developmentally altered attitudes and behavior are big reasons why it seems to many marketers that consumers are "acting more mysteriously" these days.

As people enter a self-actualizing track, they evolve into a different kind of customer. They don't think, feel, and act like younger customers. Their bundle of needs can be quite different from those of younger people even though they may buy the same brands. Ad agency executive Jon Sims, of the Interpublic agency, Mullin LHC in Winston-Salem, North Carolina, put it this way: "Both my 25-year-old son and I own Doc Martens footwear, but for far different reasons. To win each of our hearts and minds, we each need to be spoken to in our own language, appealing to our distinct value sets." Sims, Jr. is more interested in making social statements with his purchases than his father who puts comfort ahead of looks and conservative looks ahead of the latest fashions that could go out of style next year.

People don't generate their self-actualization needs. Self-actualization needs emerge as a function of personal development. They are no more created by the willful mind than are hunger pangs that signal a need for feeding an empty stomach. Self-actualization needs are primal; we have no say in what our primal needs are—only in how we address them. Therefore, you will not learn much about the self-actualizing drivers of customer behavior by surveying customers. One must be grounded in the tenets of human development in the second half of life to understand one of the most powerful forces in New Customer Majority behavior.

Had Procter & Gamble's researchers had such grounding when doing consumer research for Olestra, they might have reasoned that the ebbing of youthful narcissistic values as midlife unfolds often changes people's attitudes about their eating behavior. Some people say Olestra's side effects undermined its chances for success; however, the side effects were relatively rare and most of the time not very serious. More people suffer side effects from tobacco, alcohol, and overeating.

Makers of frozen confections also believed research indicating that aging boomers represented a huge market for fat-free ice cream, so they geared up to cater to aging boomers with their midlife bulges. However, by the end of the 1990s, fat-free ice cream sales stalled and went into freefall. Sales fell 27 percent in 2000 and another 11 percent in 2001. Meanwhile sales of full-fat ice cream shot upward.

In advanced states of maturity, people typically develop more re-laxed attitudes about life. At the same time, they seek higher-quality experiences—including higher-quality eating experiences. Most people view fat-free ice cream as inferior to full-fat ice cream. Younger people are probably more likely to sacrifice ice cream quality by eating the fat-free stuff in hopes of keeping love handles from developing, or at least keeping them from growing larger. But like Jamie Lee Curtis, many older people would prefer to eat less of the real stuff than gormandize on the fake stuff. After all, it's the rich fatty cream that gave ice cream its name and distinction as one of the world's most favored desserts. Fat-free ice cream is fake ice cream.

A casual walk through a shopping mall reveals that for better or worse, as the population has aged, people have become more relaxed about their eating. "But," one might say, "the U.S. Center for Disease Control in Atlanta says that most kids are also overweight. How about America's craze for fat-rich fast food? This self-actualization stuff couldn't be all there is to America getting fatter faster." So true.

I'm not proposing that people entering a self-actualizing track au-tomatically get fatter. For most people, the amount of weight they carry is a matter of personal choice. I'm saying that predictions about boomers doing everything they could to ward off telltale signs of aging, including wider girth, have often proven to be misleading. Jamie Lee Curtis says she has had tummy tucks and botox shots, but no more be-cause she likes her natural, aging self more each day. While not all boomers share her view, enough do that for marketing to ignore it is a big mistake. When I show Figure 5.2 to an audience, attendees are as-tonished to see just how much more relaxed people have become about their eating habits, health, and personal appearance between 1985, when the older boomers were 39 (Egad! Almost middle age! I better watch what I eat!) and 2000, when the oldest boomers were 54 (Hey, I'm only going to be here once, so don't deprive me of simple pleasures, like an occasional morsel of Godiva or a bowl of Ben & Jerry's!).

Marketing has long been heavily geared to the materialistic and nar-cissistic values that motivate the youthful spirit. Among normally devel-oping people, the influence of these values on customer behavior progressively declines in the second half of life. Recall how the Yankelovich Monitor research found that consumers now "want less stuff." How to market "stuff" to people who want less of it is one of the lessons of this

FIGURE 5.2 *Changes in Attitudes about Eating, Health, and Appearance*

	1985	2000
"People who are not overweight look a lot more attractive."	55%	(24%)
"I'd like to lose 20 pounds."	54%	(62%)
"I am always conscious of the calories in the meals I serve."	34%	25%
"A person should be very cautious in serving food with fat."	40%	33%
"A person should be very cautious in serving foods with . . ."		
• Salt	40%	27%
• Sugar	43%	25%
• Cholesterol	35%	18%
• Caffeine	32%	(21%)

SOURCE: NPD Group

book. You don't market the "stuff;" you market the experiences that the "stuff" can make possible.

Another surprising idea I share with my audiences is that while Gen Xers and Gen Yers have yet to arrive in the midlife anteroom of self-actualization, their behavior nevertheless appears to be deeply influenced by the New Customer Majority. This being so, even companies that are exclusively oriented to teens and twentysomethings can benefit from learning more about self-actualization in terms of consumer behavior. The reason is . . . well, read on.

THE "MYSTERIOUS" *PCG* INFLUENCE ON CUSTOMER BEHAVIOR

"In 1921, blue tits began pulling caps off milk bottles on front stoops throughout England to guzzle their contents. Almost overnight, relatives of these tiny little birds all over Europe followed suit. Ornithologists were stunned by how fast the practice spread. It happened too fast to be accounted for solely by mimicry.

"Might the same mysterious way in which blue tits picked up their new eating habit have some correspondence with sudden changes in customer behavior?"[3]

So began an article I wrote for the April 1998 edition of *American Demographics* concerning a remarkable change in consumer behavior: while the influence of young people's values used to percolate up into older age groups, it was now appearing that the influence of middle agers' values was trickling down into younger age groups.

I called attention in the article to British biologist Rupert Sheldrake's view that what he calls *morphic fields:* transmitted waves of influence throughout the tit species to generate rapid change in their eating habits. This is reminiscent of Carl Jung's *collective unconscious* that he said influences behavior at the deepest levels of human existence.

Talk of morphic fields and the collective unconscious may sound too much like New Age talk for some, but we now know that the brain is sensitive to a wide universe of unconsciously experienced influences. Malcolm Gladwell's best seller *The Tipping Point* explored such influences in detail.

I wrote in the *American Demographics* article about what many termed the "surprising" revival of interest in spirituality in the 1990s, offering it as evidence of subtle forces in culture exerting influential behavior on people. However, I predicted this event in *SAM* 1990 because I believed that as the population aged, a higher percentage of customers would be in the years when people are more inclined to think about their place in the cosmic scheme of things. What was more surprising to many was that interest in spirituality suddenly blossomed in younger age groups in the decade that ended with 50 million boomers having entered middle age.

The spiritual renaissance reflects a cultural shift toward a more nurturing, feminine ethos. Testifying to this in the article, I cited a 1997 *Time* cover story on spirituality in young people's music that proclaimed, "Macho music is out. Empathy is in." While hordes of youth still indulge in outrageous behavior, teens are attending religious services weekly and listening to pop spiritual music in greater numbers than seen in recent years, according to *The Wall Street Journal.*[4]

America's spiritual awakening has even touched the hard-edged world of business. The July 1, 2001, issue of *Fortune* boldly displayed these words on its cover:

God

And

Business

The Surprising Quest For

Spiritual Renewal

In the American Workplace

Surprising? Not really. This was bound to happen as people 40 and older became the adult majority, a majority whose most influential group is aging baby boomers.

The sheer weight of boomers' numbers ensures their influence on all of society as they pass into and through the autumn of their lives. Comprising 29 percent of the U.S. population and heading nearly four in ten households, boomers occupy the *psychological center of gravity* (PCG).

The PCG, which is made up of people within five years of the adult median age, has a disproportionate influence on the ethos of society. Today's adult median age is 44, which means the bookends of the PCG are ages 39 and 49. Approximately 40 million boomers make up the current PCG.

I tested the PCG hypothesis historically by going back in time to the 1960s. I found that one of the most overarching beliefs about boomers is untrue. *Boomers did not change the world during the 1960s.* Most were too young to have had such influence. Even as the 1960s ended, most boomers were still not old enough to vote. The youngest were only five.

So who did change the world during the 1960s?

The PCG of the 1960s that was made up of the so-called Silent Generation—the generation that has been called silent because it supposedly has done little to distinguish itself. The birthing years of the Silent Generation were 1928 through 1945. Its members included Jerry Rubin, Martin Luther King, Abbie Hoffman, Gloria Steinem, Ralph Nader, Jane Fonda, Stokley Carmichael, Joan Baez, and Bob Dylan—all of whom were born during the 1930s. Tom Hayden, the chief ideologue of the 1960s and cofounder of the militant Students for a Demographic Society was born in 1939. Of 125 thought leaders of the tumultuous 1960s listed on one Web site, not one was a boomer.

Most thought leaders in the 1960s' cultural revolution were members of the 1960s' PCG, which included young adults from around the mid-20s to the mid-30s (remember, the PCG is a function of the adult median age which is continuously in flux). Boomers played the role of foot soldiers marching to the drumbeat of the real revolutionaries of the 1960s. They were encouraged by Silent Generation revolutionaries to do as youth does in every generation: challenge the existing order to the extent permitted. As Daniel Levinson observed in *The Seasons of a Man's Life,* boomers could only go as far in acting out their youthful rebellious proclivities as the previous generation—the Silent Generation—permitted them.

Today's PCG appears to be influencing younger people to a remarkable degree. Members of Generation Y (older teens and twentysomethings) have been described in consumer trend reports as more concerned about work life quality than about income, and as being more responsible, independent, and skeptical than teens and twentysomethings in previous generations. A Yankelovich poll found that 95 percent of Gen Yers thought volunteering or helping people is very important or somewhat important.[5] Such strong attitudes on one's contributions to society are usually more deeply associated with midlife, when people begin thinking more about "giving back."

Another correspondence between Generation Y and the current PCG is weaker loyalty to designer labels. "While this generation has consumer power unrivaled by any preceding generation, they are not as driven by the same kind of label consciousness as Generation X."[6] Generation Y's attitudes toward labels echoes the declining label consciousness that is characteristic of people in midlife. A recent *Wall Street Journal* article puzzled over sagging interest in designer labels. Drawing from research by New York–based Brand Keys, the *WSJ* article said, "The most pronounced ambivalence toward designer emblems came from consumers in their 40s and 50s—an indication that designer-brand loyalty diminishes with age."[7]

The Brand Keys research findings are another example of a shift in customer behavior that was predictable years ago. Recall the references made from time to time in this book about how people in the first half of life are strongly influenced by their need to make social statements.

Designer labels are about making social statements, and as people move into and through the second half of life, interest in designer labels falls off because they are not as compelled to make social statements by their brand choices. The fact that Generation Y is less interested in designer labels than Generation X seems to reflect the PCG effect at work in the silent, unconscious reaches of the brains of Gen Yers.

As another example of the effect of today's more mature PCG on younger consumers, Sporting Goods Manufacturing Association's Maria Stefan told me that today's young are not as responsive to famous personality product endorsements as the young in previous generations were. Because of this, says Stefan, agents for athletes have been forced into renegotiating product endorsement contracts.

OTHER LUMINARIES (THAN MASLOW) IN ADULT DEVELOPMENT IN MIDLIFE

Maslow is far from *the* leading light in developmental psychology, though his thinking has permeated this chapter. That was a personal choice made because of general familiarity with him. The works of Carl Jung, Erik Erikson, or others could have served just as well in developing the main themes of this chapter.

Dan McAdams is another developmental psychologist whose work offers important insights into human (customer) behavior. In *Stories We Live By*, McAdams explores the evolution of identity, the source of the most influential forces in our lives. As an example of his thinking, he proposes that the primary developmental objective of young adults is to develop a social identity, for they have left adolescence with little more than an embryonic identity. Yet even upon arrival of middle age, development of identity is not complete, for there remains much work to be done on the identity of the nonsocial self—the inner self that embodies the *real self*.

If development of identity "is the central task of adulthood," as McAdams maintains, then it can only benefit consumer researchers and marketers to learn how people of all ages go about developing their identities. In young adulthood, for example, people depend on visible representations of themselves in what they buy and consume to both create and project their identities. This is not done willy-nilly, or totally as a function of free will choices. There are powerful unconscious forces at work, the knowledge of which can lead to more effective marketing.

David Gutmann is another leading light in adult development with much to share with researchers and marketers. The middle years have been an area of specialty with him. He has extensively studied the shift in affect among males toward a more nurturing self, and in females an equivalent shift toward self-assertiveness. This induces changes in lifestyles and, by extension, buying behavior.

Read the following words of Gutmann taken from the transcript of a PBS show on aging (in slightly edited form for conciseness and clarity). While reading his words, think about how rarely we see marketing messages directed to people in midlife that connect with what Gutmann says:

"In the post-parental period of life, what the French like to call the Third Age, there is a tendency for both sexes to reclaim, if you will, aspects of themselves, potentials, that were hitherto unused, hitherto on hold—subordinated, if you will, to the tests of career advancement, survival, child rearing, that kind of thing.

You see it quite dramatically in women as they come out of the closet of the domestic role. They exit from the parental [perspective] that somehow they have to live in and through their children [because] the kids can make it on their own now. You see very often a sense of liberation, a sense of 'now I don't have to be developing them; I can develop myself.'

Women come in touch with the kind of aggressivity that they previously throttled back on for the sake of children. When that passes, women reemerge. They reclaim the aggression that they used to send out of the house with their husband [who now has] retired from his macho wars and being a provider. He begins to reclaim what he used to concede to his wife, gentleness, tenderness, sensuousness, and even a maternal quality. We all know about the sort of the maternal grandpa and the tough grandma. Well, that in a sense—that stereotype has truth in it."[8]

Gutmann's words point toward some rather significant behavior changes in midlife that deserve attention in marketing executions. Keep in mind that he is not talking about what people in midlife consciously choose to do, but about the demands of personal development they are called on to answer by the voice of Nature. Conscious behavior only comes into play in how the midlife woman and midlife man respond to that voice.

Another developmental psychologist who has influenced my thinking is Cynthia Adams of the University of Oregon. Her research has revealed sometimes quite dramatic differences between how older people infer meanings from written materials, such as ads, and how 25-year-olds do. Yet, 25-year-olds can be found working on ads for financial services, travel, senior housing, pharmaceuticals, and other products intended for older people with no awareness of what Adams has found. I know from personal experience that twentysomethings in marketing can acquire the knowledge required to be optimally effective in middle-age and older markets. But I also know from personal experience that the twentysomething copywriter is not very likely to acquire that knowledge without executive and managerial leadership being brought to bear.

The point of this concluding discussion is to highlight the fact that developmental psychology offers a treasure trove of empirically tested tenets of behavior, knowledge of which can markedly improve one's understanding of customers. Without such understanding in this era of the New Customer Majority, productivity gains in marketing executions are less likely. However, those who gain grounding in the biologically rooted imperatives of midlife may experience something like Dorothy did when her worldview changed from the black and white of prosaic Kansas into the multicolor splendor of Oz. They will see aging boomers as they really are (well, most of them).

6

THE BIOLOGICAL ROOTS OF CUSTOMERS' NEEDS AND BEHAVIOR

If marketing is about attracting the attention of minds and persuading those minds to courses of action, what surefire ways are there to get customers' attention, especially because people see between 900 and 3,500 ads each day? (The numbers vary according to who is scoping the problem of getting customers' attention.) To borrow from Bill Bernbach, "*It has become fashionable* to say that ad clutter is one of the biggest problems in marketing today." Not. A great big NOT!

To understand why ad clutter is not as big a problem as many claim we must start at the very beginning of customers' perceptions—not on the television screen, the radio, or in print media. We must go inside the unconscious brain where perceptions originate.

Your brain is your mind's tuner. It picks up information sent in by the senses just as radio picks up signals from airwaves. Every thought ultimately traces back to sensory input to the brain.

Like a computer's hard drive, your brain has enormous memory capacity—in fact, more memory than any computer on Earth—but every bit of information stored in its memory banks is not *consciously* recallable. The conscious mind's memory is puny. Its RAM cannot begin to keep up with everything that enters the brain. To get an idea of this, look around you. Your eyes capture every detail as faithfully as a fine camera—every visible speck, line, and color. Your brain must limit what it sends to your conscious mind to avoid overloading it. To underscore that point, consider that only about *one-trillionth* of the information landing on the surface of the eyes ever reaches consciousness, and that is just one of five senses.

The most important task the brain carries out for the conscious mind is conducting *information triage,* a set of processes by which the brain reduces information flow to what the conscious mind can manage. Nothing gets into the conscious mind without being screened by the processes of information triage, therefore:

> Creating marketing communications that can survive information triage is the single most important challenge a marketing communicator faces.

Marketing messages that do not robustly survive information triage will not reach the conscious mind with enough force to arouse attention and generate response. *Marketing messages* refers to more than just advertising. The term includes product labels, point-of-purchase displays, sales brochures, public relations, and even the product itself, for no product fails to carry a message to the perceiver even if only provoking a yawn.

Have you ever been in a conversation at a party or around the office coffee pot when suddenly you hear your name mentioned in another conversation down the hall or in another room? Your brain heard the other conversation all along, but not until your name came up did it let your mind know about it. That's what information triage is about: determining what information has enough relevance to you that it should be sent to your conscious mind.

It takes about .2 to .8 of a second for information to travel from the senses through the brain and into the conscious mind. These are the most critical milliseconds in marketing, for this is when your message either grabs people's attention or gets dumped in the brain's recycle bin. Importantly, customers do not consciously experience your marketing messages in real time; they experience the brain's reactions to those messages.

Ad clutter is indeed less of a problem than it is commonly made out to be. The brain has an astonishing capacity to cut through ad clutter. For example, how often have you been thumbing through a magazine when you do a double take and turn back a page or two? Your brain simply took a few hundred milliseconds to alert your conscious mind to what you saw.

The more challenging clutter problem is in the brain. Ad creators strive to overcome ad clutter by using novelty and shock to crash into customers' minds. But in this age of explicitness, what can be novel or shocking anymore? Psychologist Robert Rieher says customers have become less sensitive to novelty in advertising because their brains have come to expect it:

> "The Expectant Brain of today (as conditioned by endless novelty in movies, ads, etc.) may not be easily excited or surprised . . . [novelty] may now be counterproductive. In psychophysics, Weber's Law states the stronger the stimuli, the greater the change needs to be in other stimuli for input information to be noticed."[1]

The more customers experience novelty, the higher the bar of novelty is raised for attracting attention to an ad. Ironically, foregoing novelty in favor of the familiar—such as Hallmark does in its TV commercials—often works best, especially in the New Customer Majority.

The answer to the question of how to create marketing messages that survive information triage is wrapped up in two words: *relevance* and *emotions*. To break through ad clutter strongly enough that interest is robust, attention is focused, and recallable memory is formed, a message must have enough personal relevance to evoke a strong emotional response. *Without emotional arousal the chances of a marketing message surviving information triage are poor to nil.*

EMOTIONS: THE TOUCHSTONES OF PERSONAL RELEVANCE

In ancient times, money changers and merchants used a hard black stone, such as jasper or basalt, to test the quality of gold or silver by comparing the streak left on the stone by one of these metals with that of an alloy. Emotions play similar roles in the interactive workings of the mind and brain. Using emotions as touchstones, the brain assesses the value of incoming information in terms of needs—the stronger a need, the stronger the emotional response to something that can satisfy the need. No emotional response to a marketing message means it failed to arouse emotions strong enough for the brain to think it relates enough to its owner's interests to send the message to the owner's conscious mind. This is not theory. We now know from brain research that it takes emotional arousal for a person to connect anything to his or her personal interests.

Emotions *energize* behavior. They are not vaporous puffs in our minds, but material changes in our body states. Emotions are formed by changes in blood pressure, adrenalin flow, pulse, muscle tension, salivation, and other body systems. Feelings of love, surprise, anticipation, fear, anger, and rage are outcomes triggered by stimuli in body chemistry. Many changes are too subtle to be detected by the conscious mind, yet they influence moods, perceptions, thoughts, decisions, and behavior. Antonio Damasio calls these *background emotions.*

When you have a "gut feeling" about something, the feeling literally did originate in your gut. Changes in body states signal what is important enough for the brain to bring to the conscious mind's attention. Reason plays a much smaller role in decisions than we have long thought—even less so as we age because once we enter our 30s, we make increasing use of emotion-generated gut feelings or intuition. We put more trust in first impressions, which are emotionally generated and experienced as feelings. The more we trust our feelings, the more resistant we are to efforts of others to change them. In the New Customer Majority, if you don't get it right the first time, you are less likely to get a second chance than with younger customers.

We become less rational and more intuitive as we age because the more experiences we have reasoned through, the fewer we need to reason through in the future. Previously reasoned-through experiences are encoded in what I call *neuronal macros* because they serve the same function as computer macros. With a neuronal macro in place, a mental activity that once took many steps to work through to yield a perception or thought can now be accomplished virtually instantly when something activates that neuronal macro. A more common term for neuronal macro that marketers often use is *hot button.*

The *material* brain uses the language of emotions to communicate with the *nonmaterial* mind. An emotion is how a need feels, or how an action or event that satisfies or frustrates a need feels. Feelings are the conscious mind's attempt to figure out and label what our emotions are trying to tell us.

Emotions guide us toward pleasure and away from pain by how they make us feel. People choose products for the emotional payoff they *feel* the product will provide—not for what they *think* the product will provide. Companies and customers usually operate in a dichotomy of features versus feelings, because

- most companies focus on features, while
- all customers focus on feelings.

Companies will generally find greater success in today's more emotionally directed second-half markets by focusing less on product features and more on customers' feelings. This is what the "the customer experience" that everybody is talking about calls for. However, why has the customer experience seemingly overnight become the "big" thing in marketing? Some say it is because products have become commoditized. I say it is because of the New Customer Majority, most of whose members are experiencing ebbing of materialistic influences and rising influence of experiential aspirations on their behavior.

MESSAGE RELEVANCE DEPENDS ON CONNECTING WITH THE RIGHT VALUES

Emotional arousal that is essential to product messages surviving information triage will not take place if a message has no relevance to a person. The product design, functional benefits, and economic value must have relevance, but a marketing message also must be relevant in other ways, such as in the values it projects. For instance, materialistic values play better to the young than to the New Customer Majority. Failure to recognize season-of-life differences in nonmaterial values is a big reason why many marketers have complained that customers are acting mysteriously, and why many in the New Customer Majority complain that advertisers mostly ignore them. It's not just the prevalence of younger people depicted in advertising that makes them feel this way. It's also the fact that advertising—even many ads depicting older people—reflect the values of younger people.

The Wall Street Journal recently ran a front-page story on a "surprising pattern" arising: consumers' increased attention to quality.[2] If unchanging man's values in midlife and later were better understood, this pattern would not be the least surprising. The article described today's customers as falling into two categories: those whose incomes make price the primary consideration in product choices and those who can afford to pay extra for enhanced quality. The article said that today's customers either spend $2,200 for a super grade Maytag washer and dryer unit or buy a bottom-of-the-line model at an appliance discounter. The article told how products in the midlevel price range, from household appliances and cars to wines and engagement rings, are losing out as customers buy either at the bottom or the top.

A well-known researcher quoted in the article said of this surprising pattern: "There's no aspiration to be middle class. Everyone wants to be at the top." Again, NOT!

The surprising pattern in customer behavior is not about being at the top. It is about how customers in the New Customer Majority tend to place importance on quality for different reasons than their younger counterparts do. To infer that increased attention to luxury indicates that everyone wants to be at the top is to view everyone through the materialistic lens of young people whose interest in quality tends to be more motivated by desires to make social statements. However, in midlife and later, interest in quality more often reflects an inner-directed, spiritual (of the spirit, not of religion) perspective. Luxury purchases may simply be the sign of an increased bent for savoring events by the moment. One of the hallmarks of self–actualization is *"greater freshness of appreciation and richness of emotional reaction."*[3] In advanced states of maturity, people often enjoy something for its own sake, feeling no need to impress others.

Seen through the materialistic lens of youth, a 50-year-old driving away from a car dealer in her first Lexus might appear to be expressing materialistic values. That could be—depending on her level of psychological maturity—but there could also be a more metaphysical quality in her relationship with her new Lexus than she would have had in buying a comparable car at age 30.

THE PRIMARY CORE VALUES THAT UNDERLIE CUSTOMER BEHAVIOR

The brain's information triage processes evolved over hundreds of millions of years, for they are not just a function in the human brain.

Dangling a dead insect before a frog elicits no response in its brain because dead insects are not on a frog's *survival scenario* menu of things to eat. Its eyes detect the insect, but the message does not reach the part of the frog's brain that controls its ever-eager tongue because dead insects have no personal relevance to a frog.

Survival scenarios are the sum total of everything needed for a safe, comfortable, and pleasurable existence. What makes for a safe, comfortable, and pleasurable existence revolves around what Antonio Damasio calls basic *life value*.[4] He says willful action depends first on *attentionality*—for example, an ad has to grab a person's attention before she can think about it. He then observes that willful action also depends also on *working memory*—the ability to keep track of information in the ad as a customer takes it in, manipulates it, and massages the information into perceptions, thoughts, and a final decision. But what coheres the customer's attentionality and engages her working memory? Damasio says that some basic life value—some innate force or forces—catalyze attentionality and turn on working memory.

Nothing coheres attentionality and engages working memory more forcefully than an event that threatens a person's very existence. Thus, the *most basic* life value is *the will to live,* and the most basic behavior consists of acts in service of self-preservation.

There is much more to self-preservation than dealing with threats to the continuity of life. Quality of life is necessary to make it worth continuing. Life quality depends on a secure sense of identity, connectedness to others, feelings of purpose, skills and knowledge adequate to accomplishing one's objectives, and physical and psychological health and well being.

To create marketing messages that survive information triage with enough force to cohere attentionality and engage working memory, messages *must* have some connection with basic life values, which are not determined by the conscious, willful mind. They are encoded in the chemistry of DNA. We can safely presume that basic life values, which can rightly be called *primary core values,* are embedded in our biology because they are present in everyone in every generation; thus being inherited, they are part of the biological makeup of Bill Bernbach's unchanging man.

The five primary core values that qualify as the basic life value, which Damasio says underlie all behavior, are:

1. *Identity values.* These involve self-preservation, self-awareness, and self-image.
2. *Relationship values.* These involve connections to others, institutions, and beliefs.
3. *Purpose values.* These involve meaning and validation of one's life and actions.
4. *Adaptation values.* These involve skills and knowledge necessary to negotiate life.
5. *Energy values.* These involve health, well being, and functionality.

The five primary core values form the theoretical foundation of developmental relationship marketing (DRM) that was first discussed in Chapter 4. All needs and motivations urging their satisfaction are ultimately traceable back to these five primary core values. In research mediated according to the tenets of DRM, what customers say is benchmarked and catalogued according to the primary core values matrix. Knowledge of that matrix often makes it possible to know when a research subject is leaving something out or making a statement that is not altogether accurate.

Connecting with all primary core value systems makes marketing messages powerful. Marketing messages that only connect weakly with primary core values, or that connect inappropriately for a given audience as many ads do, make it difficult for the brain to detect message relevance, resulting in quizzical looks and the question, What was that commercial about? Possibly, it can result in outright disgust with an ad as broadly happened in connection with a recent Midas Muffler TV commercial in which an elderly woman flashed a mechanic, asking "Can you fix these?" Younger people in focus groups testing the ad may have guffawed, but enough older people thought the commercial was in bad taste and it was quickly pulled. Midas learned the hard way that humor preferences change as people age (see sidebar).

IDENTITY VALUES: SOURCES OF THE MOST POWERFUL INFLUENCES ON BEHAVIOR

Identity values, or I-Values, are about the self, its continuity, its projection in time and space, and, for believers in an afterlife, the projection of the self into eternity. Nothing else so broadly and deeply influences

A *voiding the* C *ostly* B *ooby* T *rap of* M *isplaced* H *umor*

Humor preferences among different age groups is a serious matter. What is funny to one age group often is not funny to another.

In a survey of comedy performers, researchers found performers recognized striking differences in humor preferences between young, middle-age, and old. Young people favored humor based on nonsense, bodily functions, and aggression between people. Middle-age humor preferences include cerebral political, sexual, family, and aggressive humor. Older people warm most to family, political, and, yes, sexual humor, though presented differently than the young like it. The latter like their sex jokes raw and direct; older people like their sex jokes ironic and subtle. Older audience members like a kinder and gentler humor in which no one is put down or ridiculed. Out of six types of humor evaluated, performers said put-down jokes ranked first with the young. It came in last for older people who best like humor expressed in elaborated stories. Stories rank low with the young because they don't get to the punch line as fast.

customers' buying behavior and lifestyles because nothing so broadly and deeply influences each life. The 17th-century philosopher Spinoza asserted this when he said, "Each thing, as far as it can by its own power, strives to persevere in its being." He called this *conatus,* the primary life force that *motivates* each thing to persist in its existence. I-Values form the starter engine and generator of the animating forces of life.

I-Values have a dark side. They spark conflict between people from the petty squabbles of lovers to raging wars between nations. The dark side of I-Values is obsessed with control. People we call "control freaks" express the dark side of I-Values in trying to recreate themselves in other people by getting them to do as the controller would do, be as the controller would be, and think as the controller would think.

When Maslow described self-actualizers as being detached from the world, he didn't mean they had become socially withdrawn. He meant they had renounced the immature disposition to control externalities, including other people. Sometimes in my workshops I ask the audience to name the biggest source of conflict between two people. The consensus of the audience is invariably *miscommunication*. When I challenge that by suggesting that the attempt of one person to seek control over another is a better answer, audience consensus invariably shifts to agree with me. I usually see heads bobbing in assent as the consensus shifts, which always leaves me wondering if those bobbing heads recently sparred with a lover, spouse, or boss in a situation in which the sparring partner sought control over the owner of the bobbing head in some issue.

I-Values motivate people to tattoo their skin and pierce their body parts. Young people—mostly males—often put life and limb at risk doing insanely stupid things to assert their identities. People get divorced over identity issues. Women endure uncomfortable apparel to assert their identities. Religion-inspired wars are about identity.

I-Values are also the primary motivating drivers of human achievement. They encompass the *libido*—not Freud's sex-drenched libido, but the more expansive Jungian libido that drives us to recreate ourselves in everything we do. From artists projecting their identities on canvas to teachers molding students, politicians motivating crowds, and lawyers persuading juries, we all strive each day to recreate ourselves in what we do.

What higher service can you as a marketer provide your customers than to help them recreate themselves through the brands you market? For example, concern about legacy—proof after we are gone that our lives have been worthwhile—grows stronger as we move through the second half of our lives. The animating forces of what Spinoza called conatus drives us to pursue our temporal continuity through our legacy. That is why wealthy benefactors set up foundations, leave money to worthy causes, and buy naming rights to buildings on college campuses. Jump ahead for a moment into Chapter 15 and look at the ad in Figure 15.2. It is a brilliant invocation of the I-Value-generated need for a sense of immortality in marketing a watch.

I-Values operate primarily in service of the social self in the first half of life, but in the second half, they draw us more into service to the inner self. In my view, no brand does a better job of connecting with I-Values generated needs in the second half of life than New Balance.

Achieving Balance in Today's Marketplace

In the late 1980s, New Balance CEO Jim Davis noticed that sales to younger age groups were slowing, with matters slated to get worse during the 1990s when the number of 18-to-34-year-olds in the United States would fall by more than 8 million, putting a huge dent in the sneaker market. Davis reacted quicker than his competitors to that population shrinkage by turning his company's attention toward a loyal group of customers who had bought into the brand in the 1970s and were still with it as they began entering middle age in the late 1980s: boomers moving into midlife. Davis changed the marketing direction of his company toward a growing base of loyal customers who seemed ready to grow old with New Balance on their feet.

Having five shoe widths versus the industry standard of three was a decisive competitive advantage, especially among older people whose feet may have spread a bit, but New Balance's skill in connecting with the altered values of midlife has leveraged that advantage. The signature tagline "Achieve new balance" resonates with the growing desire in midlife to achieve life balance after the frenetic years of early adulthood when unbalanced devotion to career and acquisitiveness dominated lifestyle. The subtext in many New Balance ads is tend to your inner self, not to escape a complex world, but as a way of reentering it with renewed spirit.

Having famous athletes endorse their products has long been a mainstay in marketing sneaker brands. It feeds into the I-Value-generated need of the young to define their identities with a heroic mien. However, New Balance has always been an exception. Going against the grain, it makes a virtue of *not using* famous personality endorsements (see sidebar). This intuitively wrought decision made it easier for New Balance to shift its attention to older markets because it was not seen as primarily a youth-oriented brand.

Given Jim Davis's eschewing of famous personalities to endorse the New Balance brand, it might seem ironic that in recent years as the brand's popularity has continued growing in New Customer Majority markets it has been enjoying strong growth in younger markets. This development demonstrates the power of ageless marketing to extend a brand's reach across generational divides. While the values projected by New Balance resonate particularly strongly with second-half customers, they resonate with younger people as well. Also, if the idea of the psychological center of gravity described in Chapter 5 makes sense to you, it is only natural that New Balance would be in a good position to grow sales in shrinking younger markets where even mighty Nike is experiencing sales declines.

F *r o m* **N** *e w* **B** *a l a n c e ' s* **W** *e b* **S** *i t e*

Which would you prefer. . . .

Athletic shoes designed and built around the belief that better fit and better technology result in better performance and increased enjoyment of your sport?

Or, athletic shoes built around the belief that the marketing prowess of an NBA superstar can sell anything?

In today's over-hyped economic atmosphere of buy, buy, buy, sell, sell, sell, it seems that practically every product on the market is associated with a superstar celebrity endorser. Nowhere is this more evident than in the athletic footwear industry. Setting ourselves apart from—and ahead of—the pack, we at New Balance adhere to a unique philosophy which we call Endorsed by no one™. Instead of paying celebrities to tell you how great our products are, we prefer to invest in research, design, and domestic manufacturing.

New Balance presents a kinder and gentler set of values than its biggest competitors. It often expresses those values in poetically compelling ways. Ad headlines convey the spirit of an inner self, uncompromised by a narcissistic need to play to the outside world. Often, through the image of a person in a solo activity, ads project an idealized expression of the inner self. An Ansel Adams–like landscape may serve as a backdrop.

One ad headline, "The shortest distance between two points is not the point," contrasts vividly with Nike's theme that superior performance, winning, and getting there first is everything. The ad shows a man running along a road carved into the side of a mountain overlooking a shimmering sea—man *with* nature; not *mano y mano*. New Balance ads have none of the machismo that typifies sneaker marketing. Its ads promote the idea that one's worth is not measured by superiority over others, an aspiration of the social self, but by the measure of fidelity to one's true inner self. New Balance's marketing works because it connects with people in the New Customer Majority whose self-actualization needs have a growing influence on their lifestyles and buying behavior. One ad, directed to the midlife woman though the woman in the ad shown jogging down a country lane is not seen in enough detail to determine her age, epitomizes the ageless marketing idea of marketing to values, not age. The main copy reads:

> One more woman chasing a sunset
> One more woman going a little farther
> One more woman simply feeling alive
> One less woman relying on someone else.

Think back to what was said in the last chapter's closing paragraphs about how the midlife woman reclaims the independence that she formerly subordinated to others, then read again the last line of the New Balance poem to women. Click! The line settles right into place with the soul of the midlife woman.

How well has New Balance's brand of ageless marketing worked? Spectacularly. First, know that the sneaker category has been flat since the mid-1990s. Nike has not had measurable sales growth in sneaker lines domestically since 1997. However, New Balance has averaged an annual sales growth rate of 25 percent or more over the past five years.

Linking Marketing Messages to Customers' Self-Images

Customers tend to buy brands that reflect images of who they want to be over who they are. It has to do with their dreams. Recalling actor John Barrymore's words, "A man is never old till regrets take the place of dreams," marketing messages should always take into account whom people in the target market want to be. Many brands, especially personal product brands, have taglines that refer directly and strongly to this I-Value-generated desire. Two well-known examples are Calvin Klein ("Nothing comes between me and my Calvins") and Clairol ("If I've one life to live, let me live it as a blonde"). Those and many other personal product brands are I-Value-centered because they hold out the promise of helping people realize their idealized images of self. Of course, in some way, every brand connects with I-Values, for as the old saying goes, you are what you buy and consume.

Because people in the first half of life see themselves differently than people in the second half do—the former see themselves more in a social context, the latter see themselves more in a introspective context—young ad creators may unconsciously reflect their self-images in product messages directed to second-half customers and thereby fail to connect with them. For example, an ad aimed at retirees urging them to "collect the rewards you have earned" reflects a typical young person's view of retirement, not how many retirees view it. In a focus group in which retirees were shown a "collect your rewards" ad, a woman huffed, "How do they know what rewards I want? It's like they think nirvana is sitting around doing nothing but collecting rewards after you stop working. I want to be giving, not taking."

Pulte Homes' Del Webb division, developers of amenities-studded communities for independently living retirees, is the largest builder of such communities in the nation. It became the biggest by staying in sync with retirees as their self-images changed over the years.

When Del Webb opened the first Sun City in Phoenix in 1960, more than 100,0000 visitors flocked to opening weekend festivities to look over and buy homes—reportedly the largest opening weekend in history for any new community. Hordes of visitors hailed from the Rustbelt in Midwestern America. They were retired autoworkers, steelworkers, policemen, firemen, teachers, and others with modest incomes from working class America who saw for themselves a life of leisure and play in their retirement. But this image of the ideal retirement lifestyle began changing in the late 1980s. Del Webb communities began attracting more affluent, more highly educated retirees who wanted to do more than just loaf and play. Prospective Sun City residents came to sales centers with questions about volunteer activities, part-time work, and continuing education opportunities. The images of whom they wanted to be were quite different from those of the first Sun City residents in the 1960s.

Let me jump in here with a side note. You have read throughout this book that primary core values and the primary core needs they generate do not change from one generation to the next. Yet, you have just read that Sun City retirees in the 1960s wanted a different lifestyle than Sun City retirees in more recent years. What gives?

The primary core values underlying lifestyles of retirees in the 1960s and more recent years have not changed. The working class retirees that made up much of the resident population in the original Sun City communities had lived working lives constrained by limited education, modest incomes, and working lives heavily controlled by others. Upon retiring, they were able to devote psychic attention to needs that had long been subordinated to external conditions over which they had less control than would be generally true of later retirees. The latter were better educated, more affluent, and higher up the social ladder where lifestyle options are richer.

These more recent Sun City retirees have generally been more advantaged throughout their working lives and able to give more attention to their growth-inducing experiential aspirations. The earlier retirees were addressing lower-level needs in their retirement. This limited the appeal of continuing education, participation in volunteer activities, and certainly, after years of having their noses to the grindstone, part-time work. Thus, it is fair to assume that a higher percentage of today's Sun City retirees are a bit further along in their personal development. Maslow frequently pointed out that when a person is consumed by meeting more fundamental needs, he or she is handicapped against rising into higher planes of personal development. That does not mean they lack needs that manifest at higher levels. They have them, but they are nascent needs—needs that have not fully matured because lower-level needs have not been substantially gratified.

As boomers begin retiring in great numbers in the next several years, retirees' views of the ideal retirement lifestyle will continue evolving to reflect desires for even higher levels of active involvement in life than previous generations of retirees. A good friend, Marvin Tolkin, summed up the new face of retirement when he told me at age 72, after retiring as founding head of Jennifer Dale, makers of sleepwear for children, teens, and women:

> "Retirement is not about *not* working. It's about redirecting your life into other useful work."

Marvin, now 77, once recreated himself daily in his garment business. Now he daily recreates himself though a wide range of creative adventures, including extensive volunteer activities. Marvin, though not a boomer, is the epitome of the new face of retirement. Frequently traveling to distant lands with his wife Carol, he remains deeply intellectually involved in life with the unquenchable curiosity of a child. He brings years of executive experience as head of a sizeable company to senior centers throughout New York through his service as a board member of the New York Council of Senior Centers and Services. Tall, lanky, and slightly reminiscent of Milton Berle in looks, Marvin is as active as any 25-year-old. In a recent conversation with him, Marvin told me, "I feel no less energetic at 77 than I did at 27. Life is good at 77. Very good!"

I have talked for years about a very large I-Value-sourced problem that is commonly experienced in the retirement years, especially by men: maintaining self-esteem. A lifestyle of leisure and play does not promote self-esteem because self-esteem, a crucial I-Value need, is earned by being productive. It is not derived from what one consumes or from what others say about one. It comes from within as a reward for accomplishment. Companies with a full appreciation of this will do better in marketing to the New Customer Majority than companies to which it means nothing.

RELATIONSHIP VALUES: SOURCES OF OUR CONNECTIONS TO THE EXTERNAL WORLD

People need the companionship and reinforcement of others to experience a sense of well being. Relationship values, or R-Values, are the sources of that need. R-Values are also the sources of our need to have systems of beliefs—religious, political, moral, and otherwise—to guide us, and help us make sense of what we experience.

The nature of our relationships evolves throughout life to keep pace with our evolving needs. Young people are drawn toward relationships that serve their social goals, from finding intimate partners to gaining access to career opportunities and leveraging those opportunities. They tend to view relationships with a more opportunistic bent than is typical of people in the second half of life. Older people are more likely to value relationships for their own sake and often have more concern for what they put into a relationship than for what they get out of it. This imparts stability to relationships and deepens them. For this reason, *brand loyalty should be rising as the median age rises*. The disposition of unchanging man in the second half of life is to seek the safety, security, comfort, and pleasure of stable relationships.

The fact that brand loyalty has fallen as the population has aged indicates the extent to which companies have fallen out of touch with their customers and their customers' needs and desires. A quarter of a century ago, the Madison Avenue idea that people in the second half of life are more deeply committed to brands was valid. Today, according to the Roper ASW survey I will discuss in Chapter 13, second-half customers are often quicker to switch brands than first-half customers.

Customer loyalty has fallen in large part because too many companies *don't want relationships with their customers.* In the interest of cutting costs, companies minimize customer contact through technology and other means. This compromises the human interface that companies need to have in place to build and maintain loyal customer relationships. I find it astonishing that there is much talk about the economic value of keeping customers for life while companies do all they can to avoid having a human relationship with customers.

How a Bank Used R-Values to Grow Deposits from $378M to $8B in Four Years

Mark Cooper confesses to being in love with banking customers over 50 ever since he first worked with them when he was 33. Cooper, now 53, has two decades of experience to draw on to show anyone who will listen how a commitment to building strong customer relationships can produce astonishingly large dividends. I have listened to him and been amazed. Here is one of the stories Mark told me.

In early 1989, Cooper undertook a job for Midwestern-based Society Bank to put new life into its banking program for 50-plus customers. The program, called Prime Advantage, had 18,000 households signed up when Cooper took on the job, but new accounts were barely keeping up with attrition. All that changed over the next four years:

Year	No. of Household	Average $ on Deposit Per Household	Total Deposits
1989	18,000	$20,000	$378 million
1993	150,000	$54,000	$8.1 billion

How did Cooper get these impressive results?

"By building empathetic connections with our customers," Cooper said in a telephone interview.[5] "We made them feel that they really mattered to us. Of course, you have to show them. Most banks think that they should take the widgets approach with seniors, pushing free gifts, free checking, and so on. But what older people really want is a caring, stable relationship with their banker. So we gave that to them."

But Cooper had a big problem to overcome before he could deliver a stable relationship to the older customer: annual turnover of specialists who worked with older customers was nearly 40 percent. It did not take Cooper long to find out that most specialists, who were in their 20s and 30s, didn't like working with older customers. Cooper knew that unless he turned staff attitudes around, the Prime Advantage program would not go very far. He began the revitalization of Prime Advantage by launching a concentrated training program for bank staffers. At the end of four years, annual turnover of senior specialists had fallen to around 10 percent. Cooper had built a cadre of specialists who learned to love the 50-plus customers as much as he did. On occasion, specialists would turn down an offer to move elsewhere in the bank because they didn't want to give up their relationships with their older customers. Most companies are looking through the wrong end of their telescopes when they talk about generating customer loyalty to their companies. Cooper's focus was on generating staff loyalty to customers.

"My first job was to get the senior specialists, most of whom were fairly young, to understand the older customer. Sure, some older customers are a pain, but so are some young customers. The second thing I did was to incent staffers. I devised bonus programs, but at least as effective, if not moreso, were the recognition programs. We had quarterly breakfasts that were a lot of fun at which we recognized the top performers. Branches began competing with each other to see who could have the most number of people recognized at these breakfasts."

Cooper has an interesting perspective on why the Prime Advantage program was so successful. He says, "Essentially, we didn't do anything spectacularly different. We just did our jobs spectacularly well." In other words, it was not necessary to be outside-the-box creative. Just build good relationships—starting with staff—and big dividends are almost automatically assured.

To help Prime Advantage members draw felicitous experiences from the season of life through which they were passing, they received a free subscription to *Life Today*, a quarterly lifestyle magazine published by Grote Deutsch. Having seen *Life Today*, which Grote Deutsch granted companies rights to distribute on a geographically exclusive arrangement, I regarded it as the best-executed magazine for older people in the country. It covered the usual financial, travel, and health issues, but also featured human interest stories and other articles that helped cement the bond between Society Bank and its Prime Advantage customers. Each issue contained a newsletter insert from Society Bank. Cooper says, "These and other things we did were in service of the three most important things in maintaining healthy loyal customer relationships: communications, communications, communications."

Cooper is now working on a similar program for Birmingham, Alabama–based Compass Bank. He thinks one of his best customer acquisition gambits is being able to promise members of Compass Directions (the name of the program) that members get the direct telephone number of their Compass Directions specialist, as well as his or her e-mail address. "When I announce this to groups of seniors whose business we are soliciting, there is always cheering and a round of applause. Everyone is sick to the bone of automated telephone systems and their menus."

It is not uncommon to hear someone say, "Customers don't want loving relationships with companies; they just want good products, good value, and courteous treatment." I have news for people who say that. While people may not be looking for relationships that make them go all aflutter, absent feel-good experiences, there is nothing to bind a customer to any brand or company. Mark Cooper's secret is simple: "To make customers feel good, you have to first make staff feel good. When staff and customers feel good together, you can't fail. You can just sit back and count the money rolling in."

•

Some of the Greatest Brands Have R-Value-Oriented Taglines

Having a great tagline does not a great brand make. However, taglines often indicate something about a company's corporate persona—its public face. Ideally, as with the self-actualizing person, a company's *real self* and its social self are in harmony. It's called "living the brand."

R-Value-centered taglines include FTD ("Say it with flowers"), State Farm ("Like a good neighbor, State Farm is there"), and Hallmark ("When you care enough to send the very best"). AT&T's "Reach out and touch someone" is a strong R-Value-oriented tagline that is R-Value-centered. Now, however, AT&T seems more intent on promoting its technology and pricing than relationships. Saturn began its brand life as R-Value-centered, but has departed from that orientation since coming under GM's central management structure. Now, despite retaining its original tagline, "A different kind of company. A different kind of car." Saturn marketing of late has been about features, benefits, and buying incentives. It is not the R-Value-oriented brand it was at its launch.

AOL's meteoric rise was fueled by Steve Case's intuitive grasp of the power of R-Values in customer behavior. In the fledgling days of the Internet, other Internet service providers such as CompuServe and Prodigy sought to grow by serving the then oft-spoken mantra "content is king." That was a pure left brain view of the Internet and its appeal to the masses. Steve Case vanquished his competitors by taking a right brain path. R-Values are essentially rooted in the relationship-minded right brain. AOL catalyzed the formation of thousands of online communities in which people invested considerable time and energy. Over 6,000 AOL subscribers volunteered to serve as chat room moderators. There is hardly a more visible example of a brand emerging as the collaborative product of a company and its customers than AOL, and Steve Case accomplished this by building his company around R-Values and proving in the process that community, not content, is king.

Amazon.com is another company with a business model rooted in R-values. Amazon.com's founder Jeff Bezos invited customers to post their reviews of books and products, thereby collaborating with customers to build the brand. Many people—myself included—rarely buy a book or other product from Amazon.com without first seeing what other customers have to say.

PURPOSE VALUES: SOURCES OF LIFE MEANING

Purpose values, or P-Values, spur behavior that imparts a sense of meaning to a person's life and brings focus to a person's output of energy. The absence of a sense of valid purpose enervates and emotionally depresses a person, but so pervasive throughout Nature is the need for purpose to continue having a claim on life that when a perfectly healthy cell in the body no longer has a job to do—in other words, no longer has a purpose—it literally commits suicide in a process called apoptosis. John Calhoun, a researcher at the National Institutes of Mental Health, discovered that when he allowed a rat colony to become overpopulated to the point that there were too few *meaningful role opportunities* to go around, cannibalism, raticide, premature menopause, and, ultimately, the inability of females to mature into a reproductive stage destroyed the entire colony.

Having purpose is a primal need that is clearly a component of basic life value, in Damasio's terms. Yet, despite their essential role in people's lives, P-Values receive the least attention in marketing communications of any of the five primary core value systems.

When I first began working with Del Webb in the early 1990s, the company had a long-standing tradition of marketing recreation (E-Values) *exclusively*. I believed that this limited the reach of the Sun City brand because messages pushing recreation would less likely survive the information triage processes of potential customers whose retirement doesn't revolve around golf, tennis, swimming, and nightly neighborhood gatherings around barbecue grills.

It is not uncommon for retirees, especially men, to suffer the enervating effects of a diminished sense of purpose. Contributing to this self-esteem challenge is a problem addressed by a man in a focus group when he said, "We live in a society where you are what you do. So when you retire, you do nothing, therefore you are nothing."

Phoenix ad agency Lavidge Baumayr created several ads to test the idea that a virtually exclusive focus on recreation was leaving money on the table. One ad showed a woman standing in a potting shed, arms on hips, head slightly cocked saying, "Your golf courses are beautiful. But I don't play." (See Figure 6.1.) The ad generated more prospects than any recent ad had done. Why? It connected with a whole new group of people. Sun City's brand reach was extended because the ad survived the information triage processes among a large group of people for whom retirement is viewed as a time for injecting new socially justifiable purpose in life.

Not many brands use taglines that are strongly rooted in P-Values. Many of those that do are nonprofit organizations that strive to connect with people's altruistic side, such as the United Negro College Fund's tagline, "A mind is a terrible thing to waste," the subtext of which is a call for people to do good by helping young students.

One for-profit company organized largely around P-Values is Tom's of Maine. Read the following words from Tom's Web site that demonstrate how the company strongly connects with people's desires to have purpose beyond their immediate selves:

FIGURE 6.1 *Del Webb Advertisement Appealing to P-Values*

Tom's has always been a community of people grounded in respect for another, animals, and nature. At Tom's of Maine, Natural Care is a way of life that guides what we make and all that we do. We think of Natural Care as many things—caring for nature, for our customers, and for our communities. We do this by creating safe, effective natural products free of dyes, sweeteners, and preservatives; by harvesting, processing, and packaging with respect for our natural resources; and by donating 10 percent of our profits and 5 percent of our employees' paid time to charitable organizations.[6]

From its founding, moral values—doing the right thing as a life purpose—have been the foundation Tom's of Maine's business model. Reflecting on headline scandals over the previous several years involving such names as Enron, Tyco, Arthur Andersen, WorldCom, and too many Wall Street brokerage houses, one wonders why more companies don't follow the path taken by Tom and Kate Chappell, who founded Tom's of Maine in 1970. The company, which posts double-digit growth in good times and bad, marks its products up 20 to 40 percent over competing brands, demonstrating that many customers put price aside for brands that resonate with their P-Values.

In the early days of Federal Express, before it became FedEx, the determined courier coined the memorable P-Value-oriented tagline "When it absolutely, positively has to be there overnight." The original marketing targeted executives and managers who generate much of what goes into the overnight packages. However, Federal Express soon figured out that those who actually dispatch overnight packages were better message targets. The message focus was changed to put less stress on getting a package to another city overnight and more on helping dispatchers fulfill their workplace purpose by meeting their responsibilities in superior fashion.

Pillsbury's ready-to-bake brands connect with P-Values with the tagline "Nothin' says lovin' like somethin' from the oven" because the brands promise homemakers that they will help them better meet their responsibilities to their families.

ADAPTATION VALUES: SOURCES OF KNOWLEDGE AND SKILLS TO MEET ONE'S NEEDS

Adaptation values, or A-Values, concern the development of knowledge and competence to fulfill one's needs. A-Values are the primary sources of desire for novelty. Desires for novelty promote experimentation and thrill-seeking behavior, which young people generally pursue with greater vigor than older people. Cravings for the dramatic, the extreme, and the different draw young people into new experiences that broaden and deepen their learning. Learning through experimentation begins in infancy and becomes a highly creative activity in early childhood. This is what the late Carl Sagan meant when he said every child is a scientist. A-Values are the impetus of play behavior during the juvenile and adolescent years. The urge to play is Nature's way of driving the young into experiences that teach. The stronger appetite for novelty among the young makes them more prone to faddish behavior. Fads replace the routine, as well as represent a way of presenting one's self as being *in.*

As people enter midlife and move forward in age, they are increasingly more inclined to follow the routine. This serves growing desires for a simpler and more balanced life. It also is why "retro" has become increasingly appealing as the population has aged. Though experiencing novelty for learning purposes is less prominent in the second half of life, it does remain a force in behavior because novel experiences help to maintain a sense of vitality.

While learning for gain dominates the knowledge acquisition behavior of people in the first half of life, learning for personal growth and for the sheer pleasure of learning tends to be stronger in the second half of life. This is why colleges and universities across the country have been aggressive in putting together learning opportunities for older people. Marty Knowlton and David Bianco of the University of New Hampshire established Elderhostel in 1975 as a program that integrated travel and education. With more than 400,000 members 55 and older, Elderhostel works with participating institutions of learning and other organizations in every state and many nations abroad to offer the developed world's burgeoning older population with continuing education and travel opportunities.

When AARP offered travel, the director of AARP's travel programs told me that he once developed two brochures for the same destination for purposes of experimentation. The first focused on the catered services features of the tour, the second on educational opportunities. The second brochure drew the larger response, and drew especially well among single women.

Mark Cooper said that one of the strongest draws in his Society Bank program was a travel program. He outsourced the management of the program so that it didn't impose any overhead burden on the bank, but according to Cooper, it yielded big returns in membership acquisition and retention. Trip offerings ranged from local day trips to more ambitious trips abroad.

Learning is big with the New Customer Majority. Several years ago for a series of free seminars to market a Prudential's HMO product in its West Coast operations, we scheduled seminars on memory and drew standing room audiences in most of the eight locations at which we held the seminars. Older people like to learn. They like to learn more about themselves, they like to learn about others, and they just plain like to learn in general.

Messages promising people that a given product will help them be smarter, stronger, and more effective are often A-Valued-centered (though they can be I-Value- or R-Value-centered as well). A-Value-centered brand taglines include Apple's "Think different" and also its "The power to be your best," *New York Times'* "All the news that's fit to print," the U.S. Army's "Be all you can be," and *Forbes'* "Capitalist tool." They are all about becoming more competent.

ENERGY VALUES: SOURCES OF OUR FUNCTIONAL POWER

Energy values, or E-Values, generate behaviors that promote physical and psychological health, and enhance functional performance and well being. They give rise to behavior that conserves and renews energy, and are the impetus for recreational play, which is different from A-Values-driven play for learning purposes. E-Values also generate desires for change of pace, changes in activity, and rest and relaxation. Finally, E-Values play the lead role in lifestyle behaviors related to health and fitness.

E-Value-generated behavior in the first half of life often seeks renewal of energy through escape from the dailyness of one's life. Hiking, bungee jumping, partying all night, and other nonroutine activities help young people recharge their batteries. In contrast, with the coming of midlife, people typically begin more often seeking to recharge through productive pursuits such as gardening, genealogy, volunteer work, eBay, craft hobbies, and time spent with grandchildren.

Industries devoted to meeting people's E-Value-generated needs include health products, vacation resorts, games, entertainment, and, of course, the sin industries from booze and soda pop to tobacco and candy.

E-Values lie behind much of our behavior that is oriented to the pursuit of sensuous pleasures, without which, well, life would hardly be worth living. While young people may regard themselves as highly sensuous, *sensual* probably better defines the focus of their pleasure desires, for it is the term that is more closely associated with sex. *Sensuous* is the term more closely associated with all the senses. Perhaps because of their lesser preoccupation with things and greater focus on experiential pleasure, the lifestyles of members of the New Customer Majority would seem to be more sensuously grounded than sensually grounded. In fact, in *Healthy Pleasures,* psychologist Robert Ornstein and physician David Sobel report that a regular diet of sensual pleasures, together with a positive outlook on life and time spent helping others, was a better predictor of health and longevity than such lifestyle indicators as diet, smoking, exercise, and alcohol consumption.

A key distinction between adults in the first and second halves of life lies in subtle distinctions between self-indulgence and self-expression. Self-indulgence is hedonistic; self-expression is existential.

Hedonism is the pursuit of escape through loss of a sense of self by preoccupation with what catalyzes pleasure. Drugs, drinking, and wanton sex are extreme examples of pleasures that diminish or suppress altogether the sense of self. The very object of those pursuits is to get lost in pleasure. Listening to music turned up so loud that physiological responses overwhelm sense of self is a bit more benign example of pleasure seeking in the cause of experiencing escape. Operators of nightclubs and watering holes for young people know that sound too loud for intimate conversation appeals to the young. Loudness provides escape from the dailyness of life, but also from the self.

Self-expression, in the sense that I am exploiting the term here, is existential because it is about making the self one with what is being pleasurably experienced but with full consciousness of the experience. It is about experiencing the total, unified self, as Maslow would say, without the edge taken off by mind-numbing imbibing or distraction. In the simplest of terms, it is about smelling the latte and basking in its uplifting transformation of the self. It is a return to the gift that children have: gaining maximum pleasure from minimalist sources. This is not possible in a hedonistic state because the pleasures partaken overwhelm the subtle things from which the more mature mind takes infinite pleasure.

What you should take away from this discussion of E-Values in terms of second-half markets is that better connections will more often be made with older customers by emphasizing self-expression rather than self-indulgence because the mature mind seeks, in Erik Erikson's words, *vital involvement*. Disengagement is the wont of the younger, less-experienced, less-developed mind that more often needs escape from conditions that hold it hostage in the ordinary course of things. Escapist activity is in service of sanity unless it becomes an obsession.

A CLARIFICATION

It may seem that the brands I used to exemplify a strong connection with one particular primary core value also could be connected to another. For instance, I cited Pillsbury's ready-to-bake products as P-Values-centered. Could it just as logically be linked to E-Values, which involve food behaviors, or R-Values because of the family connection? Perhaps; but while "somethin' from the oven" is food and for the family, the subtext of the tagline connects most strongly with Purpose—meeting one's responsibilities to one's family.

Because no primary core value system operates independently of other primary core value systems, no brand can avoid linkage to multiple core need systems. However, every brand should have a primary core value system connection, and collateral marketing messages should never be in conflict with that primary connection.

In the next chapter, I describe how primary core values exert their influence on behavior differently over the course of life in response to certain developmental objectives and life story themes that are characteristic of each of the four seasons of life.

7

SEASONS OF A
CUSTOMER'S LIFE

When my son Brian was about 7, he had just barely escaped with hide intact from another scrap with his sister Karen who was a bit more than two years older. I forget what the squabble was about, but I do remember trying to explain to him how people often see the same thing differently. The next Sunday's newspaper fortuitously carried a comic strip that came to my aid. As best as I remember across some 30 years of time, the strip opened with an ant coming across a large round flat object. "What is that great big thing?" it asks. "Oh, it's a giant cookie," it says.

A duck waddles into the scene and says, "My, what's that? Oh, it's a big cookie."

Then a dog appears and observes, "What a nice cookie."

Next, an elephant lumbers by and asks, "What is that?" With a squinted eye cast downward, the pachyderm exclaims, "My! A wee little cookie."

In the final frame, a worm sticks its head out of the earth and cries, "Just my luck! All those cookies around and I didn't see a one!"

I showed Brian the strip. He got its point immediately. Some people never discover, even after many decades of life, what my son did at age 7. They are like the 11-year-old son of a colorblind friend. The boy cannot cognitively grasp how his father can see an apple but not see that it is red. The 11-year-old thinks everyone sees the same thing when looking at the same object.

THE FOUR SEASONS OF LIFE

No two people perceive a product message exactly the same way either. Each person's perceptions are colored by inherited traits, life history, present life circumstances, and by his or her *current season of life*. Almost everyone recalls revisiting a place for the first time since childhood and being a bit amazed at how much smaller it seemed than remembered. In similar fashion, many of us remember our grandparents, who might have been in their 50s or 60s when we were young children, as looking very old. We carry that memory into adulthood and as the years mount up and we become grandparents, we think we look much younger than our grandparents did at the same age. However, odds are that to your 5- or 6-year-old grandchild you look pretty much as old as your grandparents looked to you at the same age.

No adult would argue that a 25-year-old doesn't see things differently than a 15-year-old. Less appreciated is the fact that 45-year-olds see thing differently than 25-year-olds do, and 65-year-olds see things differently than 45-year-olds. All that being so, it's important when creating marketing messages to know how people differ in their perspectives by season of life. There is a great deal of predictability to these differences. This chapter identifies some of those differences.

No exhaustive research is needed to learn about season-of-life differences between people in how they process information. Developmental and cognitive psychologists have done the basic research for you over many years. Because these differences show up in every generation, you can safely rely on what developmental and cognitive psychologists already know.

Fifteen-year-olds, for example, typically have a perception of reality that is steeped in fantasy. A 15-year-old knows in his heart that he is going to do great things—be a movie star, big-time athlete, world-class scientist, great surgeon, or an exemplar in whatever he does—because life will simply break in his favor. In contrast, the 25-year-old knows to the core of her being that what she accomplishes will be of her own doing, not the fortuitous result of fate breaking her way. She has grown out of the fantastical worldview of a 15-year-old, and now sports a romantic worldview, one that is heroic and bigger than life. The world is her oyster and she is going to harvest many pearls.

The 45-year-old's outlook on the world and himself has changed dramatically from what it was at 25. He no longer views life from a romantic perspective. Gone is the heroic notion that he can conquer any challenge to which he puts his mind. From time to time, his spirits are dampened by feelings that there must be more to life than what he's getting out of it, even though he suffers no unmet material need, is financially secure, has many friends, and is ostensibly the master of his own destiny. Perhaps he's accomplished more than he thought he ever would, but for some reason feels a sense of emptiness. "There must be more," he plaintively muses on occasion.

The 65-year-old, now far beyond fantasy with no pretensions about conquering the world and having found the life balance and simplicity she sought in midlife, is more sanguine. She is agreeably reconciled with the idea that meaning and purpose, together with life satisfaction, come from within—not from what happens or does not happen in the external world. She has achieved social autonomy. A need for others is no longer a centering focus. Having attained that state of social emancipation, she embraces others for who they are, not for what they can do for her. Paradoxically, as her dependence on others subsided, her appreciation of others has grown stronger. She now likes many things better and appreciates them more, and what she doesn't like is rarely a serious bother. She just shuts it out of her consciousness. She learned over many years that keeping something unpleasant in the mind pollutes it and keeps a person from having pleasurable experiences with things more worthy of thinking about.

Each of those four people reflect worldviews that have evolved in a remarkably consistent pattern from one season of life to the next, and generally reflecting the following themes, by season:

- *Spring* (childhood). This season is characterized by fantastic, magical themes.
- *Summer* (young adulthood). This season is characterized by romantic, heroic themes.

- *Fall* (middle adulthood). This season is characterized by realistic, introspective themes.
- *Winter* (late adulthood). This season is characterized by ironic, paradoxical themes.

To ensure a clear understanding of what we mean by *worldview*, it's worth reflecting again on Danah Zohar's definition:

> "A theme which integrates the sense of self, the sense of self and others, and the sense of how these relate to the wider world—to Nature and other creatures, to the environment as a whole, to the planet, the universe, and ultimately to God—to some overall purpose and direction . . . A successful worldview must, in the end, draw all these levels—the person, the social, and the spiritual—into one coherent whole. If it does so, the individual has access to some sense of who he is, why he is here, how he relates to others, and how it is valuable to behave."

The characteristic worldview of each season influences how a person "integrates the sense of self, the sense of self and others, and the sense of how these relate to the wider world." This is not to suggest that everyone in the same season of life has the same worldview—or even one similar. However, no one can seriously argue that the worldviews of children and adolescents are not generally fantastical and magical or that young adults' worldviews are not generally romantic and heroic. Few middle-agers would deny being more realistic than they once were, and most elderly would subscribe to the idea that life is filled with more irony and paradox than imaginable when their worldviews were circumscribed by the certainty of youth. Psychologist Dan McAdams sees those season-of-life attributes as *personal myth themes*—themes that guide us as we act out our continuously evolving life stories from one season of life to the next.

Marketing messages can evoke strong emotional responses when they resonate deeply with people's worldviews. Nike's "Just do it!" resonates strongly with the young who see few barriers and are inclined toward immoderate self-expression. In contrast, New Balance's "Achieve new balance" deliberately plays to the midlife worldview that values moderation in self-expression and recognizes limitations.

In the last chapter, we examined the five primary core value systems that are present in our makeup at birth from which arise our needs and motivations. Our objective in this chapter is to lay the foundation necessary for understanding how these five systems lead to evolutionary changes in worldviews, values, needs, and motivations throughout the four seasons of life.

WHY SEASON OF LIFE INFLUENCES PERCEPTIONS

Each person's life is a story. You should never forget this as a marketer because when you advertise a product you are auditioning for a role in customers' life stories.

We live out our lives as personal narratives in which plotlines and characters change according to our needs in the season of life through which we are currently passing. Anticipating these changes for marketing purposes is made easier by understanding two facets of personal development, each of which greatly influences customer behavior:

1. Developmental objectives
2. Developmental catalysts

Developmental objectives. Each season of life has set purposes that determine how primary core needs become manifest. We have no control over that. They are engraved in our DNA. We do, however, have a say in how we respond to those needs. The main developmental objectives by season are:

- *Spring* (the first two decades of life): acquiring basic intellectual, emotional, and social skills needed to enter adulthood and navigate through it with reasonable success.
- *Summer* (the second two decades of life): completing development of the social self, which includes integration into social networks and stepping into roles that serve one's vocational, social, and personal aspirations.

- *Fall* (the third two decades of life): advancing the inner self to a higher quality of self-expression, which involves its integration with the social self to yield a more resilient and balanced personality.
- *Winter* (the remaining years of life): reaching a transcendent state that infuses one with a quiescence that both deepens life satisfaction and dampens the discomfiting impact of troublesome conditions the future may bring.

Development catalysts. Achieving a life season's main developmental objective depends on primary catalytic agents that make things happen to actualize that objective. The main developmental catalysts are:

- *Spring:* Persistent yearning for play through which learning takes place. The play imperative draws toddlers, older children, and adolescents into modeling life. Children and youth have the license to try roles, ideas, beliefs, and situations normally without fear of penalty for mistakes. College students throw big thoughts around over beer in their dorms without fear of being wrong. They play with ideas as part of their learning just as 6-year-olds do with their Tonka trucks and Barbies. However, thoughts modeled in the wee hours of the morning that seem so momentous as the beer runs dry are forgotten upon entering the real world after graduation when playtime is over.
- *Summer:* Yearning for work, the means by which a person satisfies a consuming focus on becoming someone socially and vocationally. Earnings generated by work support desires to make social statements that give material proof of a person's accomplishments; thus summer is the season of acquisitiveness.
- *Fall:* Yearning for life balance and meaning. The focus changes from *becoming* someone to *being* someone. The inner self, long submerged by an outer-world-directed agenda, aches for a simpler life. The quest for life satisfaction in fall shifts progressively away from a focus on things to a focus on experiences.
- *Winter:* Yearning for reconciliation with the world, self, family, and friends. This is a time for squaring life's sweet moments with its bitter, for making peace with self and with all others.

The table in Figure 7.1 summarizes these season-of-life themes.

FIGURE 7.1 *The Four Seasons of Life and Our Life Stories*

SEASON	DEVELOPMENTAL FOCUS	DURATION	SURVIVAL FOCUS & MAIN LIFE STORY THEME
Spring	Basic development	0 – 22±	**Play *(learning)* Fantasy theme:** "Everything will ultimately break my way." Dei ex machina —"There will always be someone to help me get out of trouble."
Summer	Social/vocational development	18± – 40±	**Work *(becoming somebody)* Romantic, heroic theme:** "The world is my oyster. There is no holding me back because I can do anything I set out to do."
Fall	Inner self development	38± – 60±	**Work-play balance *(search for meaning)* Reality theme:** "There *are* limitations; I can't do what I thought I could," or "I've done better than I thought, but something is missing. Who am I, *really?*"
Winter	Climax of development	58± – ?	**Life reconciliation *(making sense of life)* Ironic theme:** There's some good in every bad, and some bad in every good, nothing is black and white, and little that is certain; *c'est la vie!*

To fully appreciate the powerful though generally subtle season-of-life influences on customer behavior, it is necessary to get beyond the common view that we consciously fully plot out our lives. We may work out the details, but Mother Nature has already charted the general plotlines and themes of our lives before the umbilical cord is cut. For instance, by determining our gender, she imposes on us a major scheme of influences. Should she be ambiguous about our gender, that too will be a factor in the plotlines and themes of our life stories. However, despite bitterly wrought claims to the contrary in the 1970s and 1980s, it is now conclusive: differences between genders extend beyond the organs of reproduction into the brain. Male and female brains *are* different, with each person's behavior influenced by predispositions that are characteristic (not absolute, but *characteristic*) of his or her gender.

Once we get beyond the illusion of individual omnipotence over the directions of our lives, we can begin to understand ourselves and our customers better. There are things that just are. For example, before we have drawn our first breath, laws of genetics have already determined our native intelligence, which the renowned psychologist Howard Gardiner views as consisting of seven separate intelligences: linguistic, musical, logical-mathematical, spatial, bodily-kinesthetic, intrapersonal, and interpersonal. We can build on what we are born with, but we cannot add what we were not born with to our basic makeup.

A master growth plan designed by Mother Nature is also in place at birth. Like a city's master growth plan, some things will inevitably be different as the master growth plan gets developed, but the core elements of the master growth plan remain an influence on behavior. A few months after birth, and in accordance with that master growth plan, we begin turning over. A little later we start crawling, then taking our first tentative steps, and forming our first words. Between ages 3 and 4, we have acquired enough words to express our desires, but beyond that, in the space of just a few months we have mastered the basic rules of grammar—a feat that takes the typical adult three or four years to accomplish. By 7, our prefrontal lobes in the brain are complete enough that we can for the first time cognitively grasp the concept of time and consequences of our actions in the context of time. A few years later, we begin our transformation into adolescence, an event marked by sea changes in physiology, psychology, and behavior.

No one doubts that developmental changes throughout infancy, childhood, and adolescence influence behavior in predisposed ways. However, developmental changes occur throughout all of life, whatever age we are, to exert predisposing influences on our behavior. Despite the insistence of our human egos that we are in total control, the truth is that we are not. Until we have the humility to admit that, we will fall shorter than we would like in understanding others and ourselves. This is part of what Maslow meant about the self-actualizing person being "ego-less," being able to let go so perceptions of reality are purer, unadulterated by the ego's agenda and biases.

The goal of this chapter is to make a persuasive case that some of the strongest influences on behavior—customer and otherwise—are the innate forces of personal development as inscribed in the master plan of growth that we bring with us as we enter into the world. We may exercise control over our responses to what that growth plan contains, but the developmental drivers of behavior are there in any event. For example, the flood of hormonal changes that marks adolescence is a developmental event that gives rise to desires for sexually oriented behaviors among others. Though we may choose our responses to those desires, we have no control over their presence. We might distract ourselves or otherwise suppress our consciousness of desires, but that does not mean that we can prevent them from influencing our behavior. In the first place, even when we distract ourselves from a desire, the action has been influenced by the desire we seek to suppress. We've all experienced a desire that we would rather not have that keeps popping up in our consciousness. Then we finally give in and the desire goes away—*for a while.*

The desire to simplify life is another motivation that can be triggered by developmental forces. Trackers of consumer trends say this desire is becoming more widespread in customer behavior, often tying it to such externalities as 9/11, war jitters, and economic disorder. However, the desire to simplify life is also a primal need that begins asserting itself more strongly after the child-producing years. It is not a desire born of contemporary conditions or the complexities of modern life. Ancient religious and philosophic writings extol the virtue of withdrawing from a worldly bound existence after the child-producing years.

The season-of-life model of the evolution of behavior across the lifespan forms a framework to guide consumer researchers and marketers in planning and executing their tasks. Researchers can shape questions to research subjects around the developmental objectives and development catalysts of the season of life through which customers are passing. Marketers can create messages that reflect aspirations characteristic of the season of life through which customers are passing. Basing marketing strategies and executions on the developmental objectives and catalysts of customers' seasons of life will make marketing communications more relevant and, thus, more likely to survive information triage.

Too often marketing messages lack congruence with the needs and values of customers in a given season of life. Refer back to the New Balance ad that began, "One more woman chasing a sunset." It is unquestionably directed to women in midlife, though it will also resonate with men. The ad is about the meaning of life, which makes for a metaphysical or spiritual ad. Around the time the ad ran, Nike ran an ostensibly spiritual ad showing a Lakota Indian against a night sky announcing a long run he was planning to make the next day in the land of Paba Sapa in the Black Hills—"our church." He goes on to say that in spite of being tired, he will do it anyway, "for all Lakota." Thus he projects a machismo affect that compromises its putative spiritual theme—unless it was intended for adolescent and young adult markets, in which case the ad works. But it doesn't work as well for the more introspective middle-age markets with which New Balance so skillfully connects.

KEEPING PACE WITH THE CHANGING CUSTOMER

The path of psychological maturation laid out in DNA coding is the backbone of developmental psychology, as well as the backbone of developmental relationship marketing. People in the CRM space talk a great deal about the importance of working to keep customers for life. However, the left brain-dominated thinking behind this has been more about presenting the right products in the right way to customers. It takes a lot more than that to create loyal customers for life, or at least through a *full* season of life. There must be an emotionally forged right brain connection that conveys an empathetic perception of customers. Empathy—identifying with and understanding another's circumstances, emotions, feelings, and motives—is *absolutely* essential to keeping customers for life. To understand another person's circumstances, emotions, feelings, and motives—especially motives—requires understanding where that person is in his or her evolving life stories.

The basic premise of DRM outlines the most critical dimensions in personal development that are constantly in a state of flux. Understanding what goes on in these dimensions will make it easier to create the empathetic connections with customers that make them long-term customers.

THE BASIC PREMISE OF DEVELOPMENTAL RELATIONSHIP MARKETING

Stages of psychological maturation tend to predispose the general character of a person's behavior in five dimensions:

1. *Worldview.* This is the perceptual lens through which people see and connect to the outside world. The better the alignment between a marketing message and customers' worldviews, the more likely the marketing message will connect with customers.
2. *Needs.* These are deficiencies that often create physical and psychological discomfort until satisfied, such as when we are hungry, need companionship, or crave relief from boredom. No research is needed to know what customers' deepest and most basic needs are. That information already exists in the annals of behavioral science.
3. *Motivations.* These are urges to action. They are influenced by DNA-borne traits, personal life history, socioeconomic profile, and people's subjective responses to their experiences.
4. *Approach to needs satisfaction.* This concerns risk tolerance and impulse resistance. The young generally have higher risk tolerance and lower resistance to impulse buying than older people who are more prone to taking the tried and proven path.
5. *Thinking style.* This is about how people mentally process information. The thinking styles of young adults generally call for more directness in messaging while the thinking styles of older adults generally call for more deference and less absolutism in message style.

How Solid Is All This?

Understanding the processes and milestones of psychological maturation offers a penetrating look inside the consumer psyche at all ages.

However, in the sense that believing is seeing, unless a person believes that the foundations of customer behavior are not conscious, he or she will peer into the lens I am holding up for all to see through and see nothing.

At a sales workshop in which I was a trainer, I was describing unconscious influences on our behavior when with the suddenness of a thunderclap, a woman shot up out of her seat and yelled, "Mr. Wolfe, you may not know why you do what you do, but I am fully aware of why I do what I do." She created such uproar that she was escorted out of the room by her boss, who suggested that she might look for another line of work, as she was more interested in preserving her beliefs than in learning how to better understand customers and their behavior.

It takes true humility to be truly human. Putting on airs about how much we consciously shape our lives is not useful. We may have the ability to shape meaningful outcomes in our lives, but that control is limited by rules and potentialities embodied in our genes and in the unconscious realms of the brain. Acknowledging this is essential to a full appreciation of the hidden forces that play a major role in shaping customer behavior.

Traditionally, little attention has been paid in marketing to the underpinnings of our needs and motivations in our genes. The engines of action that drive the basic four Fs of survival—*fight, flight, feed,* and *reproduction* (as they sometimes joke in neuroscience)—are indelibly programmed in DNA code that defines us first as organic beings and last as human beings. Because many urgings thrust into our conscious minds by our brains are season-of-life sensitive, we can often know a surprising amount about a person merely by knowing his or her age.

By now, you may have a number of questions and, perhaps, even some challenges to parts of what you have read in this chapter about the seasons of life. I would like to anticipate some of these questions and challenges in a question and answer format.

Reader: Are you saying that everyone experiences the season-of-life factors that you have laid out in this chapter?

Author: Yes, but not necessarily consciously, and not necessarily with the same degree of influence. I have described the path of psychological development encoded in our genes. Within a preset range of options, how each person follows that path is unique to him or her. But everyone is inclined by genetic inheritance to take the same general path. Along that path, everyone meets up with the same developmental milestones, generally in the same time frame. We see this among children. They generally do the same things—turning over, crawling, walking, talking, etc. —within the same time frame because of preset triggers in their DNA. We don't stop evolving at age 18 or 21, or even at 40 or 50. The general direction and pacing of our lifelong evolution is a function of DNA performance.

Reader: But, you're not saying that everyone develops at the same pace or that everyone reaches the same level of development?

Author: Absolutely not. People who have not done very well in reaching their psychological maturation goals in one season of life will struggle with meeting the psychological maturation goals in the next season of life. But even so, they will pass the same milestones as a person who is doing better in personal growth; they just won't be able to actualize their developmental potential as well.

Reader: All this has been interesting, but how do I make the connection to marketing?

Author: Read the rest of the book! Seriously, everyone knows that to get another person's attention and confidence it helps to show the other person that you understand his or her circumstances, feelings, motives, and actions. Most traditional marketing is based on research involving relatively few people and generalizing research results to the many. Many customers fall outside those generalizations. Many of those customers, if approached differently than generalizations indicated, could add up to a sizeable chunk of potential sales not made. By marketing to values, rather than to age, and with sensitivity to season-of-life factors, you will extend your brand's reach.

Reader: Aren't you overlooking the role that cohort effect plays in a person's development? I mean, however genes influence our behavior, there are also the events that we share with our peers during our growing-up years.

Author: I'm not overlooking cohort effect. Cohort influences concern *how* a person responds to needs and motivations, not the nature of his or her primary needs and motivations. I would say this, however, the cohort effect card is overplayed, something that you will read about shortly.

Reader: What about differences in background like growing up poor or rich, or growing up in New York or Tokyo, or growing up in an all-American household or one that has been shattered by divorce or even violence?

Author: All of what you mentioned would influence the style and intensity of response, but the primary core needs will be the same for everyone, as influenced by season of life.

Reader: I don't know if I buy everything you've said, but I have to admit that a lot of it makes common sense when I think about it.

Author: Thanks. No one agrees completely with anyone on any issue of substance, and when we talk about human behavior, we're certainly into an issue of substance. But I'm trying to present in this book common sense ideas that are fortified with well-established tenets in developmental psychology and new insights from recent brain research. You will, of course, adapt to what I say in ways that reflect your own individualism. That's cool. An important philosophic plank of DRM is that it is not prescriptive, but suggestive. It is an analytic and decision guidance system that follows a set of basic principles. I see DRM as open source software of sorts, to which each person using it adds to it by dint of their own creative input.

INTERLUDE

While writing the first two parts of
this book, I've been nagged by thoughts of how much we short-cut critical thinking with the mindless use of labels, such as *boomers* and *seniors,*
and with vague concepts like "generation" and "cohort effect." I wondered where I might best address these thoughts. To get them off my
mind and break the pace of this book for a moment, I'm inserting this
interlude to discuss these thoughts.

ON LABELS AND OTHER BARRIERS
TO CRITICAL THINKING

When my daughter Stephanie was 7, she looked up from the comics
one morning at breakfast and asked me to listen to her read the Calvin
and Hobbes strip aloud. Calvin complained to his imaginary tiger friend
that "they" don't name a generation "until you get really old—like 20."
Stephanie then said with a quizzical look on her face, "Daddy, I don't
understand. Isn't a new generation born every day?"

At age 7 she had pointed out the obvious that probably few of us
ever see. Instead we clump together people born over an arbitrarily cho-

sen number of years and give them all-too-clever names. We then make monstrously broad generalizations that have scant foundation in reality.

While conducting a workshop in 1996, the year the first boomers turned 50, I asked for two volunteers, one born in 1946 and another born in 1964, the bookends of the boomer "generation." A balding man with a bit of a widened girth approached the podium; a trim, well-groomed 32-year-old man followed him. Before I could say anything, someone from the audience got the point and shouted, "They're twins!"

I asked each man to talk about his plans for the next five years. The 32-year-old said he wanted to get into the top echelons of his company, buy a bigger house, and start working fewer than his customary 12 to 14 hours a day. The 50-year-old in effect said, "Been there, done that. I'm easin' up now. Making my life simple. Gonna retire in a few years and I'd like to get some practice."

Each man was at a very different time of life, with different aspirations and goals, yet both are called boomers, members of an age cohort who supposedly have much in common because . . . well, just because they are boomers. Remember, we're told over and over, boomers were shaped by the same events growing up. Not. I'll tell you why in a bit.

We label things for practical reasons, but do so at the risk of inhibiting critical thinking, resulting in giving more meaning to a label than reality justifies. The meanings given to the label *boomers* have been enlarged far beyond the boundaries of reality.

We do much the same with the label *senior,* but because we've already dealt with that label, we don't need to spend any more time on it. The purpose of this brief interlude is to challenge the extent to which we use generational labels and the connected idea of cohort effect.

GENERATIONAL PERCEPTION GAPS

Marketing today is hampered by *generational perception gaps* that arise when people widely separated by age see the same thing but assign different meanings to it.

The age differences between those who dominate the creation of marketing executions and the "average" consumer is growing, probably costing companies billions of dollars annually because of generational perception gaps that lead to marketing executions that fail to do their expected jobs.

Companies spend more than $200 billion annually in advertising and billions more in research, consulting, and other services to support marketing. How many of those dollars are wasted because marketing executions do not connect with customers due to generational perception gaps?

Various reports peg the average age of ad agency account representatives between 28 and 30—about the same it has been for years. This means the typical account executive is 14 to 16 years younger than the current adult median age of 44, and 20 to 22 years younger than adults 50 and older, who represent 44 percent of all adults.

Chapter 1 documented the sharp decline in marketing productivity since the New Customer Majority began emerging in 1989. I think it is more than just coincidence that as the median age of adults has risen without a corresponding increase in the average age of product message creators, marketing productivity has fallen. Yes, other factors, such as the Internet, have impacted advertising, but I still think much of the problem arises from generational perception gaps.

Some people may feel these remarks are condescending toward young marketers. They are not. They simply reflect the empirically validated fact (as well as common sense) that people see things differently at different ages.

Think about how a typical 16-year-old sees a 30-year-old. The 30-year-old is *too old* to remember being a teen. In the 1960s, youth memorialized this idea by repeatedly warning each other "Don't trust anyone over 30."

To a 28-year-old ad account executive, age 50 seems as remote generationwise as age 30 appears to a 16-year-old. That means a 28-year-old marketer working in 50-plus markets is likely operating beyond the boundaries of his or her *natural ability* to perceive many things the same way a 50-year-old sees them. Education and training can help remedy the problem, which is why I italicized *natural ability*. But few young marketing professionals have been trained for working in second-half markets. As a consequence, messages for second-half customers more often than not reflect reality as seen through the lens of young adulthood.

WHAT IS A GENERATION, ANYWAY?

Developmental psychologist Daniel Levinson understands the problem of generational perception gaps. In his book *The Seasons of a Man's Life*, Levinson formulated a definition of *generation* that makes more sense in some crucial ways than do the generational labels of boomer, Gen X, Gen Y, and Millennials.

Levinson's research found that in terms of a person's sense of affinity with others and the ability to identify with and relate to them, a person's generation consists of people who are within six or seven years of his or her age. This means that from a *subjective* perspective, the age span of a generation is 12 to 14 years. People, who are between 7 and 15 years younger or older than we are, comprise a *half-generation* according to Levinson. They are not our peers, but not of our parents' generation, either. We relate to them more as we might relate to a much younger or much older sibling. We usually perceive people who are 20 years younger or older than we are as being a full generation removed from us, unless they are 40 years younger or older, in which case they are at least two generations removed from us.[1]

By Levinson's reckoning, no one in the New Customer Majority belongs to the 28-year-old account executive's generation, and most are at least a full generation removed.

Let's apply Levinson's thinking to the so-called boomer generation that spans 18 years. As was evident in the differences between the two boomers in my workshop, the oldest and youngest boomers fall into two separate generations. Also, because cohort effects supposedly give people who feel generationally connected a certain like-mindedness, Levinson's research challenges much of what has been said about boomers. Specifically, if his claim that generational affinity applies to people within six or seven years of one's age, it is nonsensical to talk about the *boomer market* as though it were one monolithic market, because they did not all grow up experiencing the same seminal events.

By Levinson's reasoning, babies born between 1946 (the year the first boomer was born) and 1952 had one foot in the so-called Silent Generation and the other in the Boomer Generation. Babies born between 1958 and 1964 (the year the last boomer was born) had one foot in the Boomer Generation and the other foot in the Generation X generation. Only people born between 1952 and 1958, numbering around 25 million—not 78 million—and accounting for only a third of boomers, had both feet in the Boomer Generation.

So, when people talk about marketing to the "aging boomer market," they are talking about marketing to an illusionary market. We ought not to forget that *boomer* is a marketing term borrowed by marketers from Landon Jones' 1981 book, *Great Expectations: America and the Baby Boom.* Thus, boomers were not named as such until the oldest were 35 and the youngest were 17. So, it's not surprising that many boomers don't think of themselves as boomers, and even resent being called such. For sure, few boomers born in the 1960s feel they belong to the same generation as boomers born in the 1940s.

Levinson defined *generation* from the individual's perspective, not a marketer's. It was not a crisp definition calculated to make it an easier frame of reference in building statistical models. When you apply that definition to the 18-year cohort called boomers a much different picture emerges of the cohort effects—historical experiences that influence people growing up together—shared by people born between 1946 and 1964. Leading-edge boomers (born between 1946 and 1952) have a very different historical foundation for their values and views on life than trailing-edge boomers (born between 1968 and 1964). Leading-edge boomers have a clear memory of the JFK assassination, but trailing-edge boomers don't. The youngest were not even born yet. By the time trailing-edge boomers reached middle school, leading edge boomers had shaved off their beards, cut their hair, started wearing bras again, and put away or thrown away their folk art jewelry to take their place in the establishment they formerly scorned.

So let's stop inhibiting critical thinking by extending the meaning of labels far beyond their actual significance.

THE PSYCHOLOGY OF CUSTOMER BEHAVIOR

Bit by bit, the idea that we have near absolute control over our lives through the mechanisms of consciousness, constitution, and free will is being eroded by genetics, evolutionary psychology, and neuroscience. This is a shocking development, for it means that much of what we have thought about ourselves is wrong. However, some people will deny the validity of revolutionary insights that are redefining our self-perceptions merely because they don't like what they mean.

The ideas of Copernicus and Galileo met with the same resistance some 400 years ago. Today, nearly everyone accepts those ideas with no second thought. I say *nearly everyone* because, yes, some people who, despite growing up with modern schooling, still believe the Earth is flat and hanging fixed in space like a disk on a string with the sun spinning around it. If you don't believe me, search for "flat Earth" on Google. You may be surprised by the results.

At some time in the future nearly everyone will accept without any second thought the astonishing discoveries that science is now making about our behavior. For awhile, however, expect resistance due to general discomfort with the idea that we are not who we thought we were and because no mental models exist in common consciousness that allow people to comfortably adapt to the new paradigm of human behavior.

This new paradigm does not destroy the idea of self-determination, but it does present a new picture of how free will operates. In this new view, the exercise of free will depends on output from the brain that is beyond the reach of the conscious mind. If we think about it with a clear and open mind, this only makes sense. The conscious mind does not have enough working memory to hold everything in place at one time, so the unconscious brain, which works much faster than the conscious mind, must do a lot of work for our conscious selves. It generates instant responses when there is no time to think through an urgent situation and it often thrusts unreasoned, unbidden, but on-target intuitive insights into our conscious selves. The conscious mind can still veto much of what the brain proposes through its exercise of free will, though not everything because your conscious mind doesn't have enough RAM to review everything the brain does on your behalf.

Most of this book revolves around the unseen, unconscious influences on behavior. But that is only a part of what researchers and marketers should know. Many important things take place in the conscious minds of customers about which researchers and marketers need to know.

The next two chapters are about the contents of the conscious minds of second-half customers aged 45 and above. They are based on research conducted by the Seniors Research Group of Market Strategies, Inc., under the auspices of the Mature Market Group of J. Walter Thompson Worldwide. Robert E. Snyder, senior partner and director of the Mature Market Group, has written the two chapters that lie directly ahead.

These chapters are presented with full realization that what people tell researchers in surveys, the main source of information presented in these two chapters, is often not the whole story and sometimes not a true story at all. Nevertheless, much can be inferred from what customers tell researchers that can be important to marketing success. In any event, marketers must take into account what people think is true, even if it is not wholly true. Remember, to get a full 360-degree view of customers it is necessary to integrate biology with psychology, because *biology plus psychology equals behavior*. The next two chapters thus explore the psychological sector of a full 360-degree view of a large block of the New Customer Majority: customers 45 and older.

8

VALUE PORTRAITS

A Matter of Values for the Fall and Winter Seasons of Life

As a seasoned marketer, I can confirm David Wolfe's provocative statement that "marketers must take into account what people think is true, even if it is not wholly true." Often, people draw well-reasoned conclusions based on experience and assert those conclusions as fact without understanding their experience is less than universal. After all, any individual's universe is defined by personal judgment informed by experience. Marketers, like consumers, aren't immune to making judgments based on what their experience tells them are "obvious" facts. To begin, I offer the following illustration from my own experience.

Some years back, I was involved in the direct sale of products used by schools and nonprofit groups to help raise much-needed funds. (No doubt this was a result of my having been a high school music teacher for a number of years!) Interestingly, I learned more about human behavior during my years as a salesperson than I did in all my years of teaching. Each year, the company I worked for would recruit rookies either to replace those who had not been successful or to open up new geographic territories.

Having achieved some degree of success in the sales world, I soon found myself with the title of "sales trainer" and confidant to many of the rookies. Many skilled salespeople did not have a clue how to tell others how to reproduce what they themselves had done. What I possessed was the ability to impart easy-to-use knowledge that made sense to the rookies.

One of the goals of a salesperson in the fundraising business is to find leads and turn them into prospects. Generally, this is a simple process. Every elementary school, every middle school, and every high school is filled with prospects who lead groups that need to raise money. This was obvious to all who entered the business, especially those of us who had been band directors or coaches.

Other prospects included individuals who ran Little League baseball leagues or community football leagues. One spring, I was trying to teach one of my best rookies about the importance of these types of prospects and I thought I had accomplished my task well. I provided this person with ideas of where to look and how to find them. I gave her names of leagues found in most every city in the United States. A week went by and during my next scheduled "manager" phone call my rookie said to me, "There are no leagues in my area!"

I was stunned. I had no idea that a city the size of Pittsburgh had no Little League baseball and no youth football. I was perplexed at first, then amused, by the notion that my rookie had the only territory in the United States that had no youth sports. I explained to my rookie (who was actually diligent and successful) that I was sure that Little Leagues did indeed exist in her area. She continued to insist that they did not. Of course, with a little help and direction, I was able to help her find her prospects.

I share this story in order to draw a very clear analogy regarding why the study of human values and their influence on decision making have been greatly overlooked. If you are a marketer looking for insights as to why humans behave the way they do, you would first look for the obvious. As with the example above, the rookie salesperson was able to see the obvious leads—elementary, middle, and high schools. However, when it came to finding the not-so-obvious, the rookie salesperson, having no experience in Little League or youth sports as a child, was unable to see that these entities did exist.

After a week of trying to find these prospects, she concluded that they did not exist in her area, or her world. She is a smart person, but her personal proof was based on her own limited experience. When it came to finding Little League sponsors, there were no obvious buildings standing on the corner shouting to the rookie: *"Stop Here. Make Sale!"*

That rookie became my wife, Stephanie. To this day, when we can't find something we are looking for, the joke between us is "I guess there are no leagues in my area!"

With regard to human behavior, the ability to see the obvious is indeed a good thing. In this scenario the elementary, middle, and high school prospects represent the guideposts that have directed marketing's messages for the past 50 years. These guideposts include the obvious preliminary criteria: age and income. These criteria are the "schools" in our scenario. They are obvious because they represent tangible quantifiable data. You can't miss it; it's a two-story building with a big stadium out in back. The ability to see the not-so-obvious is vitally important for a change in perspective. Change always stems from new ways of thinking. A clear departure from past behavior is required. The marketing world is not exempt from this principle.

Marketers, like my rookie salesperson, make decisions based upon experience. Experience is based upon a history of successes and failures. From these experiences, we derive our "understanding" of current events. Experience includes all of the external, internal, and genetic stimuli our senses receive. These stimuli shape our attitudes and our values, which become the subliminal guideposts that inform our decisions no matter how important or unimportant the decisions might be. Unless we choose to raise our awareness by looking for new clues, new ideas, and new leads that will eventually alter our path, we ultimately make decisions based only on the "guideposts" we have already acquired. This is good and this is bad.

The Good

Guideposts, or values, created by experience are good. Without such a system we would be living in a constant state of chaos. Values guide our behaviors and help us make decisions. In fact, they become a subconscious "traffic cop" that enables us to function within a degree of routine by setting boundaries which, in turn, help us determine when to say yes or no in any given situation. Values indeed control much of our day-to-day behavior. (See Figure 8.1.)

FIGURE 8.1 *The "Traffic Cop" of Human Behavior*

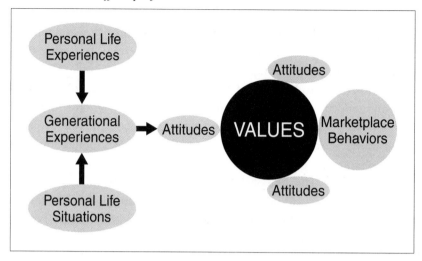

Values act like switches—they are on, off, or in neutral. Marketers want to flip those switches from off to on or from neutral to on. But in many cases, marketing campaigns do just the opposite. Those who are in the Fall and Winter seasons have acquired a greater expanse of experience and, as David Wolfe has shown, literally "think" differently than those in the Spring and Summer seasons. Values an individual uses to make decisions in the Fall and Winter of life will not only be consistent but they will also remain stable. This means that regardless of the particular experience this individual might be having in the moment, his or her values will more easily guide that individual through a new experience whether it be disconcerting or positive.

What is the goal of marketing? In the most simplistic sense, it is to deliver communications to human beings and encourage those human beings to respond to a message in a "positive" manner. This positive behavior is defined by those paying for the delivery of the communications as either an inquiry or a purchase. Before printing, sending, or broadcasting this message it is critically important to determine which words and images will produce the desired results. All communication will return results. But receiving the desired positive result is the goal.

Demographically based marketing focuses on the "obvious." Consider this analogy: when using only the obvious (e.g., age, income) the message will be directed to an ocean of individuals by necessity. Adding the filter of life stage events, it is possible to turn this ocean of individuals into a sizable lake. Even if the correct words and images are used to attract that part of the lake to which the product or service is best suited, there remains tremendous waste in purchased media space. However, if the words and images used in the messaging correlate directly to the important values of the target market, then the response will increase and the lake becomes a more manageable swimming pool.

Which is more important, the message or the size of the target audience? Regardless of the target market size, if the message does not resonate with the individuals, then market size is irrelevant. If the message does resonate with a portion of the target audience, then some degree of success is achieved.

Using values as a foundation upon which demographics can be overlaid, it is possible to narrow the size of the market even further, turning the ocean-size market into a swimming pool size target filled with very good prospects. This approach is certainly more cost effective and will yield greater positive behavior given a product or service actually has relevance to human needs. Additionally, instead of making the general assumption that most individuals experience specific life events at a certain chronological age, assume instead that those with similar values will respond in a similar manner to particular words and phrases.

By using words, phrases, and even images based on values, these messages will communicate best with individuals who possess these values, regardless of age, race, religion, and life stage! The ramifications are clear. Marketing messages that are based on values first will reach consumers of all ages who share similar values. Taking the example even further, this means that marketing response rates will not only be higher, but those who respond will also pose a more "qualified" inquiry. Consequently, marketing based on values is more cost effective. As an example of how marketing based on values works, consider the following:

A man who becomes a father at age 60 will need diapers for his baby as will a man who becomes a father at age 35. The difference is the 60-year-old will make buying decisions based on more solidified and consistent values than will the 35-year-old. Yet the younger father will respond to the messaging because it will resonate with him due to life events. By using values as a map to navigate the sea of demographics, values become a highly predictive tool for creating messages that will specifically appeal to the 60-year-old father as well as to the 35-year-old father. You get the best of both worlds when marketing to values.

The Bad

Advertising messages, as well as communication tactics, have a high probability of missing the mark with the New Customer Majority unless those who write copy and create graphic design (many of whom are in the Spring or Summer season of life) have had an *afflatus* (awakening) to understanding the values and thinking process developed by those in the Fall and Winter seasons of life. Why?

We each view the world through the lens of our own cumulative experiences and subsequently created attitudes and values. We also make judgments and lead our lives based on our view of the world as it appears through the values "lens" those experiences provide for us. Unfortunately, we also view another person's world through the same lens created by our own set of values and beliefs. In one-on-one conversation we are able to negotiate the value differences with much greater ease than when speaking to groups. When trying to communicate to a "mass" target audience, we use our lens or our "team's" lens, to guide our actions. These lenses are the basis for all judgment—right or wrong.

Those in the Spring and Summer seasons of life then use their own less-expansive experience base and thought process to develop marketing tactics and messaging. Unfortunately, the bandwidth of experience supporting these creations does not encompass the depth and breadth of the individuals in the Fall and Winter seasons of life.

The trap that develops is easy to spot but not easy to correct. Worse than sweeping generalizations made about a particular group or target market are conclusions drawn from misleading associations from various sets of "facts." These facts are generated through primary and secondary research as well as anecdotal information. Consequently, the marketer on a marketing team makes a contribution to the creative process based on information that limits his or her view and understanding of the underlying motivations driving the target audience. In this scenario, the marketing team becomes hopelessly bound to develop messages and communications based on a less-than-full, and often inaccurate, view of the target market. However, the marketing team will be totally convinced of their work's merit and validity. The curious thing is the marketing team that produced this message will not even understand why it did or did not generate the desired response.

The only way to solve this problem is to become aware one exists. The marketer must become aware there are other ways to view human behavior. He or she must realize, as my rookie salesperson did, that there are "leagues in my area" even though they may not be readily apparent or visible. Finally, the marketer must have the drive to diligently search them out.

The previous paragraphs could be summarized by the adage you may have read many times before: If you keep doing what you have always done, you will get what you have always gotten. In marketing terms, we continue to use the same tools we used yesterday (i.e., the last 50 years) hoping to achieve different results in a world that has not only experienced significant demographic shifts but has also experienced significant shifts in thought processes as individuals change seasons of life.

SO, HOW DID WE REACH THIS STATE OF MARKETING THAT EXISTS TODAY?

Since the founding of the world's oldest advertising agency, J. Walter Thompson, in 1864, those attempting to advertise or promote a product have been looking for ways to communicate with a "target" market. *Mass marketing* became highly successful following World War II. Although advertisers have given themselves far too much credit for the impact of messaging developed for various products, no one can deny the tremendous success that many companies and products have garnered as a result of these mass communication efforts.

During the 1950s everyone needed *and wanted* a house and a car. Everyone wanted an electric washing machine, and the convenience of prepackaged foods was irresistible. The simple mix of new products offering timesaving convenience with individuals who longed to enjoy new families and experiences is a phenomenon not likely to repeat itself again during our lifetime. The discovery by researchers and marketers that consumers could be understood and more accurately targeted by advertising communications through the use of demographics (mostly related to age and income) would prove to be the key to all marketing communication during the final 50 years of the 20th century.

In the sales world, we try to make a distinction between salespeople who are "order takers" and those who really understand the psychology of communication, motivation, and desire. Sales are easy when the prospect is highly motivated, or has a high desire, to own the product (or service) and the product (or service) is one of the few that will satisfy this need. In this case, you really don't have to do much selling. You are an order taker. Nothing wrong with that! Essentially, the old marketing philosophy is this: If you get the message out to everyone (mass market) you are going to make sales. Everyone wins.

Age, income, and similar demographic data represent the easy "prospects" in our search for leads that will help us understand human behavior. When you have good prospects that turn into sales, there really is no need to look for or even consider other leads that would further explain human behavior. After all, the result of using this gestalt of demographically based data worked—sales were made and the cash flowed.

RESULTS OF 50 YEARS OF DEMOGRAPHICALLY BASED MARKETING

Books have been written about the differences between the various generations. Research has been conducted with regard to the various life stages, which many of us over the age of 50 have faced or will face during our remaining years. Yet, these new insights beyond demographics have not really changed the way we think about consumers. Years of research and marketing based on demographics have created stereotypical images of various segments of the population. These stereotypes are so ingrained in our thinking that it is difficult for the marketer to conceive there might be new ways to view human behavior that would completely break these stereotypes.

Marketers have a tendency to declare "There are no leagues in my area." Translated, this means I don't see any new evidence that may prove to offer new insights that will lead to radical new ways to view human behavior. Why?

The hardest thing for each of us to do is admit the current marketing strategies we are using may be based on old ideas (not old data) and, consequently, may be the reason for fewer numbers of leads produced from even greater advertising dollars. There is good reason to be cautious when implementing new ideas. When treading onto new ground, one always has to be concerned with the outcome. What are the consequences? If I *individually* take the risk and I am wrong, I could lose my job!

As researchers have become more sophisticated in their approaches to understanding human behavior, it would seem likely that new methods of marketing and creating advertising communications would have evolved over the past 50 years. While strides have been made, when all the bells and whistles are stripped away, the strategies of today's advertisers are similar to those used in the 1950s.

In recent years, companies that advertise consistently are reporting that marketing costs are rising and the return on investment is falling. Yet, even with this evidence, the advertising industry continues to do the same things and expect better results. One might even project that marketers are doing the same things and hoping for the same results as last year.

Customer Relationship Marketing (CRM) efforts, once considered the panacea for increasing sales and capturing lifelong relationships with the customer, have been yielding less-than-satisfactory results. As the marketing world enters the new millennium, it would be logical to open its collective mind to new and far-reaching ideas that would turn the marketing world upside down as the Internet has done for the world of technology.

The Internet has literally forced a fundamental change in strategies for technology. Companies are scrambling to be connected at lightning speed. It has happened quickly and without regard to size or depth of brand equity held by any company. The Internet is brand blind. The Internet is age blind. Think of it this way, what the Internet is to technology, the New Customer Majority is to marketing. Yet, the shift in thought with regard to human behavior, motivating underlying values and brain science, has not really even started. This shift in thought needs to be as dramatic as the technological shift. However, as changes in social thought occur slowly over time, it will take a concerted and sustained effort to create lasting change in the way we view individuals who have reached the Fall and Winter seasons of life.

Ad Industry Numbers and Trends

The current status of marketing and advertising in the United States can be summarized as follows:

- We have all been placed into buckets according to age, income, and generation.
- It is generally assumed that because we are a certain age, read a certain magazine, or are a part of a generational label (GIs, boomers, GenXers), we are very much alike others within that same generation.
- The advertising world is dominated by youth. Companies with products to sell are generally mesmerized by the *need* to capture the youth market. The reasoning is this: In order to preserve our market share for the future, we must capture them while they are young. Research supports the notion that this is nonsense and yet companies and advertisers continue to do as they have always done.
- Those over age 50 are, for the most part, labeled as "spill over" according to those who place media buys for major advertisers.

This ability to see the obvious is indeed good and this current status is clearly based on the "obvious" way of thinking we have discussed. It has helped marketers sell products for the past 100 years. When it comes to understanding human behavior (or shall we say customer behavior), we have found the obvious and we have used it. We have reworked it. We have repackaged it. We have invented programs to redesign it. Finally, we have clung to it because although it is not as effective as it once was, we don't believe it's broken.

The ability of marketers to see the unobvious leading to new insights of human behavior will be the key to successful marketing to the New Customer Majority for the next ten years. Why ten years? Because it is improbable these new insights will become as ensconced in the marketing world as demographics have. If we look back to our original scenario, let's consider exploring our territory once more for unobvious prospects that present new insights into human behavior and decision making.

BREAKING THE AGE LABEL

Take a moment and read the statements in Figure 8.2. In the empty box to the left of the statement provide your best guess as to the age of the person who is making this statement.

In the statements in Figure 8.2, except for a few clues in some of the statements, it would be difficult to say whether the person was 45 or 73. Yet each of these statements does represent a certain value, which is important to the person who said it. The particular value may not be obvious at first. These not-so-obvious values retain a much higher level of importance in understanding a person's potential behavior than does age.

Age is merely the label we each carry throughout life. It allows others to assume we have certain interests or may be inclined to try certain activities. These assumptions certainly shouldn't be ignored or considered irrelevant. Earlier, David Wolfe established that a child 2 years old has certain needs and a child 12 years old might enjoy certain activities. But, as we move through the Fall and Winter seasons of our lives, the chronological predictor becomes mottled. Yet, when those in the Spring and Summer seasons of their life create communications to market products or services to those in the Fall and Winter, it is very likely they will use age as an assumptive device to create marketing messages which will surely "ring true."

The fact is, the conclusions we reach using this process often don't make sense. That is, they are spurious. But, like my rookie salesperson, the "assumer" is not inclined to look for the unexpected but more inclined to ignore a contradictory bit of information as irrelevant, and thus status quo wins.

MYTHS OF AGING: SPURIOUS CORRELATIONS

According to Hans O. Melberg of the University of Oslo:

The problem of spurious correlation is large in the social sciences. Using the term *misleading* or *illusory* correlations is better because it is not the correlation itself that is spurious, but the

FIGURE 8.2 *Assessing Age Based on Value Statements*

	1. "I have a guardian angel who watches over me wherever I go. I thank God for everything that happens in my life. I always try to help people. I'm directed to them and offer whatever kindness I can."
	2. "...your goal in life is to be on top. You know? I consider myself in charge of my own life. So I'm on top of things."
	3. "I am blessed with many friends. They call me all the time and we are always going out to lunch or dinner. They take me wherever I have to go. It really makes life worthwhile."
	4. On the subject of grandchildren: "We're very involved, as involved as we can be. Almost as involved as we were with our own kids. I never missed one of [my son's] Little League games. To me, my family was everything."
	5. "When I get up in the morning ... I'm angry. Angry because I don't have the time or the money to do everything that I want to do."
	6. "I live plain. My house needs a lot of fixing up. But, I'm very frugal. People think I save money, but I just shop well."
	7. "I do believe in God ... there are times in life that He has had to have been there watching ... I mean something happened and everything worked out. ... I talk to him every night ... you have to believe in something like God ... to just have everything be worthwhile. I don't know. If I didn't have Him to believe in then it would be silly."
	8. "I'm my own man. No one ever gave me anything and I direct my own life. I am a leader and expect to be followed. I never had a problem with this and got along well with people. I always look for a clear, right choice and push for it."
	9. "If I buy a new boat—because I love to go fishing and boating—I want to put it in the water right away. I want to go out and use it. ... It is exciting because it's something brand new ... and it will be my first experience with it ... It gives me a feeling of success. ... I feel very successful that I have set a goal and then I accomplished that goal. ... I want to call my friends and say, 'Hey, I finally saved up the money. I bought this new boat I've been talking about for so long. Come on over. Let's go out and let's use it.'"

	10. "I really try not to be negative and try to be objective and fair about things. So many people are dirty, dishonest, always breaking the rules. It really makes me angry. We all should receive our fair share, according to our needs."
	11. "I think my friends celebrate me. They truly do. Last Christmas I treated myself to a full carat brilliant-cut diamond pendant for Christmas and it was absolutely gorgeous. And my friends were very, very . . . they were just thrilled for me. My sisters thought I was a bit wasting my money. They're far more cautious. They think I'm probably going to outlive my money."
	12. "Reading makes me more aware than others. My mind is always searching. There's a lot out there to take advantage of and I'm smarter than the 'average bear.' Slow people really frustrate me. They don't have what they need to know. Being quick mentally is something that defines me."
	13. "I ask a lot of questions. So whether that's questions of individuals who I think are more knowledgeable, or going and doing research at the library or on the Internet . . . to make myself more knowledgeable about whatever that issue or situation is. And then, based on gathering all of that data, trying to decide what I feel about it."
	14. "I still get up at 4:30 every morning and get ready for whatever the day may bring. I'm always ready for whatever may come. My friends think I'm daring and impulsive, but I'm just ready."
	15. "Normally, I like to be in charge. I guess it helps your self-esteem. . . . I like to be respected by others. I like to be known as an expert or know what I'm talking about so that when I talk to people they take what I say as truth, or whatever; not to be questioned . . ."

inference from the existence of an insignificant correlation to the existence of a significant relationship that is spurious.

Marketing is a social science. The opportunity to reach conclusions based upon misleading associations is great indeed. According to Mr. Melberg, in order to deal with misleading associations, we have three options:

1. Downplay the mismatch or degree to which there is a mismatch

2. Admit that the problem is serious, in which case we must accept the rather disappointing conclusion that the scope for reliable knowledge is not very large
3. Admit you are wrong and try a different approach to knowledge

However, if you are an account service person in an advertising agency and you happen to see a spurious correlation in a new advertising effort, you don't dare speak up. You might lose your job. Don't rock the boat, it's still floating and you're on it.

The topic of aging is captured in numerous statements that contain misleading associations. Like most myths, the ones about aging include a confusing blend of truth and fancy. A few of the most misleading associations are listed below. As Rowe and Khan have indicated, these axioms and others like them usually have some link to reality, but are nearly always in significant conflict with recent scientific data. These phrases represent the lens through which those in the Spring and Summer seasons of life view those in the Fall and Winter.

Misleading associations linked with aging:

- As you age, you will most likely get sick.
- As you age, you will lose interest in intimacy.
- As you get older, you become less and less likely to try anything new.
- Older people lose control of bodily functions.
- Older people cannot function in the work place.
- The older individual can't understand today's technology.
- The older you become, the less likely it is that you have a social life.
- The older you become, the more you will need help to make decisions.

Misleading associations linked to leading-edge baby boomers:

- You aim to keep your ego fed.
- All you care about is you.
- You are rebellious.
- You are not a money saver.
- You don't read newspapers.
- You are fixated on retaining your youth and good looks.

The public, in general, and advertising people, in particular, are programmed with these misleading associations that, in turn, lead their values "lenses" to perceive aging as a *bad* thing: Once you're past 40, you're over the hill and out of the game. However, if you talk with most healthy older people, you'll learn there are many positive things about aging. In fact, Rowe and Khan speak to "successful aging [as] dependent upon individual choices and behaviors . . . attained through individual choice and effort."

Many advertising people—copywriters, art directors, account executives, and media buyers—subscribe to these misleading associations not because they choose to, but because there has been no education encouraging them to challenge their beliefs and discover new information that could change the advertising and marketing messages and strategies. It is easier for young staffers to stick with what they know and understand (i.e., what appeals to them personally). These misleading associations about aging perpetuate the creation of off-target messages resulting in higher costs of generating new leads and new sales. Maintaining these misleading associations also perpetuates the alienation of those in the Fall and Winter seasons of life and does nothing to enhance market share and increase potential revenues.

It is not impossible for advertising people to reexamine and reeducate their received, if limited, notions of aging. Crafting successful communications to the New Customer Majority fully engaged in making those individual choices and efforts that will result in successful aging calls for a new type of understanding on the part of advertising people. Younger account executives and creatives, especially those more than 20 years removed from what they define as their "generation," are capable of showing an amazing amount of empathy when their values lenses are refitted for a long view of consumers 45 and up. Understanding the values of this consumer group is an exciting new way to get "beyond the numbers" of traditional ways of categorizing those in the Fall and Winter seasons of life.

In the next chapter, we will take a more specific look at the research that resulted in detailed portraits of those age 45-plus who share similar values. We will also take a look at real sales training perspectives and marketing challenges where values have played an important role in crafting approaches and successful creative solutions.

9

VALUE PORTRAITS

A New Approach Toward Appealing to Individuals in the Fall and Winter Seasons

Value Portraits® are the results of new, unique studies that classify mature Americans (defined here by chronological age 45 and up) with similar value systems into distinct groups. Members of each group share a mind-set that reinforces a predisposition to behave in a certain way and underlies specific attitudes (e.g., purchasing certain products or services).

Traditionally, companies have relied on attitudes, opinions, demographics, and life stages to predict consumer behavior, but these can and do change over time due to life events and circumstances. Although members of any generation are linked by the shared life experiences of their formative years, it is not the experiences and events that have meaning, it is the attitudes, beliefs, and values that have been created as a result of these events that is important. In his landmark book *Man's Search for Meaning*, Viktor E. Frankl clearly demonstrates the validity of this statement: The key to capturing the hearts and minds of the mature audience lies in first understanding the values they find to be important and second to understand the values they hold which are least important.

As indicated in the previous chapter, misunderstanding an individual's core beliefs and underlying values will result in stereotypical communications based on the *creator's* personal beliefs and values. A misunderstanding occurs because we each view the world (including its material contents, interactions with others, and observations of others behaviors) through our own frame of reference or *values lens*. This is why it was difficult for my rookie to find those leagues.

WHY VALUES?

Values are not held distinctly or separately, but as part of an integrated belief system, according to Shalom Schwartz and Wolfgang Bilsky:

> "Values guide actions and judgments across situations; attitudes and opinions, on the other hand, are "domain-specific" (beliefs about a particular object within a particular context). Although attitudes and opinions affect behavior, they are likely to change throughout one's lifetime. Values, on the other hand, are deeply engrained, remarkably stable, and change slowly, if at all, over the course of life. Moreover, values constructs are relatively few in number and are largely universal. Values can be defined as (a) relatively stable thoughts or beliefs, (b) about desirable behaviors or ways of living, (c) that transcend situations, (d) guide decision making, and (e) are ordered by relative importance."

If you are a marketer or work in the field of advertising, you should be craving to find out more. This is the information that can create an awakening. This is new information that can change marketing strategies, even marketing tactics, if we just know what those values are, who has them, and their relative importance to the person who holds them. This is the *not-so-obvious* information referred to in Chapter 8.

Looking at human behavior through values-based segmentation research is not only logical but it is also statistically accurate. The key difference between this segmentation and others based on life stage or demographics is that values don't shift—life stage and demographics do. Even attitudes shift. Values, on the other hand, are virtually constant in the guidance they provide for each of us.

In fact, if one were to view each Value Portrait or segment, as a different solar system, then each would have a different combination of values at the center representing its sun. Around these values revolve not planets but words, phrases, and images that easily flow through the "lens" for that segment. There are also negative values or values that *repel* each segment. These might be considered the black holes of this universe. If the creative images, words, or even communications tactics used are the wrong ones, then the lens repels those words and images akin to how the like poles of a magnet repel one another. In other words, marketing communications may get tossed into the black hole, not necessarily due to poor product features or benefits, but because the words and phrases used were repelled by that person's universe of values. The message simply could not get through their personal values lens.

For this reason, values offer a robust approach to market segmentation. Value Portraits inform marketing strategy in order to

- identify market segments with the strongest affinity to product and service offerings;
- develop more effective programs by underscoring the important values of consumers in each target segment;
- effectively position products and services by emphasizing attributes that are linked to the values of a particular segment; and
- identify new product opportunities and/or modify existing products to be consistent with consumer value profiles and emerging trends.

J. Walter Thompson's Mature Market Group and Market Strategies' Seniors Research Group have conducted five separate studies of adults 45-plus to determine if a person's life events, situations, and generational experiences shape their core values. These studies determined that these customers can be categorized into distinct segments to help predict their marketplace behavior. Creative and media can be matched to the segments to provide different approaches to match differing needs, lifestyles, and life stages.

These studies were conducted over a two-year period and encompassed two separate studies for those age 62 and above and three separate studies for those ages 45 to 61. For the sake of this chapter, we will refer to the 45-to-61 age group as leading edge baby boomers. The interesting part of these studies is that when the values are overlaid onto the demographics, we find that age patterns are almost identical among Value Portraits or segments. In the 62 plus group age was more demonstrative than in the 45-to-61 group but only slightly. What this means is that although the segments might look the same demographically, they are distinctly different. This supports the idea that age is one of the least reliable predictors of human behavior. A synopsis of the methodology used to conduct this research can be found in the Appendix.

VALUES HELD BY AMERICANS 62 AND OLDER

Dozens of attitudinal questions were asked in order to gauge the importance of more than 34 different values to seniors. For the sake of clarity, these distinct values were summarized in 13 dimensions, ranked from most to least important as follows:

1. *Self-respect.* This is of utmost importance to mature Americans. They believe in integrity and perseverance. Self-respecting seniors also tend to value self-sufficiency and independence.
2. *Family ties.* These are also very important to seniors. Seniors with strong family ties consider their families a top priority. They are genuinely interested in the welfare of the family and each of its members, no matter where they may reside or how frequently they see them, and are willing to make sacrifices for them.
3. *Faith and religion.* Expressed as a spiritual connection to God and the community of believers, faith is virtually as important to mature Americans as their family ties. Many are guided by religious principles, taking comfort in their religion and the sense of a divine purpose in life.
4. *Warm relationships.* These are highly valued by mature Americans. Seniors are emotionally supportive and loyal and consider friendship a top priority.
5. *Kindness and compassion.* These are values that go a step beyond warm relationships. Compassionate seniors value forgiveness and honesty and emphasize helping others. They believe in social justice and equality for all people.
6. *Intellectual curiosity.* There is a segment of the aging population that exhibits a high degree of *intellectual curiosity*. These seniors pursue knowledge, paying attention to changes taking place

around them. They enjoy mental challenges and look to understand rather than accept what it is they are investigating.

7. *Health and well being.* These are important values, but not at the top of the list as one might expect. Wellness-minded seniors are likely to lead healthy lifestyles through diet, exercise, and avoiding health risks. Seniors that value health and well-being strive for inner harmony and tend to have a positive outlook on life.

8. *Fun and happiness.* Seniors value fun and happiness similar to wellness. Seniors who value happiness maintain positive outlooks on life. They enjoy variety and tend to lead active lives.

9. *Conservative attitudes.* Many seniors are conservative in their approach to living. They are respectful of tradition, authority, rules, and social institutions. Conservative seniors also value politeness and civility.

10. *Financial security.* Many seniors also value financial security because they are concerned about having enough money to sustain their current lifestyle and take care of unforeseeable circumstances.

11. *Power and recognition.* Some seniors value power and recognition because they prefer to take the lead rather than follow orders and seek the praise and accolades from others.

12. *Excitement.* The rush of excitement does not just belong to the young. There are seniors who crave thrills and adventure. They tend to be spontaneous and rebellious.

13. *Material possessions.* These are important to some seniors. They value owning status symbols. Materialistic seniors are conscious of brand image and how others perceive them.

VALUES HELD BY AMERICANS 45 TO 61

Again, dozens of questions were asked in order to gauge the importance of more than 34 different values to leading-edge boomers. For the sake of clarity, these distinct values were summarized in 14 dimensions. The dimensions were ranked from most to least important for the entire group. You will find many similarities among these and those listed in the previous section. In fact, much of the difference lies not in the values themselves, but in the language used to describe the value by the younger group.

1. *Altruism.* This is of the utmost importance to leading-edge boomers. They believe it is important to help others who are less fortunate and consider it their moral obligation to help the needy. They place a strong emphasis on honesty.

2. *Family Ties.* These are also extremely important to boomers. They place a very high priority on maintaining family ties and consider family to be the major source of satisfaction in life. They are extremely loyal to their friends and family and are willing to make sacrifices to help them. They also equate love with deep friendship.

3. *Intellectual curiosity.* This is another extremely important dimension. Many boomers enjoy intellectual challenges and problems requiring in-depth thought.

4. *Psychological well being.* This is very highly valued by boomers. They take pride in their independence and are satisfied with their achievements and their lives overall. They have a positive outlook on life and high self-respect.

5. *Spirituality.* For many boomers *spirituality* is very important. They believe in a greater purpose and feel part of God's plan. Religion plays a part in guiding their life.

6. *Balance.* Many boomers value *balance* because they feel a strong connection to nature and spend their leisure time outdoors. They also focus on maintaining their physical health and understanding and improving their inner self.

7. *Leadership.* This is important to boomers because they have a high sense of self-motivation and persistence in everything they do, as well as a desire to take on leadership roles in group situations.

8. *Civility.* Boomers also value *civility* because they feel it is important for people to be polite and show proper etiquette and manners. It is easy for them to forgive others. They are also inclined to respect authority and conform others.

9. *Warm relationships.* Some boomers consider *warm relationships* a priority because they like to belong to and be involved with their community. They place a high value on having close friends and often rely on them.

10. *Excitement.* Leading-edge boomers who prefer to indulge themselves and seek enjoyable activities value *excitement.* They tend to be impulsive, spontaneous, and daring and often do something crazy to spice up the week.

11. *Regret.* Those who feel *regret* are concerned about their financial security and wish they had done a better job of saving for their later years. They tend to feel sad, lonely, and anxious much of the time.

12. *Conservatism.* This is seen as important to some boomers because they are respectful of traditions and cultural roots. They place an emphasis on social justice issues such as equality.

13. *Recognition.* This has importance to some boomers because they crave social recognition and praise from others. They value owning status symbols and are conscious of brand image.

14. *National security.* This is of least importance to many boomers. Those who value national security are concerned about terrorism and would like to see more money spent on national defense.

DISTINCT GROUPS ASSOCIATED WITH VALUES

Regardless of the age group, the critical and most important factor in understanding the power of this research is that while the values you have just reviewed exist for all humans, they exist in different groupings and different degrees of intensity depending on how individual experiences have shaped individual beliefs. To restate this most important construct:

While the human values are constant, what varies from one individual to the next is the relative importance one places on different values, depending on one's background and life circumstances.

Following is a synopsis of the various Value Portraits, which appeared as a result of this research. The first grouping is for those age 62 and up (see Figure 9.1). The second set groups individuals from 45 to 61 (see Figure 9.2). As you read, you will find Value Portraits that are nearly identical in both age groups. The reason that we have treated the groups separately is that the collective experience of each age group is

FIGURE 9.1 *Value Portraits Americans 62+*

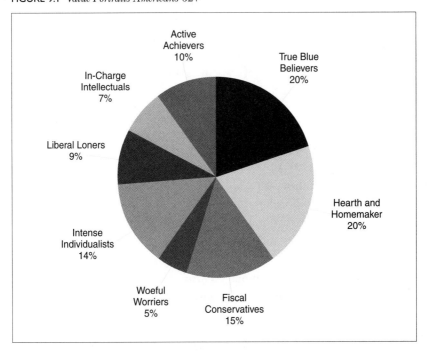

FIGURE 9.2 *Value Portraits Americans 45–61*

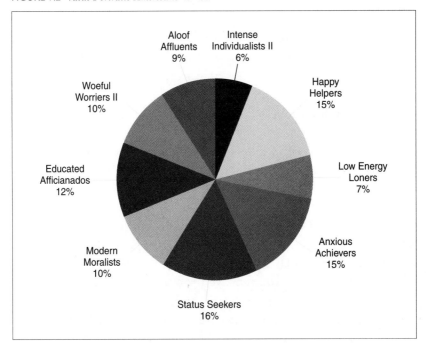

different and has created some differences in how each group describes what is actually the same or a very similar value.

Figure 9.3 shows how the Hearth and Homemakers defined two different values, and how the Happy Helpers defined the same values. These resulted in two different Value Portrait descriptions based on each group's interpretation of the same values.

Woeful Worriers (5 percent) never recovered their fiscal confidence after the depression, but they retained their faith in authority. They are

FIGURE 9.3 *Value Dimensions*

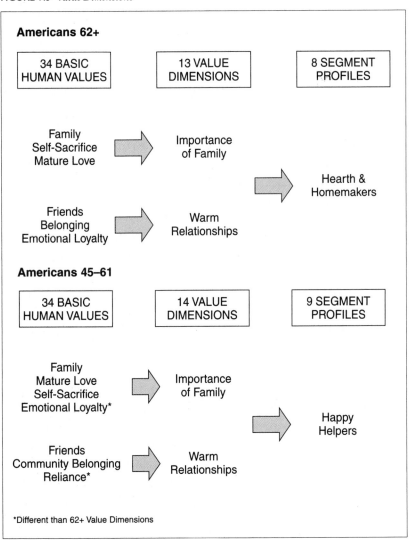

Americans 62+

| 34 BASIC HUMAN VALUES | 13 VALUE DIMENSIONS | 8 SEGMENT PROFILES |

Family
Self-Sacrifice
Mature Love → Importance of Family

→ Hearth & Homemakers

Friends
Belonging
Emotional Loyalty → Warm Relationships

Americans 45–61

| 34 BASIC HUMAN VALUES | 14 VALUE DIMENSIONS | 9 SEGMENT PROFILES |

Family
Mature Love
Self-Sacrifice
Emotional Loyalty* → Importance of Family

→ Happy Helpers

Friends
Community Belonging
Reliance* → Warm Relationships

*Different than 62+ Value Dimensions

comfortable with order and routine and shy away from excitement and risk—even if they are dissatisfied.

Liberal Loners (9 percent) find it difficult to become a part of the human family. They appear to fit a bleeding-heart stereotype, but they focus on their own independence, concerns, and needs, leaving little energy for family or friends. (Statement 10 in Figure 8.2.)

Fiscal Conservatives (15 percent) are aware that they are admired for their accomplishments and for their possessions. They shop for quality over value, but manage to find the bargains. Wary of change, they focus on tradition and family pride.

Active Achievers (10 percent) have enjoyed all aspects of their lives. They don't see themselves as "old" and don't plan to join the older ranks, regardless of their chronological age. They are well educated, socially involved, and usually well to do. Nonconformists, they enjoy excitement. They are often divorced and may lose touch with their families. (Statement 14 in Figure 8.2.)

True Blue Believers (20 percent) are often the moderates. They are religious but not zealous, compassionate not overindulgent, happy not giddy, smart not brilliant, conservative not inflexible. They are fulfilled by families and friends and satisfied with themselves. (Statements 1 and 3 in Figure 8.2.)

In-Charge Intellectuals (7 percent) are lifelong readers and thinkers who keep up with change and are secure in their abilities, opinions, and perceptions. Their personal relationships may be casual. They expect more of themselves than others expect. (Statement 12 in Figure 8.2.)

Intense Individualists (14 percent) see the world as unforgiving and a tough place to live. They have a pioneer's resourcefulness and self-reliance. They assume a leadership role in their families and communities. They are unsentimental and uncompromising. (Statement 8 in Figure 8.2.)

Hearth and Homemakers (20 percent) keep their family and friends at the center of their lives. Their religious congregation is the center of their community. Often caretakers and volunteers, they're happy and see their lives as rewarding. (Statement 6 in Figure 8.2.)

Woeful Worriers II (10 percent) are generally depressed people who have a strong tendency to focus on putting the needs of others before their own. They sometimes make family members happy at the expense of their own happiness. They are dealing with progressive medical conditions that limit their activities. Even on medication to treat depression they can feel anxious when getting up in the morning as they contemplate going through the same dreary round of tasks and responsibilities. They often feel conflicted, knowing that they need some time to themselves to pursue creative activities, but also feel a stronger pull to provide for the needs of others. Aware that others may view them as cold and quiet, they try to be positive and focus on good things about the future. For this group, the future appears to be a very uncertain place and their natural tendency is to think about bad things that could happen to them.

Low-Energy Loners (7 percent) tend to be perennial outsiders, socially isolated and depressed. Life generally feels empty to them in which each day is like another "string of zeros." They are often bored and struggle to identify something in their lives that could truly be called exciting. If the opportunity presents itself for them to "break out of the mold" of a daily routine they may agree to do things in which they have no real interest, just to break the monotony of day-to-day life. Low-Energy Loners often have few friends and those friends they do have are likely to describe them as depressed or kind of crazy. Members of this group are very anxious about the future. They often worry about their current financial situation, and they do not see any avenue of improvement, considering the limitations imposed by such factors as geographic isolation, illness or injury, declining health, and the demands of homemaking, spouses and children who often leave them feeling underappreciated. (Statement 5 in Figure 8.2.)

Aloof Affluents (9 percent) are idealists with high standards of conduct and performance who feel most comfortable when in charge of the activities around them. They are natural supervisors, directors, and workaholics who believe that accomplishment is all about being the "top dog" in everything they do. When they are not in charge, they feel like a "fish out of water" and tend to withdraw and become quiet. In such situations, they are likely to wonder if, under someone else's leadership, the project will not turn out as well. Members of this group have a strong tendency to believe in their own intuition and gut feelings about things, rather than automatically accepting the advice of so-called experts. To an Aloof Affluent, all experts are "so-called" until they prove themselves by answering the insightful questions that Aloof Affluents are likely to ask, such as, "Why do you think your idea will get the job done better?"

and "What proof do you have?" Members of this group have a tendency to take great pride in their work and are quick to spot hypocrisy or dishonesty around them. The high principles of honesty, integrity, honor, and hard work are not just words to the Aloof Affluent, they are inextricably bound up in their sense of self. (Statement 15 in Figure 8.2.)

Educated Aficionados (12 percent) are interested in constantly learning from the best, most unbiased sources of information. They tend to be strong advocates of adult learning and continuing education. Much more likely to watch a political thriller than an Arnold Schwartzenegger movie, or read the newspaper over watching cable news, Educated Aficionados prefer sources of information and entertainment that force them to think and analyze. Members of this group prefer PBS over mainstream cable channels because they are interested in in-depth coverage of stories with as little filtering as possible from editors and newsrooms. They want to get information from insiders and outsiders and put the sources together to arrive at their own truths. They will pore over interesting articles in local and national newspapers and compare the coverage of these stories to that on international Internet news sites, such as the BBC. They also have an interest in the close-up, local world around them and will follow local stories, such as news about American Indians, to learn about indigenous cultures and ceremonies in their own areas. (Statement 13 in Figure 8.2.)

Modern Moralists (10 percent) tend to be very deterministic and focused on their relationship with God or higher power. They have a strong tendency to study scriptural texts and for fellowship with like-minded people in order to learn what God has in store for them. Many Modern Moralists view the human experience in eschatological terms, that is, with a future determined by the slow unraveling of ancient prophesies, followed by a dramatic intervention in which they will "win" by being on the side of truth and righteousness. They have a tendency to filter everything happening around them through the lens of faith, prayers, and their understanding of divine commands. They often feel that their faith helps inoculate them from many stresses that unbelievers must endure without respite. Members of this group have a tendency to believe God has turned a switch on inside them that allows them to see and understand things in the world that others miss, or, at minimum, that divine forces play a role in making impossible or unlikely things happen that are favorable for them. (Statement 7 in Figure 8.2.)

Status Seekers (16 percent) tend to be highly driven people who get a great deal of satisfaction from the stimulation of work and its rewards. What really motivates members of this portrait group to throw themselves into their work is to share their acquisitions with friends and family, whether the project is an extensive remodeling of a house, buying a Civil War antique, buying a diamond ring, or picking up the check at a restaurant. Status Seekers have a tendency to believe that everything they do is a performance for an "in-the-know" audience, everything can be an opportunity to show that they have thought out the details of a project and pulled off the performance at a high level of quality. For members of this group, the important thing is not to give in to stupid people. Status Seekers are interested in social recognition and will readily volunteer to work on important community projects, like volunteering at a battered women's shelter or at the local library. (Statement 11 in Figure 8.2.)

Anxious Achievers (15 percent) are excited by the feeling of success they get from setting goals and reaching them. But they are also reflective people who are interested in maintaining or achieving harmony first with themselves, then with those around them. They tend to analyze situations from multiple perspectives to discover the desires and motivations of others around them. They firmly believe that their own health, their family, and good friends come before money or anything else. They tend to be excited by new vistas and realizations that have the potential to change their lifestyle by shifting what they consider valuable. They may actively seek answers in organized religion. Now entering their late 40s and early 50s, they often realize that they have been impulsive in the past and are now interested in calming down long enough to hear what course their "higher power" may want them to pursue. (Statement 9 in Figure 8.2.)

Intense Individualists II (6 percent) are very focused on maintaining their independence and freedom through work and "quiet zones" they create around themselves to get recharged, such as gardening, woodworking, and small building projects. They are intellectually curious but mostly to learn things with a practical application to something they are actually doing. They are open to doing new or different things but feel a strong pull for the routine and familiar. They will try something new if they feel the activity will be an outlet for a creativity they know they already possess. Members of this portrait group tend to be very competitive and want to come out on top in everything they do, whether that means closely watching their investments on the Internet, realizing a personal dream of moving to paradise, or charting their own weekend excursions on a sailboat. (Statement 2 in Figure 8.2.)

Happy Helpers (15 percent) are nurturers, comforters, and caregivers of family and a wide circle of friends whom they consider "adopted" family members. Happy Helpers have so many friends they can be overwhelmed by so many people depending on their "broad shoulders" for comfort, empathetic listening, and advice. They know their children will call them right away to discuss problems because they have proven to their children over time that they will never be judgmental or let their own feelings run ahead of giving sound advice. Happy Helpers feel a strong pull to contribute to organizations that help the less fortunate, believing strongly that others need a little extra help to get on their feet. Unselfish giving, listening, being depended on—for Happy Helpers these attributes are all tied to the idea of being honorable, following through on their commitment to be the Rock of Gibraltar when others are being flailed about by storms. (Statement 4 in Figure 8.2.)

AGE BLIND, VALUE CLEAR

The impact of a values-based segmentation on media planning can and will be felt. Knowing the media habits of the 62-plus population is important. By determining the media habits of the Active Achievers or the Intense Individualists, for example, media placement and tactics can be more targeted and thus more cost effective.

The values-based segmentation has excellent potential to help those marketing to the New Customer Majority. It can help marketers achieve greater insight as to which words and phrases to use and which to avoid, generally, and in each universe. Finally, the end result of using values-based research is that it will result in marketing to an "ageless" market, thus eliminating chronological age as the sole basis for one group viewing another.

For instance, Active Achievers and Intense Individualists place a very high value on thrills and excitement. This explains some of those "odd" individuals that don't fit into the stereotypical view of this population. These market segments are the ones skydiving and trekking off to some remote place on Earth to visit a hidden temple. Interestingly enough, we know there are younger individuals doing the same thing. Why? Because values cut across all age groups.

If a 45-year-old and a 65-year-old aspire toward the same value, then messages based on that value will communicate to both.

As the leading-edge boomers begin to age chronologically, every company in America is trying to scramble to grab this market. There are so many numbers, so many life stages, and so many different types of boomers that trying to make sense of it all can be confusing, costly, and fruitless.

One of the key functions of research based on Value Portraits is that it provides an unchanging baseline against which all known demographic information can be categorized and evaluated. Now marketers can take the known information and look at it through the values lenses of their target market instead of filtering the information through their own biased eyes.

PORTRAITS VALUE AND SALES

To illustrate how Values Portraits can be applied in real world applications, consider the creative examples and case history that follows. We begin with a contribution from Jackie Stone, partner with the Mature Market Group, part of J. Walter Thompson Worldwide. Ms. Stone is directly involved with consulting and training a variety of clients' salespeople. Though they work directly with consumers, salespeople are often "blinded" by their own assumptions (values lens) regarding the buying habits of their customers. Jackie Stone is immediately involved with helping salespeople remove their blinders as she fosters a new type of understanding for those she trains. Using her own experience as a consumer, and looking dispassionately at herself through the lens of Values Portraits, Ms. Stone relates the following, telling story.

Having read of the different Values Portraits, and without knowing Ms. Stone's specific age, enjoy her story and draw your own conclusion as to which Value Portrait best defines her.

Like most people, I dread the process of shopping for a car, but because I like to get a new car every few years, it's a process that

I go through more often than I'd like. Because selling and teaching others how to sell is my passion, I choose to make the car buying experience more of a research project to learn more about the sales skills of others.

My most recent car buying experience was a prime example of how people make decisions based on their values, and how salespeople miss the mark if they don't look through the values lenses of their customers.

I am a very busy person who travels four days a week, then tries to get caught up with life on the weekends. I am very task-oriented and I like to get things done. I am decisive, impulsive, and have a dominant personality. I appreciate people who have a sense of humor, are intelligent, and communicate well. I don't shop around for a bargain because my time is valuable to me. I make buying decisions based on what looks good, rather than price, but I don't like being taken advantage of. The values that I possess are ones of power, recognition, thrills, and excitement.

I lease my cars for three years and my lease was expiring in the next few weeks. Being the busy person that I am, and dreading this process as I do, I left the task of shopping for my new car until the last minute. I had to find a car and I only had a short period of time in which to do it.

To the savvy salesperson, I am not a tire kicker—I am a hot prospect! Not only that, but I am very direct. I walk in and tell the salesperson that my lease is expiring. I want a black car with a sunroof, a spoiler, and a good sound system (because of my values, I want to look good and enjoy the driving experience). I drive the car and ask the salesperson how much my monthly lease payments will be, but I also make it clear that I don't want to go through the "good cop, bad cop" routine where the sales manager comes out and meets with you, then they go back and forth with the finance department on price (I want to be in control and I don't like tradition and authority). I generally tell the salesperson: "I have to leave, please call me with the price."

I followed this routine at several dealerships—I was looking at a Toyota Camry, a Saturn, and an Oldsmobile Alero, simply because I like the way those cars look. I also did it all in one day to get it over with.

At the Toyota dealership, I was greeted by a saleswoman. During the test drive, I found out that she used to be a nurse and recently switched careers. She was personable and seemed to want to do a good job, but I learned more about her than she did about me. Although I had volunteered information about myself, she didn't ask me much more about myself than I offered.

When we got back to the showroom, I saw a black Camry with gold pin-striping and told her that I liked the way that detail looked. She said, "Oh, you don't want that. It's $600. It's not worth it." I wanted to tell her to go back to nursing because I had just given her a buying signal and she completely ignored what was important to me and tried to sell based on her own values. Nevertheless, I did sit down with her and got the price, which seemed reasonable, but by the time I got home she had already called and said she made a mistake on the price and it was going to be higher.

My second stop was at the Saturn dealer, where I was also greeted by a female salesperson. She sat down with me and asked me what was important to me, how often I drive, if I mostly drive for fun or for work, what kind of music I like, and what I wanted my payments to be. In other words, she genuinely attempted to find out what I valued so she could meet my needs based on those values. She wanted to sell to me the way I wanted to buy. I appreciated the way I was treated and respected her knowledge and professionalism. She showed me exactly what I wanted, and, as requested, she called me back within an hour with the price, which was slightly below what I wanted to pay. I wanted to buy a car from her but I also wanted to investigate the Alero before I made my final decision.

At the Oldsmobile dealership, I was greeted by a man and I went through the same introduction that I did at the other dealerships—telling him I wanted a black Alero with a sunroof and a sound system. I wanted to know how much the monthly payments would be and I didn't want to spend hours in the process. We test drove a car and I liked it very much, however, the salesperson was terrible. He didn't ask me anything about myself, but I found out that he was new to the area and he had relocated to my hometown from Florida due to a fight with his wife.

He told me a few things about the car—technical equipment kind of things that I don't care about—but couldn't answer any of my simple questions ("What does this button do?"). Although I was skeptical about his level of knowledge, I liked the car so I asked him to call me with a price. He called the next day and said that he couldn't tell me over the phone and that I had to come in and talk to the finance manager.

That was exactly what I didn't want to do but I decided I wanted the Alero so I went in. He sat me down in his office, wrote up the paperwork asking me my name, address, etc., which I had already given him but which he had misplaced. Then, he disappeared into another office. I sat alone in his office for 15 to 20 minutes and then walked out, with the receptionist hurriedly paging my missing salesperson. He did call me back, apologizing for taking so long, but he still would not give me a price over the phone. He said I had to come back in.

So, what did I do? I liked the way I was treated by the salesperson at the Saturn dealership but I really liked the way the Alero looked; I just didn't want to deal with the salesperson there. Because my power and recognition value is high, I want what I want, and I want to do it my way.

I called the manager at the Oldsmobile dealer, telling him exactly what happened with the inept salesperson there, and how I wanted to buy, emphasizing the fact that I was a hot prospect and I would lease the car if I could just find out how much my payments would be without going through hell to do it.

The manager called me back within an hour with a price. As I intended from the start, I returned to the Oldsmobile dealership, signed the papers, and took delivery of the car the next afternoon. The manager apologized for my experience with the salesperson and asked if my experience with him had been satisfactory, which it definitely had been. The manager listened to what I valued, sold to me the way I wanted to buy, let me be in control (or at least think I was), gave me the exact car I wanted, and, most importantly, respected my desire to do things quickly and conveniently. I would buy a car from him again and have already referred him to some friends.

For me, this car leasing experience really confirmed the importance of values-based selling. Once someone takes the time to find out what you value in life and sells based on those values, you will buy and you will feel good about your decision.

From Jackie Stone's story, it is not difficult to see the critical flaw in two of the three salespersons' approaches to her as a consumer. Despite being told, in no uncertain terms, what she wanted and how she wanted it, two salespersons wanted to see her only in their own context and through the lens of their own values and experience.

Many times, it is only through an appeal to a person who has attained some degree of authority through greater expertise, experience, or simple ability *to hear,* that the buyer attains a degree of interaction that respects his or her values and results in a commercial transaction satisfactory to the buyer and the seller.

As Jackie has illustrated, communication is often a one-way street with the buyer ending in frustration. Though no mention was made of the ages of the unhearing salespersons, the jump from them to an unhearing marketing and creative staff of an unspecified age is not a long one. There is a saying that goes "Older you may become, but immature you can remain forever."

Conversely, let's take a look at an example of a marketing team at the Mature Market Group that includes a range of ages from early 30s to late 40s, but who, through the lens of Values Portraits, crafted a very successful marketing campaign for a retirement community in need of a mature understanding and a real solution to a difficult marketing dilemma.

CASE STUDY: THOMAS HOUSE

Thomas House is a Washington, D.C., retirement community housed in a former apartment building. The building was acquired in the 1970s by Baptist Senior Adult Ministries (BSAM), a not-for-profit corporation affiliated with the American Baptist Churches in and around the District of Columbia. Thomas House began operations as a continuing care retirement community (CCRC) in 1975.

In the late 1990s, BSAM was acquired by American Baptist Homes of the West (ABHOW), one of the oldest and largest operators of CCRC's in the country.

At the time of acquisition, Thomas House was suffering from several real barriers to its success as a retirement community, frustrating its efforts to attract the very people it was uniquely positioned to best serve. The blunt facts contributing to its low occupancy rate included its location, a common negative perception of its very elderly resident base, and marketing materials that were somewhat off-target and not working.

Thomas House is located in a part of Washington that had declined to a very seedy state over the years. It is located in what is known as the Thomas-Logan area (or the 14th Street Corridor). However, this neighborhood was definitely on the rebound as rising housing costs and limited residential options within the District of Columbia spurred the neighborhood's gentrification. New restaurants and galleries had begun to move into the area and many of the rental units in the area's brownstones were being purchased as condominiums.

With an average resident age of 84, Thomas House was not perceived to be an "active adult" retirement community. Thomas House consists of 144 residential apartments and 53 licensed nursing beds. The community has not provided assisted living services, another barrier to marketing to today's senior.

Thus marginalized, Thomas House faced a real challenge in bringing in new, younger, and healthier residents. While much of its poor reputation was definitely not deserved, the retirement community needed to communicate and present itself in a different way in order to pull itself from a sales slump.

The collateral material and ads used by Thomas House over the years were typical of many retirement communities. They presented a somewhat condescending picture of life—certainly much less vital and active than real life. They needed a new look in their advertising that represented all of the true living activities a residence in an urban setting could provide.

The true challenge for Thomas House and the Mature Market Group had several features, but the face of it was best described as the task of repositioning Thomas House in the marketplace and to prove itself with new sales against future resident attrition.

The marketing and creative team at the Mature Market Group has no small experience with CCRCs. Its approach has always been to position these clients not by selling their amenities or their health-related services, but by selling the *intangible benefits* derived from those important features the retirement community lifestyle offers. Also, the Mature Market Group's experience maintains a creative approach that is based on the understanding that a retirement community is defined more by its residents than by its "bricks and mortar." The first marketing and creative step had to begin then with a sure understanding of the current residents of Thomas House and how those residents could inform a marketing message to attract new prospects.

The residents of Thomas House were quick to respond to a survey undertaken by the Mature Market Group. When questioned about their hobbies, opinions, and preferences, their responses revealed a rich, full description of their lives. The mostly female population is very proud of their former positions within the urban working world of the nation's capitol. Many of the residents are self-identified "Government Gals" who came to the city to meet the bureaucracy's need for clerical help during World War II. With time and experience, they moved into higher positions of influence and came to consider themselves Washington insiders, privy to secrets and associations with the powerful spanning many years and many administrations.

While a smaller population than the Government Gals, the male residents of Thomas House shared a similar history of work and life in the city, experiencing its shifting fortunes from decade to decade. Along with the self-aware, independent women, the men consider themselves Washington insiders as well. Generally, most Thomas House residents remain fully engaged, to the limits of their physical abilities, with the rich cultural and intellectual life of the capital.

In addition to this vivid characterization of the residents of Thomas House, there are some credible assumptions that can be made about the residents of any CCRC. Given the costs to maintain residency in such a community—from the initial buy-in to the monthly maintenance and fees—income levels are reasonably predictable. Taking that financial wherewithal into account, it is fairly reasonable to assume that Thomas House residents were planners and savers throughout their adult lives. Also, these residents are not living with family members, indicating either an attitude of independence or emotional distance from or lack of close family ties. They are not especially bound by an emotional attachment to their former homes, thus they are not determined to "age in place." Further, they possess a fair degree of financial savvy evident in recognizing the economic advantages in becoming residents of a continuing care community. This savvy also suggests a very rational approach to the fiscal and physical realities of aging.

As you now have a familiarity with the various values, traits, and personalities represented by Value Portraits for age 62 and up, I'm sure you can begin to recognize what Value Portraits best define the existing residents of Thomas House. It is easy to see the residents of Thomas House, both immediate and potential, fall mainly into the In-Charge Intellectual and Active Achievers Value Portrait, and, to a lesser extent, the Liberal Loners. This is the conclusion the marketing and creative teams arrived at when they applied the insights the Value Portraits research provided them.

The important task before the marketing team relied on accurately addressing the questions of how then to craft a marketing effort to attract new, younger, and healthier residents. Among the three Value Portraits represented, the most important similar values were intellectual curiosity, financial security, power and recognition, and fun and enjoyment of life. For the creative team, they needed to determine how to design work whose visuals didn't rely on or emphasize the values of family ties, and write copy that didn't mine the typical veins of tradition and authority, and health and well-being. The emotionally freighted appeal of puppies and grandkids wouldn't cut it with these people. Likewise, Value Portraits research results informed the creative staff's belief that typical depictions of golfing grandpas and aerobic grannies risked totally alienating new prospects who shared the values of In-Charge Intellectuals, Active Achievers, and Liberal Loners.

For the Mature Market Group, the most meaningful marketing solutions lie in messages and images that speak directly to prospects' sense of their own intellectual prowess and cultural literacy. The exercise of the mind, the appeal of city living and its convenient access to such long-established cultural and intellectual life-defining resources was the genuine opportunity Thomas House offered, as its health and security amenities were already in place and could be taken as a given.

With a creative focus informed by Value Portraits research, the task of challenging the popular, negative perceptions of Thomas House in its primary market area remained. With Thomas House, as well as other retirement living options in general, it is a fact that people planning a move to a continuing care retirement community can take months to make a decision on where to relocate. Often, such decisions are postponed until a health crisis or a perceived threat to their personal security and autonomy becomes real. Taken into account, these unfortunate motivators can and do foster misconceptions about who lives in retirement communities and why.

Then too, there is the challenge of perception versus fact. When directly questioned, people after the magic age of 30 tend to see themselves as anywhere from 10 to 15 years younger than they actually are. In dramatic contrast to the youngster who wishes to appear older and mentally mature, adults tend to picture themselves in a personal context of physical and intellectual vigor that can be at odds with their appearance and normal physical limitations. On visiting a CCRC populated by individuals who are obviously frail or ill, the prospective resident mentally recoils thinking, "I'm not like all these *old* people."

The only way a retirement community can counteract these negative perceptive influences is to make a real effort to bring residents in at a younger, healthier age. Much refined, this was part of the issue the Mature Market Group needed to address in changing the perception and reputation of Thomas House.

THE MARKETING PLAN

For overall strategy and tactical applications, it was time to put the conclusions drawn from Value Portraits research to the test for Thomas House. Working with their client, the Mature Market Group's team came up with a plan to bring special, intellectually oriented events to Thomas House itself. By opening itself to prospective residents in a way that was low-pressure and seemingly sales-neutral, the prospective resident could form their own opinions regarding the physical environment of Thomas House *in situ*. Rather than seeing a run-down "home" populated by "patients," the prospect could enjoy an intellectually stimulating event such as an art exhibit or a book signing following a reading by and discussion with the book's author in the company of actual Thomas House residents. There would be no piano sing-a-longs, but there would be stimulating subjects to discuss with interesting people in an attractive pleasing environment.

Using the information gathered from actual resident surveys, a series of events was developed and scheduled. The events were advertised through public relations activities both in print according to resident reading preferences and through a radio buy on local National Public Radio (NPR).

Thomas House residents had indicated a very strong affection and preference for certain NPR programming. As NPR doesn't accept flat-out commercials, sponsorships of resident preferred programs such as *All Things Considered, Car Talk,* classical music blocks, and a wonderfully titled, very popular program called *Songs for Aging Children* were arranged through a two-week period, including weekends.

Collateral materials for the events were designed and developed for both direct mail and print media. Some examples can be seen in Figures 9.3 through 9.7.

As you can see, these pieces were somewhat visually sophisticated and subtle in design and message. Conventional wisdom maintains older consumers have the time and interest to read and absorb much information. However, postcards and print advertising can't and shouldn't belabor their message with a surfeit of copy. Individuals in the Value Portraits the marketing team identified as potential prospects for Thomas House value their time and are proud of their intelligence. They find

FIGURE 9.3 *Direct Mail Postcard*

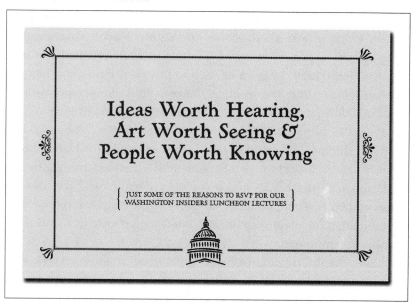

FIGURE 9.4 *Direct Mail Postcard*

FIGURE 9.5 *Direct Mail Postcard*

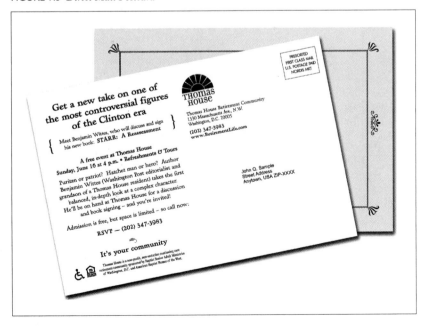

FIGURE 9.6 *Print Advertising*

Congressmen, Senators *&* Ballerinas

{ JUST A FEW PEOPLE OUR RESIDENTS CONSIDER FRIENDS }

Now, retirement doesn't have to mean leaving the community and lifestyle you love: because you can join the diverse, interesting accomplished people who have made Thomas House their preferred choice for a rewarding retirement.

Because it's located in the heart of downtown D.C., Thomas House lets you take full advantage of all the world-class culture and local flavor you're accustomed to: from Capitol Hill to the Smithsonian, from sports to the arts.

And, because it's the only continuing care retirement community (CCRC) in downtown, you'll have the peace of mind of knowing that a complete range of quality care you can count on is always available, should it ever be needed.

Variety, comfort, convenience, security ... with thoughtful services and exceptional amenities, to help you make the most of every moment, in the city you've always loved.

It's where you want to be. It's the way you want to live. It's your community.

See for yourself. Call us today at **(202) 347-3983** to join us for a complimentary luncheon and tour, as our special guest.

It's your community

1330 Massachusetts Ave. N.W.
Washington, D.C. 20005

(202) 347-3983

www.RetirementLife.com

 THOMAS HOUSE

Thomas House is a nonprofit, non-sectarian continuing care retirement community sponsored by Baptist Senior Adult Ministries of Washington, D.C. and American Baptist Homes of the West.

CODE

FIGURE 9.7 *Print Advertising*

Museums, Galleries & Openings

{ JUST A FEW PLACES OUR RESIDENTS HAVE BEEN SPOTTED }

With all the attractions and advantages of one of the world's great cities at their doorstep, who would dream of leaving it all behind for some distant suburb? Certainly not the active, interesting residents of Thomas House – and they're waiting to welcome you to D.C.'s most rewarding retirement lifestyle.

As the only continuing care retirement community (CCRC) in downtown Washington, Thomas House has it all, in the heart of it all – and our residents enjoy the diversity of life in the city.

Whether enjoying all the culture and excitement only the District can offer, or relishing our own special combination of outstanding amenities and services, Thomas House residents are busy living the lifestyle they've always dreamed of, in the city they've always loved.

And, because a full range of health care is always available, they know their future can be every bit as carefree.

You know you love it ... so why leave it? Find out why Thomas House is D.C.'s favorite destination for a fulfilling retirement. Call today at **(202) 347-3983** to join us for a complimentary luncheon and tour.

It's your community

1330 Massachusetts Ave. N.W.
Washington, D.C. 20005

(202) 347-3983

www.RetirementLife.com

Thomas House is a nonprofit, non-sectarian continuing care retirement community sponsored by Baptist Senior Adult Ministries of Washington, D.C. and American Baptist Homes of the West.

overstatement or a lack of subtlety in some print advertising mediums off-putting, if not insulting.

There is a time and place for collateral materials that are more information rich and offer a more visually oriented presentation. The marketing team realized there was much more of the Thomas House story that needed to be related and elaborated upon by vehicles that played both to the prospects' sense of themselves visually (remember the perception of being 10 to 15 years younger), vitally (remember the residents' values of intellectual curiosity and lifelong learning), and intellectually (remember their relative disregard for authority, convention, and tradition).

Figures 9.8 through 9.10 take a look at examples of collateral materials that addressed those very things.

FIGURE 9.8 *Thomas House Letter*

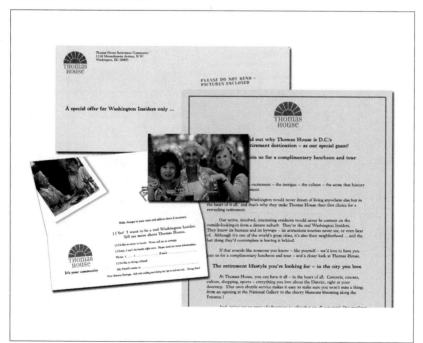

FIGURE 9.9 *Thomas House Brochure*

FIGURE 9.10 *Thomas House Newsletter*

RESULTS

The Mature Market Group's approach to rebranding Thomas House through the efforts of its marketing and creative teams strongly resonated with the management team at American Baptist Homes of the West. The enthusiastic implementation of the plan and its components brought a level of excitement that both invigorated their sales efforts and the residents' perception of themselves and their home.

Attendance at four lectures/events drew a total of 159 new prospects, an average of about 40 each event. Some of these prospects converted to actual sales. The response to the direct mail efforts is a concrete, measurable quantity. Sales leads have doubled since the inception of the program indicating a real, positive shift in the popular perception of Thomas House as a retirement option. Thomas House is a real-world validation of the meaningful insights Value Portraits can contribute in a marketing effort to those in the Fall and Winter seasons of life. Through the lens of Value Portraits, the Mature Market Group was able to create a marketing message that was relevant to and resonated with the target audience.

CONCLUSION

As David Wolfe has presented so convincingly, there is a growing crisis created by marketing efforts that cling to limited ways of seeing the New Customer Majority as a market entity. No single approach or dictum of demographics or segmentation promotes a completely clear view of consumers anymore. As we continue to educate ourselves as marketers, we must get beyond the "obvious" in our perceptions of the marketplace.

At the Mature Market Group, our Value Portraits research is proving to be an innovative, effective new lens through which to view the market segment we specialize in, understand, and communicate with. As part of the 360-degree view of customers David Wolfe is exploring, the psychological import of Value Portraits offers a contributing component that, along with biology, creates that sum total of consumer behavior.

CONNECTING WITH REALITY

People get more interesting in the second half of life. They have more of a story to tell. They have chapters describing dreams that came true, and chapters about dreams that fizzled out. They have chapters on unwanted challenges that came their way that they overcame, and chapters on unwanted challenges that got the better of them. Some of the most poignant scenes in their life stories are about their growth through childhood, wholly dependent on parents and other authority figures, into the first awkward steps as adolescents seeking emancipation from dependence on and control by others. Their stories chronicle their first steps into adulthood, fortified by an audacious view of their competence and what they would accomplish. Their stories reveal that as careers began maturing and personal lives continued evolving—not always as they thought it might years earlier—they came to the threshold of midlife where they first stared into the face of *real* reality and began experiencing a change in consciousness that dissolved the unbounded romanticism and heroic mien of earlier adulthood.

This is when their stories really get interesting. This is when they take up issues they wouldn't have dreamed taking up at 25, such as the big Ws in life: *Why* am I here? *What* is my future—not as a spouse, a careerist, but as *me*? *Who* am I really? *When* will I feel complete and satisfied with life?

Interesting people are more complex than less interesting people. The reasons why they choose brands and companies are more complex than the reasons of less interesting people. They have more stories to draw on in making their choices. The chapters in Part Four connect with the realities of second-half customers that make them so interesting—and so complex as customers.

10

LIFE SATISFACTION
The Missing Focus in Marketing

Companies spend bundles trying to measure customer satisfaction. However, few spend a dime probing customers' *life satisfaction*. It seems to me that an authentic customer-centric company goes beyond the limited boundaries of customer satisfaction—which is a product-centric concern—to take a role in promoting customers' life satisfaction.

Satisfaction can be viewed in terms of two time-based categories: episodic satisfaction and ambient satisfaction.

Episodic satisfaction is fleeting and superficial satisfaction. It can last a minute, an hour, a day or two, or maybe even a week or so, but sooner or later episodic satisfaction fizzles out, sometimes leaving us with that day-after-Christmas feeling that kids experience. Maslow was talking about episodic satisfaction when he discussed his *grumble theory* of personal growth. He observed how we lust after something, diligently apply ourselves to getting it, experience a brief spell of euphoria, then find that what we wanted so badly and worked so hard for stops giving us the pleasure it first did. Then we start grumbling for something new. This recurring scenario, he said, leads us to new experiences that may contribute to our personal growth.

Ambient satisfaction is enduring and profound. It must be present to experience life satisfaction. It is a prevailing mood of comfort about one's life. Unlike episodic satisfaction, which can be shattered in an instant by some untoward event, ambient satisfaction is durable. It not only resists threats to its existence, it protects a person against psychic erosion by adversity. This becomes particularly beneficial in later life when chances of progressive, debilitating illness are greater and the incidence of death among friends and family increases.

People can frequently experience episodic satisfaction without having life satisfaction. Those whom Robert Snyder calls Woeful Worriers in Chapter 9 have happy times at family gatherings, among friends, and on outings to the theater, athletic events, or perhaps a shopping mall. However, they do not experience life satisfaction. Even frequent instances of very strong episodic satisfaction cannot produce life satisfaction. Manic personalities have very intense highs, but no ambient satisfaction.

Life satisfaction correlates with maturity. People in self-actualizing states invariably have a deep sense of satisfaction with their lives. Their life satisfaction is *internally* developed. It does not depend on material goods, money, or even others, though severe deficits in those departments can inhibit life satisfaction. Life satisfaction only becomes possible when negotiations between the social self and the inner self lead to the conclusion that satisfaction with life is not dependent on what happens to a person but on how a person processes what happens.

This chapter offers practical insights into the topic of life satisfaction that companies and their marketers can draw on to become active collaborators with customers in advancing their quality of life beyond any contribution a product might make. But before getting into that, let's parse the common view of customer satisfaction.

THE THREE DIMENSIONS OF CUSTOMER SATISFACTION

Gary Solomonson, a marketing and operations consultant serving the retirement housing industry, is big on "walking around the market" to learn about customers. On visits to client communities, Solomonson asks residents, "Do you feel that you are getting your money's worth?" It's a simple straightforward question that elicits simple straightforward answers.

Solomonson credits the answers he gets with helping him better understand the basis of the satisfaction (or dissatisfaction) of residents, which he says is more complex than he once thought. He claims that the stark honesty of his opening question lets residents know that he is sincere about wanting to learn the truth about how they feel.

"I learn much more than any survey could tell. And even if I asked them face-to-face if they were satisfied or happy living in the community, many would tell me what they thought would please me. It's like asking someone, 'How do I look?' Most people will hedge their answer to avoid offending the questioner."

Solomonson's question is a good one to ask in the planning stages of a marketing campaign: What will make customers feel they are getting their money's worth? It might prove useful to have everyone on the marketing team—outside agencies included—to write down what they think would make customers feel they are getting their money's worth. I guarantee that you will get divergent answers.

People in second-half markets often go well beyond price and product performance in determining whether they are getting their money's worth and, as Solomonson learned, it is a more complex process than is usually the case with younger customers.

Despite all the money spent on customer satisfaction research, there is a dearth of understanding about customer satisfaction, especially among older customers. Phillip Cooper, a marketing professor I met at Loyola College before he passed on, lamented to me, "There is a deplorable lack of information derived from in-depth research that shows how customer satisfaction evolves, takes shape, and is maintained. This has been a major focus of my research and of a handful of others in recent years, and we have a paucity of literature to draw from."

In the DRM marketing framework, customer satisfaction is parsed into three dimensions:

1. Functional performance desires and expectations
2. Social reinforcement desires and expectations
3. Consequential experiential desires and expectations

Where is price, you might ask? To a large extent, and especially in second-half markets, satisfaction with price is a function of the three sets of desires and expectations listed. A product that doesn't measure up to customers' desires and expectations in those three categories is overpriced at any price. Also, because the focus of this chapter is customers' *life satisfaction,* there is no point in discussing the issue of price because it makes no contribution to life satisfaction.

Functional Performance Desires and Expectations

Meeting customers' desires and expectations of a brand or company's functional performance depends on how well companies and brands fulfill both *explicit* and *implicit* promises to customers. It also depends on how closely aligned company intentions are with what customers hope for and expect. Because they are focused more on moving products than on deeply pleasing customers, most companies suffer a paucity of understanding about what really does generate customer satisfaction. In the first place, not everything worth knowing about customers' desires and expectations can be uncovered by conventional research for the simple reason that customers have unconscious desires and expectations. No survey or traditional focus group can do well in that regard. I got a good lesson in subtle desires and expectations some years ago when I owned a company that managed condominium and homeowner associations.

I learned that some of the most competent property managers did not get management contract renewals as often as some lesser skilled property managers. To find out why, we hired a squad of college students to interview client boards of directors. They returned with a stunning finding.

"Mr. Wolfe, you have two contracts with each board. You have a *legal* contract and you have an *emotional* contract. Deliver fully on the legal contract, but fall down on the emotional contract and forget a contract renewal. But if you deliver well on the emotional contract, and short of something egregious, you don't fully deliver on the legal contract, the board will probably renew the management contract."

We then gave all managers psychological tests to see how personality might be a bigger factor in contract renewals than we previously recognized. It turned out that managers with the best contract renewal record tested highest in self-confidence, felt less need to impress others with what they knew, and tested highest in empathy. Those three attributes will help any marketer to be more successful in fulfilling the emotional contract with customers.

Every product and service is coupled with both a legal and an emotional contract. Take the brand that tattoo artists are very familiar with. How many brands literally get under customers' skins the way Harley-Davidson does? Harley-Davidson may not have the highest performance ratings, but its empathetic connections with customers overcome that. (Chapter 14 describes how Harley-Davidson first built an empathetic connection with its customers.)

Harley-Davidson's delivery on the emotional contract is its competitive edge. It is not only fun to experience the sound and ride of a Harley, but also to simply experience the ownership of a Harley, whether one rides it or not. I have heard that some people who feel they can no longer safely ride their Harley keep it anyway. They park it in a garage where they can pay it visits and polish it from time to time because the joy of owning a Harley never goes away.

Companies that design products from a customer-centric perspective, as the accounting software producer Intuit knows, are likelier to experience high levels of customer satisfaction with the functional performance of their products.

From its earliest days, Intuit worked from a customer-centric perspective in creating its flagship product, Quicken. It all began one day when visionary Intuit cofounder Scott Cook watched his wife paying bills. She didn't do it like an accountant would. Cook, who entered the accounting software space for individuals and small businesses after others had pioneered it, made simplicity and intuitiveness, not gee-whiz sophistication, Quicken's hallmark. To deliver on that, Intuit involved customers in designing Quicken. Says Cook, "One thing we do know that people want: simplicity. We know they want us to take the complex stuff they hate to do—stuff like doing their taxes, keeping their books, and getting a mortgage—and make it drop-dead simple."[1]

Intuit's researchers worked like anthropologists work. They went into people's homes and offices to observe them in real-life settings. Cook noted in an interview, "What customers want is not always something you can discover with feedback, doing a survey, or holding a focus group."[2]

Cook's customer-centric philosophy paved the way for Intuit's stellar performance, enabling it to vanquish even the mighty Microsoft, one of the few companies ever to do so. Microsoft, with typical intensity, sought to dominate the field. However, failing in its objective, it tried to buy Intuit. Federal regulators nixed Bill Gates' plans, and Intuit remains the 800-pound gorilla in its category.

Marketing guru Seth Godin, who coined the term *permission marketing*, says, "Most products are good enough today." In other words, most companies are satisfying the legal contract. It is the emotional contract that companies are widely failing. Today, because of what Godin says about product parity, the emotional contract is virtually the only arena left for establishing a competitive edge. We've all heard a lot of noise about how important the customer experience has become. The customer experience is about the emotional contract.

Social Reinforcement Desires and Expectations

People do not willingly buy products that make them look bad or that are in conflict with their self-image. To make sure that they look good to others, people in first-half markets depend on cues issued by their peers. However, as people move into midlife and beyond, looking good to others, at least in the sense of making big favorable impressions, begins to be less important. By age 60, people generally—there are exceptions, as always—become relatively impervious to peer influence on their buying behavior, especially those who are well along the path of self-actualization.

A different kind of social influence comes into play when people get their first AARP membership solicitation. Commonly, people who have celebrated their 50th birthday shy away from products that are associated with older age, which is why many people throw away AARP's first invitation to join 35 million other people aged 50 and older. The brand manager of a well-known nutritional supplement with a name indicating that it is for people over 50 told me that if his company had to do it all over again it would choose a different name. He said research indicated that many people in their 50s do not buy the product because they perceive it as a symbol of being over the hill.

Aversion to associating with age-based products poses a daily challenge to extended services retirement communities. A 78-year-old, concerned with being associated with *old* people, might walk into a retirement community sales center and announce, "I am not here for myself, you understand. I am looking for my sister (sometimes it's his mother!). I'm not ready to retire yet," notwithstanding that he might have said his final goodbyes to his office 15 or 18 years earlier.

A famous case of a product being spurned by older customers because of an *age stigma* originated in the kitchens of Gerber a few years ago. After learning that a number of older denture wearers bought baby food for their own use, Gerber created a line of pureed foods for them and rolled it out under the inelegant name Singles. The product never got off the ground. Its failure was foreordained by behavioral subtleties among older people that traditional research might not reveal. It's hard to image a denture wearer in a focus group saying, "When I buy Gerber baby food for my sore gums, no one thinks I'm buying it for myself. They think I'm buying it for my grandchild. Heavens! If I bought Gerber Singles, everyone would know that I'm toothless!" My dentures-wearing mother would never have confessed that to a researcher.

Affinity shampoo also had an inauspicious launch for similar reasons. It was first marketed for "over 40" hair. The sought-after market rejected it. However, Johnson & Johnson saved the brand by repositioning it in ads showing the quieter, mature, special kind of beauty that women in midlife can project, doing so with no reference to age.

Campbell's Soup tried tying a product to age with its Senior Singles—Soup for One. That one was dead on arrival.

Our society's long preoccupation with the idea that beauty, vitality, excitement, and sex are reserved for the young promotes the idea that after 50, if not in the 40s, age becomes a steadily progressing liability. Consider how many laws reinforce that idea by coupling the words *elderly* and *handicapped,* as in "for elderly and handicapped persons." How often does one see public conveyances that post "For elderly and handicapped persons" on certain seats? As long as age and handicap remain somewhat synonymous, many older people will have an aversion to products and services associated with "old" people. Rule number one in ageless marketing:

Market to values, not to age.

The fastest way to kill a brand's chances in older markets is to tie it to age. But, you may ask, aren't some products by their nature age-specific, such as Medicare policies? I was involved in designing a series of television ads that were essentially ageless for PacifiCare's Secure Horizons Medicare brand. The credit for solving the problem of adapting age-less marketing to an inherently age-specific product goes to Brenda Forrest of Portland, Oregon, a former art director with McCann-Erickson who struck out on her own. Her solution was to first present PacifiCare in a voice-over as "for people from 0 to 64" in the first half of the 60-second spots. Then the spots introduced its Medicare brand, Secure Horizon, with the voice-over stating it was "for people 65 and older." This projected the idea of continuity, as in "Whatever your needs, PacifiCare will meet them for a lifetime." Forrest never used those words because the stories she told in the commercials said it all.

The spots started out with a typical family scene, in a park in one case, at an art festival in another. The characters were established in the first 30 seconds in a scene from early family life, but with older people included. In the second half of both commercials, the older people who had been introduced in supporting roles in the first 30 seconds now moved to front and center as the main characters.

The first commercial opened in a park showing a dad with his three children. Off to the side, the grandma was doing a crossword puzzle. The two older kids were doing somersaults, but the youngest, about three, was not able to get one going. Dad picked her up by the heels and tried to move her through the motions of a somersault. When the second segment began, the grandma put down her puzzle, went over to the little girl and did a slowly developing somersault so the little girl could see how it was done. The little girl followed suit, executing an awkward but complete somersault. That commercial engaged a metaphor to reflect a powerful force in people's lifestyles and product choices: independence. While the dad tried to control his daughter through a somersault (making her dependent on him), the grandma showed her granddaughter how she could do it on her own (independence).

In the second commercial, a family, together with its grandma and grandpa, are shown at an art fair. As children line up to get their faces painted, one of the older kids bumps a little girl of about three out of line. That symbolism of being outside the mainstream carries over to the second segment when the little girl is shown on the sidelines while other kids are whooping it up in a folk dance. Grandpa sees her all alone, looking pensive, goes over to her and brings her into the middle of the dance floor where they dance together. Showing the little girl getting bumped in the first half of the commercial was a conceit intended to create an empathetic connection between the little girl and older people watching the commercial. Remember from Chapter 3 my 57-year-old friend being bumped aside at a cosmetics counter when the clerk chose to serve a twentysomething woman out of line? The empathetic connection set up in the first segment was reinforced in the second segment as the little girl stood a bit lost and alone on the sidelines, a feeling not uncommon among older people.

The metaphorical presentation of two small children echoed two common concerns among older people: maintaining independence and having a meaningful place in life. Through children, PacifiCare attempted to build appeal for the Secure Horizon brand by demonstrating the empathetic understanding of older people. Both commercials were good theater, and both worked amazingly well.

A benchmark survey was conducted prior to their launches to measure awareness. Six weeks later a second survey, according to Forrest, reflected the strongest lift for an established brand that she had experienced in 25 years in major league marketing. A local columnist asked her readers, "Have you seen those PacifiCare commercials that just bring tears to your eyes?" The take-away from this tale of ageless marketing: Don't present brands based on age, even brands that are only used by older people. Values sell better. The PacifiCare commercials I've just described projected nurturing values in a family context, not a healthcare company's context.

Consequential Experiential Desires and Expectations

This is the most complex and subtle realm of customers' desires and expectations. It encompasses experiences that extend beyond the functional performance and social reinforcement dimensions of customer satisfaction. Consequential experiential desires and expectations can be subtle to the point of being beyond customers' knowing, though still highly influential on customer behavior. When well served, these desires and expectations—more than the other two sets of desires and expectations—can contribute to a customers' life satisfaction. Even a brand as mundane as a toothpaste brand can contribute to a customer's life satisfaction, as the success of Tom's of Maine suggests, as we discussed in Chapter 6. Of course, it's unlikely that a single tube of toothpaste will budge the needle on a person's life satisfaction meter, but when people buy Tom's higher-priced toothpaste primarily because of the company's sensitivity to the natural environment and to human values in the workplace and community, a tube of toothpaste and its replacements may be like a single brick in a great wall in which every brick counts. Every tube of Tom's toothpaste counts in some people's edifice of life satisfaction.

Leon Schiffman, director of the doctoral program in marketing at Baruch College, City University, New York, succinctly summarized his research findings about older customers' consequential experiential desires and expectations: "They buy experiences, not products or services."[3]

MISCONCEPTIONS ABOUT OLDER PEOPLE THAT CAN BE COSTLY TO COMPANIES

As people move into the Winter of life around the age of 60, many report more satisfaction with their lives than they experienced as younger people. Of course, not everyone who gets old arrives there in a life-satisfied state, but according to numerous studies, higher levels of life satisfaction in later life are commonplace. That surprises many younger people because, "Life satisfaction for the elderly is too often measured in terms of objective conditions like having enough money and being in good health," says Monika Ardelt, a University of Florida sociologist who has conducted studies on the relationship between wisdom and life satisfaction. "I found that developing wisdom in one's later years has a far greater impact on psychological well-being."[4]

Regrets over lost youth and what might have been do beset some people in advanced age, but not people in advanced states of psychological maturity. The latter are generally free of fears about a future that holds the prospects—*though not the certainty*—of growing disability. They are suffused in a continuum of life satisfaction that is found only infrequently among young adults, as Maslow explained in his writings.

Having experienced substantial satisfaction of materialistic and social aspirations, the mature adult is more resistant to advertising that reflects the narcissistic and materialist ethos that widely dominates advertising. The mature of mind and spirit devote less energy thinking about "things" to buy and more to the pursuit of experiences that enrich one's being. They have less desire to escape the routine—a big imperative among younger people. Like my friend James who discovered new and exciting things about himself and life in his coast-to-coast bike trip at age 55, the truly mature delight in making new discoveries about the routine (a vignette of James's bike trek appears in Chapter 15). Some human development specialists see this behavior as reflecting a child-like affect that echoes more respectfully the perennial idea about a return to second childhood in later life. This is a poorly understood dimension of the Winter of life, and because it represents what customers in Fall are working toward, it means deficient understanding of the developmental purposes of midlife is pervasive in the marketing community.

Marketers create product messages promising young people a wide range of satisfying experiences spanning the gamut in youthful lifestyles. However, in marketing to retirees, too much focus is placed on ceaseless empty "fun," carefree lifestyles, services that promote dependency, and on sundry soulless experiences that dull the mind or are only for the dull of mind. Life satisfaction does not come from self-indulging activities or from being waited on at every turn. It comes from living a life of purpose and meaning. So, let's blow away some of the condescending misconceptions about the later years of life that cost companies untold amounts of money in marketing mistakes, as happened to Gerber and Campbell's a few years back.

Don't Take the Romance out of Life

People, regardless of age, have romantic experiential aspirations. Romance is not the private domain of the young. It is a need all people have all their lives, especially when defining romance as being about an *adventurous spirit and enthusiasm for life*. But let's focus for a bit on sexual romance.

It's amazing—no, sad—how many people believe that sexuality and old age are incompatible in "normal" people. This is probably a throwback to adolescence, when the young have difficulty imagining their parents "doing it," and horror, certainly their grandparents couldn't be "doing it." Once those images are in the mind, they are fortified by the unremitting focus on youthful sexuality in advertising and entertainment that solidifies the notion that sexual pleasure is a privilege of being young.

I have from time to time used an ad for Hennessy in workshops to make the point that sexuality and aging are not incompatible. The ad shows two people in their later 20s or early 30s in a rustic cabin before a roaring fire, he, bare to the waist and she, bare-shouldered with a blanket pulled over her bosom. In the foreground is a bottle of Hennessy that has just been removed from Christmas wrapping. The intent of the Hennessey ad is not to sell the product. Rather, the ad sells an experience by invoking the prospects of a romantic evening of sensuous *and* sensual pleasure, before a glowing fire, enriched by the sharing of snifters of Hennessey. The headline's double entendre "The civilized way to unwrap," refers directly to the just-unwrapped Christmas present of Hennessey, but indirectly to the bare bodies of the couple.

Presented in color in the original, the ad is in soft, sepia-oriented tones. The heavy rustic stonework in the walls provides a juxtaposition of "a primitive image" with the word *civilized* that appears in the headline. Good storytelling!

After I present the ad to an audience, I ask a pivotal question: "How many of you—be honest now—can see a 75-year-old couple in place of the young couple in this ad?"

Inevitably, members of the audience respond with such comments as "Of course not," "Well, it depends," "Maybe," "No!" Sometimes two people turn to each other and start arguing. One can see the substitution, but the other can't. Others object to the idea of even considering showing older people baring their skin.

A woman in one audience said, "Such an idea is demeaning to older people." Another woman responded directly to her: "My first reaction to Mr. Wolfe's question was the same; but then I thought the problem about older people shown in sexy poses is mine, not theirs."

I flip to the next slide. It shows a picture from a *Time* magazine article on the "new senior." A half-dozen older men and women, all bare-shouldered, are partying in a hot tub. Audience response is a mixture of gasps, giggles, and laughter. An actual picture of half-naked older people works in their minds better than the imagined picture I invited them to conjure up by mentally substituting a 75-year-old couple for the young couple in the Hennessy ad.

After showing the photograph of six people in their 60s or older, I present an ad for hot tubs that features a well-seasoned couple enjoying themselves with two glasses of wine (and an unspent wine bottle to the side). This picture works for the audience, too. A cardinal point has been made in this interesting exchange with the audience that is expressed in the famous line from the defunct Pogo comic strip: "We have met the enemy, and it's us." One of a marketer's worst enemies in older markets, especially Winter markets, is a mind filled with misconceptions about older people that when woven into marketing decisions can lead to costly mistakes.

Sixty, Sexy, and Susceptible

In 1981, Marcella Bakur Weiner and Bernard D. Starr published one of the first major works on sexuality among older adults, *The Starr-Weiner Report on Sexuality in the Mature Years.* The report was based on interviews with nearly 1,000 older people. Weiner says of the interviews, "There was a flowing of feelings and attitudes expressing a desire for intimacy and romance."

Jim Moore, of Moore Diversified Services, a market research firm in Ft. Worth, Texas, tells of the time when the subject of sex in later life came up in a focus group. One prissy older woman said, "It's disgusting the way sex always creeps into conversations. It's not everything, you know." A pert, vivacious woman, who appeared to be in her 70s, countered, "I don't know about that, dearie. I kind of like a little tingle now and then."

In *Love and Sex After 60*, Dr. Robert N. Butler, former head of the National Institute on Aging, and psychotherapist Myrna I. Lewis, write of the presumption that sexual desire automatically disappears with age: "thus an older woman who shows . . . interest in sex is often assumed to be suffering from mental problems . . . older men [interested in sex] become 'dirty old men'."[5] Many people in their 70s, 80s, and even into their 90s maintain active interest in sex which they act on.

Professor Ian Philp, National Director for Older People's Services for the British government, said at a conference on aging held in London in 2001, "Sexually active older people live longer and stay healthier than their celibate counterparts. Sex can help elderly people stay healthy like any exercise, yet it seems that the sexual interest remains particularly strong in elderly women."[6] I have a friend who can testify to that. An elderly uncle called him from the extended services retirement community he lived in and cried out, "You've got to get me out of this place. The women are driving me wild." Some women regard men as precious commodities in these communities because the male-female ratios may be as extreme as seven or eight to one.

THE FOUR FACES OF THE NEW SENIOR

Most assuredly, travelers through life's Winter have experiential aspirations that go far beyond the pleasures of sex, travel, and golf. In *SAM* 1990 I included a brief that I drew up for an agency to guide it in creating marketing messages for older markets. It was entitled, "The Four Faces of the New Senior." A bit revised, you can read this brief in the sidebar (and yes, I know I was making broad, sweeping generalizations; however, I did so consciously for the purpose of helping an ad agency rid itself of broad, sweeping, *negative* generalizations that promote inaccurate stereotypes of older people).

The Four Faces of the "New Senior"

The First Face: Creativity and Intellectual Involvement. The New Senior is a member of the most information-driven segment of our society, when information is not related to livelihood. New Seniors' favorite TV consists of news shows and documentaries. They are big readers of newspapers and magazines. They travel to expand their intellectual horizons, rather than for the escapist reasons that often motivate young people to travel. They sign up at colleges and universities by the tens of thousands. New Seniors are creative about shaping their lives and have deepened their intellectual involvement in life. They employ this bent in their consumer behavior, not only when buying for themselves, but when buying for their grandchildren. More than a third of all juvenile books sold are bought by grandparents.

The Second Face: Experience and Wisdom and the Desire to Share Them. The idea that retirement is a time for living a never-ending vacation is an anathema to New Seniors. They want to give back. New Seniors represent a massive source of volunteer talent. As Erik Erikson observed, the final responsibility in the last decades of life is *generativity*—giving attention to the incoming generations. People often talk about the experience and wisdom of older people, but generally ignore their *desire to share it.*

The Third Face: Vitality and Productivity. We see a 75- or 80-year-old who is "active" and say "Isn't she remarkable." One 82-year-old woman said she was tired of being referred to as remarkable. "I am just an 82-year-old version of my 22-year-old self—hell, I was always remarkable," she exclaimed.[7]

Most seniors want to continue producing something of value—it's the only route to self-esteem. Self-esteem does not derive from one's consumption activities. The overemphasis on leisure in marketing senior living environments is contrary to this image of productivity. A 1986 study by SRI, International, found over 80 percent of seniors felt too much emphasis was placed on recreation in marketing senior communities.

The Fourth Face: Compassion for Others and Concern for the World about Them. Seniors are our best citizens. They vote at a higher rate than any other age group and are more heavily involved in "good works" than the rest of the population. While one may argue, "That's because they have more time," it may be because they care more. Otherwise, they would do what most nonseniors erroneously think they do—play full time and love it.

The Four Faces of the New Senior provides a contextual framework from which to draw ideas for creating imagery of older people according to what they feel honestly represents them. Project the images they inspire and they will infer from your marketing executions that you have an empathetic understanding of them.

LIFE SATISFACTION: THE MOST POWERFUL MOTIVATOR OF SECOND-HALF CUSTOMERS

The late Phillip Cooper and George Miaoulis, also a professor of marketing, observed in a professional journal more than 15 years ago, "While all marketing situations contain a life satisfaction ingredient, that ingredient becomes more pronounced later in life. As people gain more possessions and have more experiences with them, they come to understand that life is not only about possessions. *Life satisfaction becomes their dominant goal.*"[8] (Italics added.)

If Cooper and Miaoulis are right, many marketers have been missing a sure bet by ignoring life satisfaction in shaping marketing strategies and executions. In fact, by ignoring it, the wrong things tend to get stressed, such as when the physical properties of something, rather than the possibilities of something, dominate an ad. As said before in this book, on average the appetite for "things" ebbs in the second half of life, with spending for "things" peaking out around the late 40s.

That might tempt some to say, "See, I've been telling you that young markets are where you should put your marketing dollars." Yet, even with less per capita spent each year in most categories after age 50, the number of people beyond their peak spending years is so large that people 50 and older still collectively spend 60 percent more than adults under 45. Also, I believe there is more money to be made in Fall and Winter markets than companies are making because marketing to second-half markets is often grossly ineffective and even counterproductive. *SAM* 1990 carried a passage aimed at putting the value of older markets in a proper perspective:

> Older markets are not so much additional markets in the total scheme of things as they are *replacement* markets. The value of older markets to businesses in today's economy lies in their role in providing alternative markets to the traditional youth and family markets, as those latter two markets decline in number and total buying power. If U.S. business leaders realize this and take creative action to make up for revenues lost in younger markets by capturing older markets, then the economy will ease more slowly into its new, lower consumer-spending configuration.
>
> Creative action taken today in penetrating older markets will allow for a smoother landing after the heady growth we have enjoyed for nearly a half a century. I firmly believe older people, within limits of financial prudence dictated by their individual circumstances, can generally be induced to spend more than past history indicates. To the degree this occurs, however, it will be due to a much better understanding of the psyches of

older consumers than currently exists. It is in their behavior patterns, not their numbers or their affluence, that will influence their future contributions to the consumer economy.

While per capita spending peaks by age 50, spending winds down slowly. People don't suddenly stop spending as of their 50th birthday. They still buy a lot of things. For example, they buy things:

- To replace things they already have and still need that are in disrepair or obsolete
- To maintain the lifestyles to which they have become accustomed
- To make gifts to others
- To gain access to experiences made possible by the purchase of a "thing"

Note that the last reason ties into to the third category of consumer satisfaction—consequential experiential desires and expectations. Older people generally will spend more—sometimes much more—for products and services that serve as a gateway to experiential pleasures they covet. While they may be constrained by issues of affordability, they are not as constrained by price as they were earlier in life. They might leave the grocery store with fewer bags now that the kids are in college or out on their own, but they may have left just as much money at the checkout counter.

Why Second-Half Customers Are Likelier to Experience Life Satisfaction

Some twentysomethings and thirtysomethings may want to quibble with the idea that life satisfaction correlates with psychological maturation and is generally found only among older people. However, in her book *The Pathfinders*, Gail Sheehy reported that of 60,000 questionnaires probing the issue of life satisfaction, not a single young person met the measure of all five conditions that she maintained are characteristic of people enjoying a continuum of life satisfaction. None of the five conditions necessarily involve either "things" or purchased services. They include having:

- A clear sense of direction in life
- A sense of having achieved important goals
- An overall satisfaction in the way major life crises have been handled
- A general pleasure with personal growth and development
- Rare feelings of feeling cheated or disappointed by life[9]

Sheehy's "Hallmarks of Well-Being," as she termed them, may not have been scientifically derived, but they are consistent with the work of numerous adult developmental psychologists who have addressed the subject of the continuum of life satisfaction.

Clearly, the picture that emerges of people who enjoy a continuum of life satisfaction is that they are self-sufficient, self-confident, able to get over life's rough times in one piece, and are comfortable with themselves, others in their life, and life in general. This picture applies most frequently to people beginning in the mid-to-upper 40s, according to Sheehy, with no age at which the feeling of well-being decreases because of age—for emphasis, let's repeat that: *with no age at which the feeling of well being decreases because of age.*

Even severe adverse physical conditions are not the barriers to life satisfaction that many a young people would believe. Renowned astrophysicist and Nobel laureate Stephen Hawking, a victim of Lou Gehrig's disease, has been virtually paralyzed from his head down for most of his adult life. He has been unable to speak since his voice box was removed in 1985 to make his breathing easier. Yet, he has been a prodigious contributor to the body of theory on the origins of the universe while serving as a Lucasion Professor of mathematics at Cambridge (the seat Isaac Newton held). He is widely regarded as second only to Albert Einstein in his stature as a scientist.

Hawking, now 61, communicates through a voice synthesizer made gratis for him by an admiring engineer in California who promised to make it possible for Hawking to speak again, if only through an electronic voice box surrogate. With the squeeze of a finger, nearly the full extent of his self-willed muscle movement, Hawking painstakingly assembles his statements from words rolling across a computer monitor mounted on his wheelchair. The voice synthesizer gives sound to his word selections. Despite the formidable communications obstacles, Hawking's droll humor comes through his synthesizer intact to indicate that inside his twisted, frozen body dwells a man with a vibrant enthusiasm for life. Hawking once asked a reporter interviewing him to get him a cup of coffee, then apologized for the American accent, informing his visitor that the synthesizer was made in California.

To what better example can we point to show how a continuum of life satisfaction can exist even under the most severe health constraints as long as the mind is whole than Stephen Hawking.

Play Pens for Wrinkled Babies?

Even many people who work with older seniors on a daily basis don't get it. Brochures for extended services retirement housing commonly betray a poor understanding of people in the Winter of their lives. This quotation from a senior housing brochure illustrates the point: "You will find a program that encourages independence, but emphasizes care and service." That oxymoron mirrors in an oblique way the widely held impression that being older than 75—the target market of extended services elder communities—means better than even odds of being dependent on others.

I once asked a 66-year-old to review a stack of brochures I had picked up from extended services communities around the country and let me know what he thought about them. His analysis: "They all say the same thing. They promise independence in the opening paragraphs, then everything else is about how they are going to keep you from being independent. They tell you how they are going to feed you, clean your apartment, launder your linens, bus you to where you want to go, and, with a social director, decide what you will do each day."

When not viewing elderly as dependent, many people see older seniors as self-indulgent pursuers of full-time leisure. They sometimes support their views by referring to the oft-seen bumper stickers that state "We are spending our children's inheritance," and "The boss is still working, I'm not." Then they might bring attention to legions of retirees who have chosen to live in recreation-oriented all-adult communities—communities that the Gray Panthers' founder, Maggie Kuhn, dubbed "playpens for wrinkled babies."

Even that aging warrior for senior America, Maggie Kuhn, was ageist! Who would want to move into a community of nothing but "old people," as her derisive characterization of adult-only communities for retirees seems to be saying. However, throughout our lives before we re-tire, we tend to gravitate toward communities populated by people in our general age group. Why should that be any different in the retirement years? Having consulted for a dozen years with the most successful builder of communities for independently living retirees, Del Webb, I have had the opportunity to observe with great pleasure and sometimes awe how some people come to blossom as never before in communities specifically designed for their later-life lifestyles. I have heard Sun City residents say over and over, "I never knew life could be this good." Products, whether they be housing products, travel products, or whatever, that have been designed to reflect later-life lifestyles are more apt to be seen as gateways to the kind of experiential life that promotes life satisfaction. What more powerful appeal could a brand have than that it can serve as a facilitator of life satisfaction.

PRESIDENT CARTER: THE NUMBER ONE ROLE MODEL FOR RETIREMENT AMONG OLDER PEOPLE

People who think that few retirees contribute much to society obviously are unaware that retirees represent the largest block of volunteers in the nation. Civic Ventures, a national nonprofit organization working to expand the contributions of older Americans to society, represents a markedly different picture of retirees. Civic Ventures conducted a poll among older people in 1999 and found that famous retiree Jimmy Carter was the number one choice for a role model in retirement—not another retired president, Gerald Ford, who until a few years ago, spent much of his time on the links at Palm Springs, California.

Civic Ventures, founded in 1998 (by one of those self-indulgent baby boomers) is striving to help transform an aging society into a source of individual and social renewal. A recently posted blurb on its Web site said:

> According to findings from a new survey of Americans 50 to 75, they are committed to tackling the nation's challenges head on and the proportion planning to make volunteering and community service an important part of retirement has grown markedly over the past three years (now 56 percent). The poll,

conducted by Peter D. Hart Research Associates for Civic Ventures, shows that America's older population is in the midst of redefining retirement. In place of the old "golden years" notion of a leisured later life, the men and women surveyed make it clear that older Americans are poised to assume a leadership role in rejuvenating the nation's civic life.[10]

Seniors have long been America's most responsible citizens. They give the most time to volunteer causes; give vast sums of money to community, church, and other causes; and vote at more than twice the rate of people in their mid-30s and younger.

Erik and Joan Erikson, together with Helen Kivnic, wrote about the need for *vital involvement* in later life in a book entitled *Vital Involvement in Old Age*. The vital involvement they speak of is not play-time involvement widely depicted in advertising for travel, housing, and other products and services aimed at retirees. It is involvement in doing good for others. Contributions to others are *vital* to one's sense of well-being, hence the term *vital involvement.*

THE GIANT DISCONNECT BETWEEN MARKETERS AND SECOND-HALF CUSTOMERS

SAM 1990 reported a 1988 study by the Donnelley Marketing organization of Stamford, Connecticut, concerning variances between marketers' views of seniors and seniors' views of themselves. Because there is little reason to expect much has changed, we present the main findings of that report again in Figure 10.1 to spotlight how far off base marketers' views of seniors can be. Note in particular the divergence of thought about what label older people prefer, especially the differences between marketers and older people on the label "senior"—seems the latter don't mind it as much as marketers do—and the label "50+," which marketers thought older people would like best when in fact they liked it least.

With the reprise of the Donnelley report revealing a serious incongruence between older people's views of themselves and how marketers view them, we arrive at the closing of this chapter in which we set the goal

FIGURE 10.1   *Comparison of Marketers' and Mature Consumers' Views of Mature Consumers*

---

1. What products or services are of interest to older consumers in order of degree of interest? (Responses on a 1-5 scale, with 5 being highest)

Product/Service	Ratings of 50+	Ratings of Marketers
Healthcare	4.1	4.7
Financial Services	3.7	4.3
Travel	3.6	4.2
Hobbies	3.3	3.7
Education	3.1	2.9
Automobiles	3.1	2.9

2. What advertising media are depended upon most by older consumers?

Media	50+ View	Views of Marketers
Word of Mouth	3.6	4.3
TV/Radio	2.3	3.0
Magazines	2.3	3.3
Direct Mail	2.3	3.0
New Brand Trial	3.5	3.0
New Product Trial	3.6	3.0

3. What name label do older people prefer?

Label	50+	Marketers
Mature	28.3%	26.9%
Adult	25.4%	12.9%
Senior	23.7%	2.2%
50+	16.9%	43.8%
Other	5.7%	4.2%

Source: Donnelley Marketing
Stamford, Connecticut
Reported in *Mature Market Report,* May 1988.

---

of illuminating the importance of life satisfaction aspirations in second-half markets. My parting thought is that companies that try to understand the makeup of life satisfaction in the second half of life will turn one Madison Avenue myth into reality for themselves: They will have a portfolio of older customers who will not switch to another brand.

11

FAMILY CONNECTIONS AND COMPLEXITIES

The five-generation Erskine family is a microcosm of the marketplace in terms of age, with members ranging in age from 10 months to 91 years. John and Mary Erskine, both 69, are the functional heads of the family. Both of Mary's parents, her father Brad, 91, and her mother Charlotte, 89, are still living, along with John's mother Pricilla, 89. John and Mary raised three children. Jack, 48, is the oldest. Jack heads up marketing for a commercial real estate developer, and is comfortably settled into life with his college sweetheart, Margo Goldman. Jack and Margo have two children. Andrea, the elder, and her husband Rob recently made Jack and Margo grandparents for the first time.

Alice, 45, John and Mary's second child, was married years ago, shortly after her daughter Heather was born, broke up with her husband a year later, and has been single for nearly 20 years. She sells real estate in general brokerage. Peter is the youngest at age 38. He is a computer programmer and is struggling with lack of satisfaction in his job, career, and life in general, including his marriage. Peter has two children by his second wife, Alicia.

The Erskine family is an all-American family, representing all ages, including frail elderly parents needing continuous looking after, and kids in both successful and unsuccessful marriages. Some Erskines are happier than others, and some have more accomplishments than others. In this chapter, we begin to use the Erskine family as a prism to split the properties of life into seasonal spectrums to better understand the effects of season-of-life influences on consumer behavior. We begin by listening to John Erskine through the eyes of Christian Cantrell, a skilled writer who has temporarily abandoned his writing ambitions to join the more lucrative world of high tech. I know these things about him because he had the good judgment a few years ago to marry my daughter, Michelle. Around the time they were married, I asked Christian to take the story of John and Mary Erskine, whom I first wrote about in *SAM* 1990, and make them really come to life.

A STUDY OF LIFE IN THE SECOND HALF FOR WHICH THE FIRST WAS MADE

"Some Friendships You Can't Explain; They Just Are"

It's funny the way friendships are. It seems to me some are like children. They require constant attention and nurturing and then, still, you never know how they are going to turn out. Then some are like a beam of light. They'll just keep going on forever as long as there's nothing to impede them. Then, there are friendships that you can't explain. They just are, and they are the kind you just leave alone and let be.

The guy I'd call my best friend, I don't see but twice a year, three times if it's a good year. But see, we have this kind of common, hallowed ground where things happen that just can't happen anywhere else, and the friendship that has come out of the times we've had on that ground just doesn't know time and distance. Actually, I think it would be more accurate to call it our common, hallowed water instead of ground, for therein lives the sacred rainbow trout. That's where we mostly meet. I'll tie flies for a week before we go. I'll tie twice as many flies than I know I could possibly use. I do it every time, too, so I've got this case with more flies in it than all the zappers in all of Virginia. But I'm addicted and Ron's the same way. We do it to make the fishing trip seem more real, to keep the days going by and the trip coming closer and closer.

What's funny is that I don't spend all that much time in the water casting. I usually split my time between my pole and camera, for I have a passion for taking pictures of nature. I think I've developed a good eye for color and perspective over the years. To be honest with you, I'm just as happy standing on the bank of the river at sunrise with my camera as with my pole.

"Who's that guy, that landscape photographer in black and whites," Ron once asked me. I told him it's Ansel Adams, "But don't call me an Ansel Adams because I'm not that good and I shoot in color. Ansel shoots in black and white." But Ron didn't pay attention and now he calls me Ansel whenever I have my camera in my hands, but only John when I'm casting.

We like the Poconos. We've been to many places, fished many streams, but we like the Poconos and this one little cabin. It is just one big room. There's the kitchen along one wall and beds against the opposite wall and a bathroom door in the wall between. There's no place to go to be alone except the bathroom, I guess, and that's the way we like it. We go fishing to be alone together. If there were two bedrooms, we'd feel funny not taking them both up, and then we'd miss being together. That would be 7 or 8 hours out of 24 that we'd miss. Of course, we'd probably get a better night's sleep that way, getting away from each other's snoring and coughing and mumbling, but Mary says its good for me so I can appreciate what she's been going through for nearly 50 years.

Ron's the real fisherman. He's twice the fisherman I'll ever be. Sometimes when he's casting and concentrating I'll stop what I'm doing and just watch him. There's something he does with his wrist when he whips that pole that just lets his line float then touch down exactly where he knows the fish are. He says he can spot the little eddies and shady spots where the fish hover better now than he could with the eyesight of a young man. I watch him carefully, trying to figure out exactly what's doing. Then I have my camera ready for when that fly tickles the water in just the right spot to trigger the lightning strike of hungry trout.

So even though I usually catch enough to satisfy me, Ron usually gets a good bit more along with a good deal of pleasure in doing it. But it's even in the end because I do most of the cooking and he does the cleanup. To be honest, I don't even like the taste of fish that much, but there's something about pulling your dinner out of a river in the mountains.

When we first started many years ago, we would bring canned food, hamburger meat, and some hot dogs in a cooler just in case we didn't have any luck. But now if we don't have any luck, we don't eat. That's the way we like it. There's no kind of food that could tempt me away from cutting the white meat away from those needle bones and laying it down in the old black iron skillet, not while I'm out there with my best friend.

I remember we used to never talk about next time. At first we did, but then there was a time when we drove away from the cabin and wondered if we'd be back. We never talked about it and neither of us ever said anything about it out loud, but we both felt it. It was sort of a mood, a feeling of uncertainty as to whether or not circumstances would ever let this happen again. It used to ride home with us in the car like a third person in the back seat, like a nervous hitchhiker we regretted picking up. That's exactly how I felt coming back the year I was diagnosed with chronic lymphocytic leukemia only a week before the trip. I wanted to cancel going that time, but Mary pushed me out the door. On the return home, I looked at each familiar milestone, wondering if it was the last time I would see it.

That was when we were having a lot of problems, Ron and me. Just before I was diagnosed, Mary had had a lump removed from her breast. Ron's wife Margie, who has since passed away, learned from her doctor that she was at high risk for a heart attack or stroke. Adding to Ron and Sally's stress was their daughter's second divorce that was underway, and a real tough one it was. I can't explain exactly how we each were affected by all of this or exactly what we feared. Cancer, heart disease, a grown daughter's broken heart—I can only remember clearly looking back at the cabin as we pulled away that year like I was looking at it for the last time.

We didn't go back the next year. Some things got better and some didn't, but we both finally realized that fishing wasn't one of our problems and that by not going we were punishing ourselves for things that had gone wrong, things that we couldn't control. The day I decided to call Ron he called me first and said, "Let's go fishing."

Now it's always next time. Next time is all we talk about on the way home. The last time we went, I suggested we skip the cabin. I said we could take tents and then corrected myself and said we should take a tent. We would build a camp, cut wood, store water, cook with the black iron skillet over the campfire instead of over a stove. I suggested we try roughing it next time. Ron suggested I try black and white.

Mary Erskine: "People Are Like Snowflakes . . ."

One morning almost 60 years ago, as we watched the first snowfall of the season from my bedroom window, my mother told me that people are like snowflakes. I have kept her words with me ever since, playing with them, adding to them, trying to figure them out.

"No two ever form in exactly the same way . . ."

I have met a number of people through my work in the theater, but really only two who I think of as true friends. Like snowflakes, they have their own unique patterns.

Craig is probably the most creative and sensitive man I have ever known. I have admired his writing and directing for the past six years, since I first became involved in community theater. Two years ago, he was directing one of his own plays and he asked me to play a small role. I was 67 at the time, and never in my life been so flattered. I felt like an old lady who thought her beauty had faded but was suddenly asked out on a date. I remember wanting to say "no," to simply take it as a compliment and politely decline. I had never done any acting and the other actors intimidated me. Craig sensed my apprehension, withdrew the offer, and restated it as a command.

During rehearsals, he taught me how to use my own experiences as supplementary material, as "onions to make you cry," or as "gas to make you laugh." He taught me how to summon forgotten emotions, which keep us wiser and kinder the closer they are to the surface.

Tom is the set designer, and he, without question, has the best sense of humor of anyone I have ever known. He uses it to cure like a doctor uses drugs, modifying it and dispensing it in various doses and strengths. I remember during rehearsals having trouble with a scene in which I was to explode into laughter as another actor turned his back on me. I could not make the laugh convincing and spontaneous enough. Between takes, Tom came up on stage, patted each of us on the back, and offered us some encouraging words.

When we tried the scene again and the other actor tuned his back, there was a sign taped to his shirt that said, "KICK ME." It's silly I know, but I've never laughed so hard in my life as I did then. The funniest part was the other actor did not catch on at first because he thought I was still following the script. I never had difficulty with that scene again and it still sneaks up and tickles me sometimes.

". . . you'll never know just where they will fall . . . ," Mom said.

High school is a cloud and the students are drops of water that form into flakes and float and drift and settle to earth. No matter how carefully you watch them and follow them, it is impossible to say where they will land. When my best friend Liz got married and moved to Washington, D.C., I thought she had floated and landed far enough away from Boulder where we grew up together that I would never see her again. What I did not realize is that I too was a floating snowflake. In 1978, John was transferred and we moved right outside of Washington in the Northern Virginia suburbs. Liz and I reconnected after more than 30 years and we have been tight ever since.

John and Liz's husband, Mike, have never become friends and, to be honest, Liz and I don't encourage it. We like things the way they are. John and I have our joint friends, and he has his friends and his fishing, and then I have my friends and activities. It's like we live in a house with three rooms, a big room that we share, and two smaller rooms in which we each do as we please. Recently, I renovated mine. It is now a study.

I left college as a sophomore to marry John and always told myself that someday I would go back and get a degree, but I never took any steps until after Liz and I reconnected. Liz got married shortly after high school and immediately got pregnant with the first of her four children. After her last child went off to college, Liz began thinking about college herself. By the time she and I hooked up again, she was working on her bachelor's in psychology and planning to go on and get a master's in social work. If Liz could do it, why not me, I asked myself. She was my inspiration, the spark that got me headed back to school. I got started on my undergraduate degree in art history in my early 50s. Then, when I was in my mid-60s, I decided to go back to school to get my master's.

". . . they may melt in an instant or fade away slowly . . . ," said Mom.

John's father died of a heart attack 15 years ago. My father is still living, but he's in a nursing home with Alzheimer's. I volunteer there one day a week and suffer with him.

Some days he knows me and other days he doesn't believe me when I tell him who I am. I think even when he does recognize me, it's no more than a vague familiarity, for even though his lips form my name, his cloudy confused eyes betray him. To him, I am Chary as often as I am Mary. If I correct him, he may act indifferently or may scornfully object, insisting he knows his own daughter's name. Now when I'm Chary or Charlotte, my mother's name, I no longer correct him. It's so sad to see how Mother looks at him. You can see in her eyes that to her, her Brad is dead.

Sometimes I want to laugh. A nurse will tell me something he has done or said and at first I want to laugh, but only in front of the nurse because it is easier than crying. I feel guilty when I laugh because I can remember him, tall and strong and clear. He used to seem so big to me, and now he has shrunk. He is a snowflake on a cold sunny day, melting away very, very slowly.

John and Mary: On Surprises

John: As far as I can tell, there are three kinds of surprises. The first kind is the worst kind. It's the kind you know is coming. It's the horror movie kind of surprise when you know something is about to jump out but it still scares the devil out of you when it does. That's how I felt 15 years ago when my father died. I'd known it was coming, that it would have to come someday soon, but it still scared me half to death.

Mary: Twelve years ago, my mother was diagnosed with breast cancer. After that, I felt it was only a matter of time before I discovered a lump in me, so I kept looking for it until one day it was there. Expecting it all those years didn't make it any easier to deal with.

John: Then you have the kind of surprise that sneaks up on you so gradually you don't see it, and then it just sits there, watching you, waiting for you to look up and realize it's there. After the shock of my father's death, I looked up and realized that there wasn't anyone ahead of me anymore, that I was getting older and that trying not to think about it wasn't stopping it. Of course, I'd always known that, but that's not the same. Knowing something and realizing it aren't the same. You can know something all your life, but it's the realization that surprises you.

I remember the summers when I was a kid, spending those long days fishing and swimming and exploring the woods, playing games around my neighborhood, making up new games. Anything we couldn't fit into one day, we just started with the next. Those summer days didn't have names and numbers and we never kept track of them. They just kept coming, one after another, every day a new one with something new to do, until the day my mother told me it was time to go shopping. That is when I realized summer was ending and school was about to start. Once again, days would have names and numbers. I had known all summer that this time would come, but it took my mother's announcement, "It's time to go shopping," to realize it, and whether I wanted it or not, I had to get ready.

Mary: My mother was treated with a radical mastectomy. I was more fortunate and had simpler surgery. Everything went well and soon I felt physically fine, yet something in me was slow and reluctant to heal. Something in me couldn't understand what had happened to my body and why it had turned against me. I felt a kind of separation, as if my body and I were no longer one, and I felt as though I could no longer trust it.

That was one of the hardest years I have ever been through. A month after my surgery, John was diagnosed with chronic lymphocytic leukemia, or CLL, and six weeks later his mother fell getting out of the bathtub and broke her arm. I went through a period in which I thought I was losing control. I waited for the next surprise to come, for the next catastrophe to add itself to the list and spin my life further out of control. While I was waiting, things began to even out and the unwanted surprises stopped coming. We learned that John's kind of leukemia usually progresses very slowly and did not require treatment in its present stage and that some people live with it for 15, 20 years or even more. Mom Erskine's arm healed quickly for a woman of her age and my checkups indicated that the doctors had gotten all the cancer on the first try.

In retrospect, that awfullest of years brought a lot of good to me. With the help of my friend Liz, I began to realize I had not lost control of my life; rather I had relinquished it and it was up to me to get it back. I realized that what happens to you matters less than how you react to what happens. Like most people I always knew that, but it took a really bad year to make me realize what I already knew meant. That was when, after 42 years, I ended up back in college.

John: The third kind of surprise is the best. It's the kind you get to spring on someone to make them happy. It's the flowers behind your back kind of surprise, or the screaming "Surprise!" at a surprise birthday party kind. They're the kind of surprises that you have to lie about and be sneaky about to make work, and then all the lying and sneaking is justified in a single moment when the surprise is sprung.

Next May, after Mary has walked across the stage and accepted her master's in art history, and we have celebrated at one of her favorite restaurants, Galatino's, on one of the proudest days of her life, Mary and I will go home, she'll pull back the covers of our bed, and find underneath two tickets to the Hermitage, one of the world's greatest art treasure troves. That's the kind of surprise I'm talking about.

Mary: John thinks the best kinds of surprises are ones you set up for someone else. He calls them "surprise party" surprises. I hope he likes being the victim as much as he like victimizing, because next July, after I've gotten my degree, John's best friend Ron will show up at the house with a brand new fly rod for John's birthday and a note saying, "You have one hour to get your affairs in order. You are being kidnapped for a two-week fishing excursion to the greatest fly fishing waters in the Poconos. Ron has reserved the cabin for one week and the next week they will "rough it." John's real surprise will come about an hour after they have arrived at the cabin, when I knock on the door. I figure I'll cook and clean and keep an eye on them for a week and then they will move around to the other side of the mountain, in really wild country, to rough it on their own for a week. I don't know why, but Ron wants me to remind him to take along some black and white film. He knows that John only works in color. But Ron won't tell me what he has in mind.

John: I've heard Mary say that the best kind of surprise is when you do something to surprise yourself. She might be right. The thing about those kinds of surprises is that they aren't over in a moment or in an evening. They don't wear off. They become a part of you and you can always enjoy them and relive them. You always have them with you wherever you go, and all you have to do to get them back and feel surprised again is think about them.

Mary: I believe there's a surprise better than the "surprise party" kind. It's when you surprise yourself. Never in my life have I had so many opportunities to do that, to do things I never thought I could or would be able to do. I'm referring not only to big things like finally finishing college, but also about smaller things, like acting in Craig's play. I know

that the unexpected will always happen, that you can't control everything that affects your life, but I also know that there is a lot in my life I
can control, and that I have endless opportunities to surprise myself.

WHY STORIES ABOUT THE ERSKINES?

Ethnographic consumer research, in which researchers study customers in their natural settings, such as Intuit's Scott Cook had his researchers do, gives researchers a more true-to-life picture of customers.
By observing rather than by asking, often better insight into customer behavior is gained. I've let you into the Erskine family's lives to give you the
opportunity to make your own observations, as an ethnographer would.
Also, Christian Cantrell's vignettes of John and Mary Erskine are replete
with subtle insights that one might not expect from a 22-year-old writer,
the age he was when he wrote those vignettes, all of which is to say that
the youthful age of a marketer is not of itself a barrier to being able to
gain enough understanding to be able to develop marketing communications that empathetically connect with people in second-half markets,
regardless of their ages. I encourage the use of those vignettes in training
sessions, for they can help make more real the basic theories in which
one needs grounding to be optimally effective in second-half markets.

Also, while this chapter opened with a look into John and Mary Erskine's life, later in this chapter and in the next, we learn something
about their middle-aged children, Jack and Alice.

DON'T FEEL SORRY FOR JOHN AND MARY ERSKINE BECAUSE OF THEIR AGE

John and Mary have had their share of challenges in life, but in their
twilight years have achieved a hard-won serenity that at once magnifies
the pleasure they take from life and decreases their sensitivity to pain
and losses that will come more frequently and often with greater intensity in their future. Recall Mary's words as she reflected on one of the
most difficult years of her life, "I realized that what happens to you matters less than how you react to what happens to you. Like most people I

always knew that, but it took one of the hardest years of my life to make me realize *what I already knew* meant."

She knows that unwelcome surprises of the first kind John talked about hover over her, fated to pop unbidden into her life sooner or later. She knows she will soon lose her father to Alzheimer's, and that it's likely that her 91-year-old mother will soon pass. Yet both losses are apt to invoke a surprise response even though she expects them. But she is prepared.

She didn't mention it in her soliloquies, but Mary has rheumatoid arthritis, though not severe enough to keep her from carrying on with her busy life. Like John with his chronic lymphocytic leukemia, Mary is one of the more than two-thirds of people 65 and older who have at least one chronic condition. Like most such people, Mary and John move through their days as though they were in the prime of health at half their age. An ache or pain that might cause a young person to call in sick may be regarded by people like John and Mary as just a mildly irritating thing to get over and beyond.

There is no need to work in Winter markets with a "glad it's not me" attitude that leads to copy and imagery that inadvertently reflects negative feelings about old age and health many people in the Winter of life simply don't feel. For anyone bothered about growing old—and it is quite normal to be bothered by aging earlier in life—let's review how many older people feel about their age, but also how they feel about the way it is often represented in marketing.

Made wiser by all they have seen, heard and experienced, John and Mary do not have patience with marketers' entreaties that lack sincerity and relevance. They are particularly indifferent to hints that people in their season of life owe it to themselves to "rise above their age" by taking this pill or that supplement, or doing this, or going on that adventure to "stay young." John and Mary are comfortable with their age, as most people in their 60s are. Research shows that a majority of people in their 60s, like John and Mary, feel that their life quality is the best it has ever been, and this extends to self-perceptions about health.

In a survey I conducted in a retirement community where the average age was 73, nearly 75 percent of the respondents reported their health to be good to excellent. Interestingly though, only 60 percent described their spouses' health as good to excellent. And about 45 percent described their elderly neighbors' health as being good to excellent.

There's an object lesson in this: It seems that most people rate their health better than it might be, which goes hand-in-hand with the fact that most people think they look younger than they actually do.

Gerontologist Gene Cohen describes in his book *The Aging Brain* that a national survey found people 65 and older less beset than younger people by angst over health and aging, regrets about life running out, and despair that the future will never be better. The survey found that people 65 and older scored higher than people under 65 in responses to the following statements:[1]

- I've gotten pretty much what I expected out of life.
- As I look back on my life, I am fairly well satisfied.
- I would not change my past life even if I could.
- My life could not be happier than it is now.

The Erskines score high on each of those statements. The Erskines remind me of a woman in her late 60s in a focus group who said, "I can't believe how lucky I am. I wake up each morning almost feeling guilty about how good my life is." Another woman in the same group said, "I ran a meat packing plant in Chicago. I always had to be tough. I couldn't be myself. Now, since retiring at 62, I've been more me than I have been since I was a child. These are the best years!"

The Erskines are attentive to their health but don't go overboard about it. They have good family genes, but they know that they don't have many years left and are comfortable with that. They worry more about their grown children and their grandchildren than about themselves.

SOME BRANDS "GET IT" AND ARE CASHING IN BIG

John, who retired seven years ago at age 61, around the average age of retirement, might look to some people as though he's a bit of a stereotypical old skinflint. While he can afford any car he wants, he tools around town in a 13-year-old Buick Park Avenue with expectations of keeping it for another three or four years at least. He likes the car because it has served him well and was intentionally designed with older drivers in mind.

In the mid-1980s, Buick faced the fate Oldsmobile now faces. It was to be dropped by GM. However, an engineer named Ed Mertz was promoted to general manager of the Buick Division and changed the course of the brand's history. He set about redesigning Buick models with special attention to the needs of older drivers, because most Buick owners were in their 50s or older. However, instead of asking his design engineers to come up with concepts to be evaluated by prospective drivers, as was customary, Mertz ordered extensive interviews with prospective customers. The results served as both the inspiration and guidance for a totally redesigned line of cars that saved the division. In 1991, the second year the new models were on the market, Buick had the largest market share increase of any brand. Sales increased by more than 20 percent *during a recession*. Mertz proved that by inviting customers, especially older customers, into the product design process to provide practical, if not creative, input, a *Field of Dreams* phenomenon would transpire. Build it that way and they will come.

Mary drives a Lexus, which they use on longer trips. Except for the Lexus, the Erskines give the appearance of retirees bent on saving every dime possible. They moved from a 3,500-square-foot house to a 1,600-square-foot condo. John drives a car that is long past its prime. He spends next to nothing for himself on clothes. His wardrobe hasn't changed in a dozen years except for gifts he has gotten, and two pairs of shoes he bought since retiring. The Erskines watch TV on a 14-year-old 30-inch Sony, share magazine subscriptions with friends, and Mary takes cents-off coupons with her on nearly every trip to the grocery store. All this makes it seem as though Madison Avenue is right—don't spend too much going after older customers because they don't spend a lot of money. However, while many older people spend less on themselves, they spend more on others. Like many grandparents, John and Mary dote on their grandkids.

Mary's clothes-buying budget has also shrunk considerably over the past dozen or so years, but recently, she has been spending more. A big reason Mary's clothes buying fell off was that with a bit more on her bones than in her size 8 days, she found shopping for clothes increasingly frustrating as she grew older. However, thanks to a tip from her daughter-in-law, Margo, Mary discovered Chico's, a store that has made clothes shopping easier.

Chico's accent is on fun fashion that is youthful and comfortable for women over 30. "Our target customer is 35 to 55," says Pat Murphy, chief merchandising officer of Chico's. "We love her. She feels young, is active, and travels a lot. She wants to look good, but not like her daughter." Murphy says midlife markets are underserved, noting that, "Today's woman of a certain age doesn't feel old, but her figure is different. We want to give her a comfort level that she looks good—not foolish."[2]

Even though Murphy defines Chico's target customer as 35 to 55, the retailer is more an ageless marketer serving women over 30 in general. After her first trip to Chico's, Mary told John that if he was ever in a quandary about getting a gift for her, "Go to Chico's. I would like almost anything you brought home." (Actually, my wife Linda, who is only a little younger than Mary said that, but I thought I would make it Mary's line. I have tested Linda on that and never brought anything home to her from Chico's that she didn't love.)

Chico's stores reflect a more human scale than department stores do. They range in size from 1,200 to 5,000 square feet, but most are around 1,500 square feet. This intimate scale appeals to older women, many of whom find it quite disagreeable going through rack upon rack of unsuitable clothes in larger stores in hopes of finding something. When Mary called Margo to thank her for introducing her to Chico's she said, "I felt human. It was quiet. It was intimate, and they weren't pumping music that I don't like in my ears. The clerks were a bit older than in most stores so I knew right away that they could relate better to me and my needs."

Mary has problems with glare and noise, a common condition among people in their 60s and older. She found the lighting and acoustics in Chico's is "Mary-friendly." This is part of what makes her "feel human" in Chico's even though she is not conscious of all the reasons she feels more "human" in Chico's. But that doesn't matter to Mary. She just likes going there to shop and, as a bonus, getting an automatic 5 percent discount on everything she buys with her Chico's Passport card.

While Mary does not buy as much for herself as she used too, she still loves to shop—when she "can feel human." So, she stops by Chico's from time to time to see if she can find a gift for someone else. "You know," she said to John recently, "Even though at my age I have everything I need, the fact that I still love to shop, must mean that women have a shopping gene. It makes sense, doesn't it? I mean, back in caveman times, men were hunters and women were gatherers. Shopping is the modern woman's way of gathering." John said nothing. He just smiled.

RETIREMENT OFTEN TURNS OUT DIFFERENTLY THAN PEOPLE ENVISIONED IN PRERETIREMENT

The Erskines know that beyond a certain threshold of leisure activity, they get this nagging feeling that they ought to be doing something worthwhile. As John says, "Retirement? I don't know what they mean by 'retirement.' I'm busier now that I ever was at the office."

John's golf handicap is about what it was ten years ago, although he now has to get out on the links at least once a week to hold it there, which is not always easy to do because of other activities he has committed to. He is active in the local chapter of RSVP—Retirees in Service to Volunteer Programs. He also has recently been devoting a great deal of time to a local housing agency, using management skills gained from his years as regional executive VP of a hardware chain to reorganize and streamline the agency's operations.

From when we first enter vocational life, our jobs help us validate our existence. Need for validation never expires. Among retirees, activities like volunteer work, personal enrichment programs, and hobbies are not time fillers; they are means for remaining physically and mentally healthy. Research shows that even when nursing home patients are given a task as mundane as taking care of a plant, their spirits pick up, physical deterioration is slowed, and they live longer than controls without plants to care for. Among people who have heart attacks, pet owners have one-fifth the death rate of those without pets.[3] Being able to express one's life purposefully seems to have a strong connection with well-being.

Many retirees unfortunately experience difficulties finding ways to get a sense of validation. This is truer among men than women, and surely underlies the fact that people 65 and older account for 13 percent of the population but 20 percent of the suicide rate—with men accounting for 80 percent of the suicides among people 65 and older.[4] Keep in mind when marketing to retirees that validation is a widespread problem that companies can key to in older markets to demonstrate empathetic understanding. While many older people feel they are living validated lives, many of them live with spouses or have friends who don't feel that way. It is not a matter of presenting with sympathy, but in such a way that older people in general feel—validated and otherwise—that someone with something they would like to buy understands them.

THE NEW GRANDPARENTS IN THE ERSKINE FAMILY

Jack and his wife, Margo, live in tony Bethesda, Maryland, on the outskirts of Washington, D.C. Their home was built in the 1920s, and redone by Jack and Margo a little over ten years ago. They have a backyard pool, but it doesn't get used much since their youngest, Bob, left for college last fall.

Jack and Margo have been talking about selling the house and moving into a condo, much as Mom and Dad Erskine did a few years ago, over the protest of Jack. "Remember," Jack recently asked Margo, "when you and I thought Mom and Dad were really going to miss the old house? Now we're talking about doing the same thing. You know, I think I wasn't happy with Mom and Dad selling the old house *because of me.* It was *me* who had trouble parting with the house with all its memories. They didn't seem to have any trouble at all. It's funny how when you get older you find it easier to let go of things."

Margo likes the idea of getting rid of their home. "You know, with the house at the shore and, on top of that, the boat to take care of, we really ought to think seriously about simplifying our lives." Jack and Margo are *talking* about simplifying their lives—John Sr. and Mary Erskine have already done it.

Jack and Margo, boomers though they are, are following a path similar to the one Jack's parent took a few years ago. In terms of income, Jack and Margo belong to the age group with the second highest per capita income, 45-to- 54-year-olds. Only 55-to- 64-year-olds earn more per capita. But Jack and Margo's age group has the highest rate of consumer spending, though it peaks at about age 48, the age Jack and Margo now are. As their spending begins tailing off in many categories, however, they are entering a new category of spending: gifts for their new grandchild, Hillary. They have become grandparents at 48.

Grandparent spending is taking off in this decade, turning grandparents into a major consumer market, and they aren't all "old" people, either. The average age of people when they first become grandparents is 48.

There were 69 million grandparents in 2000, a number expected to grow to 80 million by 2010. Grandparents spend a median of $489 per year on grandchildren, about $30 billion annually. Lower-income grandparents spend $239 annually; middle-income grandparents spend $637; and higher income grandparents spend $840 annually. Indicative of the kind of concern that grandparents have about their grandchildren's future, 60 percent buy books for their grandchildren as compared to just 38 percent who buy toys, although that adds up to grandparents buying one of every four toys sold in America each year. Seventy-four percent of grandparents buy quality clothing for their grandchildren.[5]

The fact that grandparents account for about 40 percent of upscale clothing for kids, over a third of children's books, and 25 percent of all toys makes it clear that marketers of products for children and teens should be paying more attention to grandparent markets. The population of parents in the child-raising years may not be growing significantly, but the 16 percent increase in the number of grandparents in this decade spells new, though widely underappreciated market opportunities. I genuinely think that grandparents would spend even more on their grandchildren if marketers paid more attention to them.

Jack and Margo are beginning to think about the life they want to live as retirees, a life directed toward "enjoying the rewards they have earned." Odds are, however, that the life they will end up living will be closer in style to that of Jack's parents, and they will find life in retirement as busy as life in the career years.

Jack and Margo still have one foot in the world of family nurturing and career, but the other foot is stepping into a new dimension of life. They *feel* as well as *know* that major changes lie ahead. Still in the first half of the Fall of their lives, they continue their midlife reevaluation of life's meanings, though they are giving it less thought than they did several years ago. They are becoming more disposed to simply accepting or rejecting things on fate than to try to figure everything out. They don't know yet where the inner voices that are gently pressuring them to reorder their priorities will take them, but they have no doubt that things will be different in the future. They are hearing the voice of Nature along the road to self-actualization.

Their affluence, age, and coming freedom from family and career responsibilities will be no better predictor of their future lifestyle as "senior citizens" than it was for Jack's parents. As with the elder Erskines, personality maturity will play a large role in predisposing Jack's and Margo's future lifestyles. They have always planned for the future, but now plan it with a sense that life as retirees could be different from what they might have thought a few years ago.

Neither Jack nor Margo find the idea of aging as bothersome as it was around the time they turned 40. They are more "laid back" about more and more. They are leaving the "time is of the essence" market. Urgency rarely compels their consumer behavior. They are becoming more discretionary, "I can take it or leave it" consumers. They spend a lot of money, but much of it outside predictable patterns, except that they are more experientially oriented than materialistically oriented in their spending. Buying decisions are more often decided by the quality of the customer experience than by the product itself.

Jack and Margo are traversing the steps taken earlier by John's parents that Carl Jung called "the seven tasks of aging." In their middle years, Jack and Margo are working on:

1. *Facing the reality of aging and death.* While doing this they are discovering in the process that one becomes more alive when aging and death are no longer an overhanging issue. This imparts a richer appreciation for life that can be effectively mirrored in product messages by projecting values associated with what really matters—family, friends, faith, trust, authenticity, experiences, giving back, and having a positive outlook.
2. *Reviewing their lives.* This increases the incidence of nostalgic moments but is also necessary to reconcile the sweet and the bitter of life so that in Winter they will have the peace with self and world that the elder Erskines project. With people in midlife now dominant in the marketplace, this aging task has given rise to so-called "retro" in product design and product messaging, and has spawned an explosion of interest in "golden oldies" music, making the 45-plus population the fastest growing CD market.[6]

3. *Defining life realistically.* By doing this they acknowledge without regrets limitations imposed on a person by time, circumstances, and other people. This increased pragmatism calls for more earthy marketing images with less dependence on novelty of execution. Sensitivity rather than show works best among members of the New Customer Majority who are not into the impossible, the unachievable, and the fantastical that ensnare the minds of the young.

4. *Letting go of the ego.* This is one of the hardest aging tasks. It means giving up urges to control others, for a person who no longer tries to control others as an extension of his or her own ego becomes free. This task is key to achieving the selflessness that psychologists associate with what they call *successful aging.* Projecting people in ads who reflect this letting go of ego will resonate strongly throughout the New Customer Majority. It is a powerful value that can be effectively used in marketing cross-generationally.

5. *Finding new rooting in the self.* This means turning inward to hear one's own counsel, as opposed to basing one's life on influences from the external world. This is an essential step in gaining the freedom that awaits at the higher levels of personal growth; New Balance's marketing is exemplary in reflecting this task in marketing executions.

6. *Determining the meaning of one's life.* This is perhaps the central aging task in midlife because it is wrapped up with one's identity and self-preservation imperatives. It involves realization that life's most important meanings are not defined by others, but by self, and not measured by social or material success. Legions of people who cashed in on the dot-com bubble before it burst left their careers and retired in their 40s and 50s to set up foundations, do volunteer work, or otherwise pursue a different path than just making more money and accumulating more things. The legacy imperative that arises in midlife is a powerful imperative largely overlooked in marketing.

7. *Rebirth—dying with life.* This idea is reminiscent of the ancient idea in Christendom that one must die in order to live. In midlife, the old self is called upon to pass into the night, to die as it were, so that in rebirth a person may find new and loftier avenues for cre-

ative expression of his or her life. A few years back, Shearson Lehman ran a series of television commercials devoted to this theme, "Where do you want to be in five years?" or, in another case, "Where do you want to be next year?" The commercials brilliantly captured the idea of midlife death and rebirth. The company reported in a press release that the campaign was one of the most successful in its history.

Jung's seven tasks of aging form a scaffolding for designing products, marketing messages, promotional programs, and customer experience scenarios that will strongly resonate throughout the New Customer Majority. The marketer who projects these themes will empathetically connect with customers and help them *process their lives.*

Several years ago, I went on a weekend retreat devoted to storytelling. A Trappist monk by the name of Joseph gave a talk on the role of storytelling in our lives and with one statement dramatically altered my perspective on marketing. He said:

Storytellers help us process our lives.

Abbot Joseph observed that the greatest secular and religious leaders use stories to teach and inspire their followers. It suddenly hit me that *the most effective kind of marketing possible is marketing that helps customers process their lives.*

To help people process their lives, it is necessary to know what they are processing. What people must process in adolescence to achieve personal growth is different from what people in their 20s and 30s need to process to the same end, and so it is throughout life. Each season of life involves a set of developmental objectives that sensitive marketers can help customers achieve.

Of course, Jack and Margo would not likely come up with Jung's list of all seven tasks of aging if they were they asked about the kind of person they want to be now and in the future. However, they are nevertheless addressing each of those tasks in their own way. Everyone faces those tasks beginning in the early days of midlife, but not everyone is equally effective in addressing them. Alice Erskine has been struggling to even get started.

ALICE, THE SEEKER

Alice might be called the stereotypical number two child. "God knows, we tried," Mary sometimes says. "She just has to be her own person, as she used to say. Always being a bit different. She made those teen years in the crazy '70s tough on everyone, including herself. She now seems to be always searching for herself. Haven't heard from her in months. Still looking for herself, I guess."

Maslow said that there must be substantial gratification of needs at one level in his hierarchy of basic needs before a person is able to achieve substantial needs gratification at a higher level. Some people get stuck at a lower basic-needs level, staying there longer than most of their chronological peers. Gradually, the gulf in maturity between them and their chronological peers reaches the point where the slower-growing person becomes painfully aware that life is not delivering what he or she thinks it should be delivering. Such people are prone to regarding the source of their problems as "bad luck" or other people rather than of their own making. Honest admission of immaturity is virtually impossible. One can never see one's own face until one reaches the summits of full humanness.

Twenty or thirty years of psychologically operating at more or less the same levels of immaturity become demoralizing and drain a person's zest for life. This diminishment of spirit can dampen the kinds of interests that would make a person a significant consumer of discretionary expenditure items. Let's look more deeply into Alice Erskine's life, for it is important to understand why her significance to marketers is not great despite her good income—not great, that is, unless a marketer knows how to connect with her disturbed midlife soul and help her process her life to higher levels of satisfaction, or to at least lower levels of discomfiture.

Alice Erskine is stuck somewhere in Maslow's ladder between "safety and security" and "love and belonging." She can never fully commit to others because she runs perpetually insecure. She has not defined herself in ways that give her a comfortable sense of identity, hence a sense of really belonging. She seems condemned to a Sisyphus sentence of periodically glimpsing success in her aspirations, but falling back to try once again.

Alice, at 45, is beyond the years of dominance by materialistic aspirations without having achieved much materialistic gratification. She is particularly unfulfilled in terms of animate "possessions." To her low-simmering regret, she has no real family of her own making. Her daughter Heather spent most of her first five years with her grandparents and has spent many summers after that with them as well.

Alice owns a small condo, enjoys a respectable though not great income as a real estate sales agent, and has a moderately priced four-year-old Saturn. But, her worldly possessions are few, her expenditures for services increasingly less, and her dissatisfaction with life great. For Alice, possessions do not define her identity according to her self-image, though she once dreamed of a home in the suburbs, a husband, children, and most of the traditional accoutrements of the traditional life that characterized her childhood.

Alice is a good customer in some regards, however. Ever in search of the key to a satisfying life, Alice periodically attends seminars and retreats on self-improvement. She has a large library of how-to books on solving personal problems (How to Get A Man; How To Get Rid of a Man; How to Advance in Your Career; Why Career Is Not the Key to Happiness, etc.). What Alice has been unable to find in the natural course of life that could lead her into full mature adulthood, she is trying to find at Amazon.com.

Alice is also potentially a good travel customer. She has taken a few trips over the years, in search of the romantic, but now is thinking about trips to learn about things—culture, geography, and history sorts of things.

Apart from some basic necessities (food, clothing, cosmetics, etc.), Alice generally has no particular distinction as a consumer. What she needs and what she buys has little relationship to her age. She is of little importance to marketers targeting mature adults. She is not a mature adult and likely will not be or, in Maslow's terms, she will never reach "full humanness."

Alice Represents a Huge Market, Though a Difficult One

How many Alices—insecure, disenchanted, frequently depressed middle-agers, who are not significant in discretionary markets, irrespective of their income picture—are there? A study by J. Walter Thompson USA in 1989 projected this group at 8 million consumers. Referring to this group as Mature Singles with a mean age of 45, "they tend to be divorced or separated and 81 percent have been so for ten years or more. The group, far from being stereotypical career climbers, is instead insecure, pessimistic, alienated, and indifferent to work. Marketers will face the toughest hurdles reaching this audience, but Club Med and other vacation spots could benefit from repositioning themselves toward this group," according to JWT.[7]

If there were eight million Alices in 1989 when J. Walter Thompson did its study, there could well be more than 12 million now because of the explosive growth of the middle-aged population since 1989. That adds up to a sizeable customer segment. Of course, not all of the people whose psychographic profile is similar to Alice's are single or female by a long stretch. There are men and women, both married and unmarried, who are living through their middle years hoping against hope that something good awaits them in the future. Their numbers would be added to the 12 million Alice-types.

If our view that the most effective marketing is marketing that helps people process their lives, then people like Alice represent a bigger market than current statistics on their consumer behavior might indicate.

Before he died, the prominent American psychologist Erik Erikson sympathetically mused about all those people, men and women, whose paths through life have left them without children to give them grandchildren in their later years. For sure, many people make a conscious choice to not have children in the first place and do not regret their decision. Then there are others who wanted children but were not able to have them. Leaving those two groups of childless adults aside, Erikson expressed concern for the many millions of people now moving into their later years who will feel the absence of grandchildren in their lives as they see friends of their own age drawing pleasure from their grandchildren.

An American Express Financial Services advisor told me that she had inadvertently found a solution that would work for older people without grandchildren who wish things were otherwise. She had an unmarried client named Rosemary who entered later life without children to bring grandchildren into her life. Rosemary was unhappy about this, so she did something about it. She helped fund first one then another neighborhood child through college. They became family to her and, as she was in good health with the prospects of living many years more, she stood a good chance of someday being a surrogate great-grandmother. The financial advisor friend went on to help other clients emulate Rosemary, thus taking a proactive role in helping clients *process their lives* in fulfilling one of Jung's seven tasks of aging—finding meaning in one's life.

Don't write off the Alices of the world. By understanding the scenario of her life, a marketer can connect with her where her needs are most keenly felt. Whatever has prevented Alice from achieving satisfaction earlier in life, there are still ways in which she can find a better life than she now feels she has.

12

THE THREE LIFESTYLE
STAGES OF ADULT LIFE

Remember the old saw about how if you give a man a loaf of bread he eats for a day, but teach him to grow wheat and he eats for a lifetime? It seems to me that most books on marketing are like gifts of bread. They prescribe solutions for limited circumstances rather than teach principles that people can draw on to design their own solutions, as postmodern marketing does. The term *postmodern marketing* has recently been popping up here and there, although I'm not sure what it means. Sooner or later most fields of creativity—and I consider marketing to be one such field—seem to go through a postmodern phase without much agreement about what postmodernism is, whether manifested in architecture, dance, music, painting, or literature. In any event, this definition of postmodern marketing works for me:

> Marketing based on principles of behavioral science, in contrast with traditional marketing, which is grounded in ad hoc research and statistical analysis.

It's an astonishing trait of traditional marketing that as a discipline it has no discipline, meaning it has no generally adopted principles to guide those who have made it their profession. Some may argue that the system of the four Ps—product, pricing, promotion, place—is a principle. I would regard it as a scaffolding or framework, not a principle. In any event, it is a product-centric whatever that has less meaning in a customer-centric corporate environment where marketing is not about products but about customers.

There is no shortage of books on marketing that tell readers how to do this or that, but they tend to be tactically oriented rather than strategically oriented and devote more attention to anecdotally grounded prescriptions (illustrated by case histories) than empirically grounded principles that remain valid across time. Most books on marketing present a narrow-bandwidth view of life in the marketplace, seen from a single perspective or vantage point. The postmodern marketer views life in the marketplace from multiple perspectives to honor the fact that every customer is a multifaceted, multidimensional, multipersonality being. Not all sides of a cube can be viewed from a single position, and neither can customers be adequately viewed from one vantage point. In this chapter, customer behavior will be examined from a different developmental vantage point: the *lifestyle stages* of adulthood.

THE THREE EXPERIENTIAL STAGES OF ADULT LIFE

In the DRM school of marketing, one view of adult customers is taken through the lens of three lifestyle stages. Each lifestyle stage forms the foundation of people's dreams, aspirations, and much of the behavior that underlies their lifestyles. These three stages are:

1. *Possession experiences,* in which desires for things dominate buying behavior
2. *Catered experiences,* in which desires to be served by others increasingly take precedence over desires for things
3. *Being experiences,* in which desires for transcendent experiences increasingly take precedence over desires for things and catered services

Obviously, people pursue all three types of lifestyle experiences throughout adulthood, but possession experiences tend to dominate the buying behavior of young adults, catered experiences generally have the strongest presence in the middle adult years, and being experiences usually become most prominent near or around the beginning of the last quarter of life.

Customers who are in their possession experience years are the most popular among marketers and the easiest customers to figure out. People in the catered experience years are more complex. Customers in their being experience years are the most difficult to figure out, and enjoy the least popularity among marketers. These customers often confound marketers because their age correlates less with their buying behavior. Marketers are more accomplished in dealing in markets in which age more closely correlates with buying behavior. A 1989 J. Walter Thompson lifestyle research report anticipated a time when marketers would need an alternative to age-based marketing. Peter Kim, then senior VP/U.S. director of research said in the report, "As Americans redefine what it means to grow old, age, in many ways, will become an obsolete marketing concept."[1] Kim clearly anticipated the ultimate emergence of *ageless marketing* in the year that I finished writing a book that introduced that term to the business world.

POSSESSION EXPERIENCE YEARS: THE ACQUISITIVE LIFESTYLE STAGE

Let's look in on Jack and Margo Erskine's grown children, Jason, 26, and Liz, 24, to get a flavor of buying behavior during the possession experiences lifestyle stage.

Jason, who is married, and Liz, who is not, have fundamental needs to satisfy such as shelter, transportation, and "threads," as they would say, but they also need to make social statements in what they buy, consume, and do that reflect the lifestyle they aspire to and live. They are in the building and acquisition lifestyle stage, pursuing satisfaction of the primary psychological, socially oriented developmental objective of Summer: becoming someone.

Possession experience aspirations revolve around the inanimate (things) and the animate (my wife, my son, my dog, etc.). Jason and his wife Amy have a nine-month-old daughter, Hillary. They take great pride in telling others about the latest cute thing Hillary has done. They want everyone to know that she is unique and extra smart. A smart baby, of course, means Mommy and Daddy are smart. That's a good trait to be recognized for having in building a career and social standing.

Possession experience aspirations often lead to simple needs being satisfied at a higher cost than might rationally make sense. Amy just bought a rather pricey Mont Blanc pen and pencil set for Jason to place on his desk at his law office, though she was careful to buy a less expensive model than one prominently displayed on a senior partner's desk. Jason is aspiring to reach junior partner status before he turns 30, an aspiration that Amy intensely shares with him. A $1.98 ball point would meet Jason's writing needs just fine, but Amy decided to serve his writing needs in a way that would help make Jason look classier to his colleagues and superiors.

Jason's sister Liz just blew a tidy sum on a Michael Kors cashmere turtleneck, buying it at what her more frugal 68-year-old grandmother called a ransom price of more than $700. Liz is not yet married, so she doesn't have major responsibility needs, but $700-plus for a sweater is a bit much, her grandmother thinks.

Some possession experiences barely cause a blip in brain waves that register pleasure while others might induce euphoric joy as powerfully as an illegal substance might. Those we call *peak* possession experiences, examples of which appear in Figure 12.1.

The duration of the possession experience years varies. Some people never get beyond them. However, possession experience aspirations generally begin ebbing around the onset of midlife. The motivating forces of possession experience aspirations begin receding with social emancipation from feeling "I don't have to prove anything to anyone anymore." Carl Jung saw this happening in patients as early as age 36 but more often in the later 30s. My informal samplings indicate that age 38 is the most common year of life when people first sense the emergence of a new consciousness about self and life. Interestingly, Gauguin left his lucrative stockbroker job, wife, and six children at age 38 to go off to Tahiti to paint for the rest of his life.

Of course, some people never get beyond feeling a need to prove themselves through "things" they buy. As a result, some reach old age with less financial security than their incomes should have provided. This is how boomers were supposed to be entering later life according to many predictions that saw them as uniquely self-indulgent to the end.

FIGURE 12.1 *Candidates for Peak Possession Experiences*

- New bicycle; new motorcycle
- New car, especially first new car or first high-end car
- Home entertainment system; new photography system
- Engagement ring; other gifts of fine jewelry
- Surprise large cash bonus for outstanding job performance; outsized raise
- New fur coat
- New boat
- First home (perhaps a rented apartment); newly purchased home; beach house
- Finding a long-sought collectible
- Unexpected gifts

Also, animate objects such as
- New love
- First baby (and those that follow, too)
- Acquiring a well-connected new friend
- Acquiring a long-coveted pet

I will leave it to boomers who've passed the half-century mark to determine the worthiness of that gross generalization.

What people buy and how much they buy does not tell whether their buying behavior is materialistically based in possession experience aspirations. Wealthy people can spend great sums on possessions in later life to maintain their lifestyles, but have a lifestyle that is not grounded in materialistic values. When people enter the catered experience years, they don't automatically stop buying fewer "things." They continue buying whatever "things" are necessary to maintain the lifestyle to which they have become accustomed. Spending on "things" usually does not begin tapering off significantly until the later catered experience years.

CATERED EXPERIENCE YEARS: ENJOYING THE FRUITS OF MATERIAL GAIN

Sometimes ads intended for retirees urge them to step up and collect the hard-earned rewards of a lifetime of work. However, the middle years are when people do the most collecting of rewards, as typified by Jack and Margo Erskine's lifestyle. They are deep into their catered experience years, already feeling the tugs of materialistic aspirations weakening, but still spending liberally for catered experiences.

With "things" not giving Jack and Margo the satisfaction they once did, they now talk more and more about simplifying their lives, which means becoming less possessed by possessions. Jack and Margo live comfortably in their home (built circa 1922) that they gutted, renovated, and refurnished nearly a dozen years ago. They also have a condo in Bethany Beach, Delaware, where they dock their sailboat, an Irwin 32. But the time of big dreams about big "things" is now over.

Margo was the first to sense that getting more out of life was not going to come from getting more into "things." That was ten years ago. She was 38. A fulltime homemaker since Jason was born, she would soon see him off to college; Liz would shortly follow. With children now operating pretty much on their own (except for paying their bills!), Margo began feeling a certain emptiness. There has to be something more, she thought. But she kept these strange feelings to herself—"strange" because she had virtually everything she dreamed of having when she and Jack were married, yet, here she was with it all, feeling unfulfilled and not knowing why.

Perhaps because he was so wrapped up in his work, Jack didn't notice Margo's mood changes until several years after they began. He started realizing that something was going on in Margo's mind one evening after playing golf with Wally Baker. Wally, 42, had just separated from his wife Jill after 16 years. Everyone was shocked because the Bakers' marriage seemed as solid as the Rock of Gibraltar. "How could you guys suddenly fall apart," Jack asked Wally on the way to the 10th tee after blowing the 9th hole with a double bogey.

"It wasn't sudden. It just seems that way," Wally said. "Jill and I just drifted apart. Her job and the kids were taking up a lot of her time and she didn't have much left over for me. But then, I was so busy with my company that I guess I didn't give her a lot of time, either. Actually, she initiated the split. She said we just didn't have that much in common anymore, and thought she had enough time left to figure out how to get more out of life, but she couldn't do it with me in her life."

"How'd that make you feel?"

"Like shit at first. But then I got to thinking, maybe there's more out there for me, too."

"But you and Jill have—or had—everything. Good kids, nice house, more than enough income," Jack said. As he said that, he felt the whiff of a sickening feeling in his gut, like somehow he was feeling Wally's pain.

Later, he would realize that it was his own pain. It came from dawning awareness that he and Margo could soon be where the Bakers are now.

"Sure," Wally replied, "it looks like we had everything, but obviously we didn't. The old passion wasn't there any longer and we didn't have that much to say to each other anymore. She had her friends and interests and I had mine. We stopped communicating. We talked to transact family business, but we stopped talking with each other like we used to. Now I wonder if we ever did really communicate all that well."

When Jack went home that night he brought with him a dark quietness. Margo noticed but said nothing. Through the lens of his gloomy mood, Jack suddenly saw Margo differently than he had seen her when he left that morning for his golf date with Wally. Over dinner he thought about how Margo's hair no longer had the brilliant luster that once drew his fingers into it like a magnet so that he could pleasure himself with its silky softness. She looked older this night than she did this morning.

In the days that followed, Jack began thinking more about his life with Margo. Passion was a memory. They had changed as a couple. Their time together was less and their conversations more mundane. As with Wally and Jill, the vitality of the Erskine's marriage didn't suddenly disappear like air from a popped balloon. It seeped out slowly over time like air in a tire with a pinhole leak. Jack knew this was happening, but you can know things without realizing them. But after that fateful day on the golf course with Wally, Jack started to realize what he had known for some time: he and Margo had grown apart. What happened to Wally and Jill was happening to Margo and him.

Jack became more introspective, as Margo had nearly three years earlier. He began thinking more about getting old and dying, more about the meaning of his life, more about the meaning of life in general. Something was wrong, but he couldn't figure out what. Maybe it had something to do with Margo not being as satisfying a marriage partner as she used to be. In his funk, he looked outside of himself for something, somebody to blame. He started feeling a bit sorry for himself. He had worked hard and done well by his family, but felt that he had never done all that much for himself. He thought. "Maybe it's time for me to think more about me." Jack's long-repressed inner self, his real self was speaking to him, but he was misinterpreting what he heard. "Jack," it was saying, "You're not unhappy because of Margo or because you've sacrificed yourself to make others secure and happy. Stop looking outward for the causes of your inner pain. You have arrived at the time of life when you must look inward to find what is missing in your life to the point of discomfort." But it would be awhile before Jack realized what his real self was trying to tell him.

In Chapter 6, I told you how New Balance shoes had enjoyed annual sales growth of 25 percent or more over the past five years in a category that had stopped growing, one in which even Nike could not find growth since 1997. The credit for New Balance's stellar success goes to CEO Jim Davis for having uncanny insight that led to realigning the brand's persona with values that are particularly influential on midlife lifestyles. New Balance's signature tagline "Achieve new balance" resonates with an important plank in Jack and Margo's lifestyle aspirations after the frenetic years of early adulthood when unbalanced devotion to getting ahead vocationally and socially is the norm, and family life fills whatever time is left over. Recall the earlier-made observation that the subtext in New Balance ads often is: Tend to your Inner Self, not to escape a complex world, but as a way of reentering it with renewed spirit. In their early 40s, Jack and Margo needed renewed spirit, both individually and as a couple.

Perhaps because she was further along in reevaluating her life than her husband was, Margo was first to realize what was happening to them as a couple, so one day she said to Jack, "We need to change our relationship."

Jack felt like someone had slugged him in the stomach. He recalled Wally saying that Jill initiated their break-up. He gathered himself together, masked his panic, and calmly said, "Oh?"

Margo replied, "Yes. I think we should start dating again."

"Date again?" Jack thought to himself, his stomach churning in anxiety, his head swirling in confusion. Was this a toe-in-the-water step toward separation, he wondered.

"What do you mean date again?"

"Well, we've been pretty distant with each other and I just thought it might be a good idea to make like we were just starting out together again. I mean, let's find some time when nothing determines what we do and when we do it—friends, kids, your job—the whole lot, let's give ourselves some of the attention we've been giving everyone else. The kids are pretty self-sufficient now, and I'm sure you could carve some time out of your work . . ."

He was relieved, if still a bit confused, but reacting uncomfortably to Margo's take-charge demeanor. However, in the months ahead, Jack and Margo began putting new life in their marriage. Meanwhile, each worked silently on adapting to new realizations about their mortality, their place in the cosmic scheme of things, as it were, and dealing with other issues that move people in tiny steps away from a materialistically footed lifestyle.

Jack and Margo had entered the *midlife-crisis years,* a term coined by Erikson. Though not universally accepted as a developmental phenomenon, a broad consensus still exists that during the earlier midlife years many people undergo a major reassessment of their lives with rising anxiety about their future. This time of life is eerily like adolescence, with quandaries appearing once again about identity, purpose, and life's meanings. Relationships often get microscopic scrutiny during these cloudy and sometimes stormy days, and other life issues become more urgent. Many feel the wrenching shift of a consummate focus on *becoming* someone—the core developmental objective in Summer—toward greater concern about *being* someone—the core developmental objective of Fall. Jack and Margo felt all these things.

Following Margo's suggestion that they start dating again, the Erskines began dining out alone more often. They bought season tickets to Washington's Arena Stage and took occasional weekend trips to New York. With the idea of using multiple approaches to get their marriage back on a satisfying path, Margo took golf lessons, hoping that she would soon be able to play with Jack without embarrassing herself or risking his impatience with her less-than-enviable skill.

Refurbishing their marriage posed many challenges. There were moments of awkwardness because Margo was unready to open up fully to Jack while he seemed more tentative about getting close to Margo again. He had had strong feelings about distance and independence and sometimes felt Margo "closing in on him." But, in time, they grew solidly closer.

As they moved into their late 40s, Jack and Margo began taking on new interests separately. Jack, who had occasionally dabbled in cooking, mostly over the barbecue grill, began taking his culinary interests more seriously. He signed up for cooking workshops and found a new delight in going to Williams-Sonoma to look over what he might not already have in his already well-equipped kitchen. While Margo still did the main family shopping at Safeway, Jack began shopping for specialty foods at high-end grocers.

Margo became interested in lapidary arts and became quite interested in working with semi-precious stones. To her delight, Jack offered to photograph stones and jewelry that she put out to bid on eBay. She was making a little bit of money on her own, something she had not done in years, and it felt good. Even as she was intent on doing what she could to strengthen her marriage, she was taking a parallel path to develop herself into a more independent, self-confident person. After years of often being deferential to Jack, she was becoming more assertive. Jack didn't know quite what to make of this at first, but then began admiring his wife all the more for it. Margo at first didn't know what to make of Jack's more nurturing demeanor, reflected in part by his doing more of the cooking, but it seemed to fit perfectly with her declining interest in domestic activities.

Now, closing in on their 50th year, Jack and Margo began wondering if the condo at the shore, and perhaps even the Irwin were worth the trouble. Earlier, the boat and oceanfront condo served as a felicitous common ground for the whole family. But as the kids got older, the condo became more a burden than a blessing, especially for Margo, for whom it was just another house to clean and take care of. She had been cooking and cleaning and managing the Erskine household for a quarter of a century, and now thought it time to lessen the domestic constraints on her life. The Erskines will probably sell the condo sometime in the next five years—maybe less—and move the Irwin closer to home, to Annapolis, Maryland, just an hour away from their Bethesda home, and let someone else take care of it. Jack enjoyed working on the boat in the past, but now is more agreeable to letting someone else do the work. He will just sail it.

The Erskine's shift from a heavily materialistic lifestyle to a more experiential lifestyle is taking place in today's marketplace on an unprecedented scale. Because middle-aged adults are now the dominant force shaping the leading values, views, needs, and behavior in the marketplace, the midlife bent for experiences over things has given rise to what Joseph Pine and James Gilmore dubbed the Experience Economy in their book by that name.

MARKETS HAVE CHANGED; IT'S TIME FOR MARKETING TO CHANGE

According to the law of entropy, AKA the second law of thermodynamics, the more energy that flows into a system, the less efficiently the system operates and the sooner its collapse. Similarly, the more a person's possession experience aspirations have been satisfied, the less efficiently material things produce satisfaction, and the sooner a person's materialistic value system will collapse. As materialistic urges weaken, one begins *grumbling*, to use Maslow's word for what happens when something ceases to give its former pleasure, for experiential sources of satisfaction, first primarily in the form of catered experiences, then as often as possible in the form of being experiences.

As with possession experiences, catered experiences occur in both mundane and peak manifestations. Figure 12.2 lists candidates for peak catered experiences. As with possession experiences, catered experiences can play an important role in projecting the marks of a person's identity. In the earlier stages of adult life, possessions often say, "We are arriving." Catered experiences more likely say, "We have arrived!" They mark the first stage of *being* someone versus *becoming* someone.

BEING EXPERIENCES: TOWARD THE LAST OF LIFE FOR WHICH THE FIRST WAS MADE

Advertising directed toward retirees often talks about the "golden years," the "prime of your life" years, and the "best years of your life." I am in those years, but like many of my peers, I grimace when I see such words in ads. They are patronizing, and my peers and I know that they are used for the sole purpose of selling something. The advertiser is not interested in us as human beings, only as consumers. The advertiser has not established the empathetic connections with us that would give it the license to speak that way. I would like to give people who use those words in ads an assignment. I would like them to write a two-part essay. First, they would have to explain why *they* are not living in their "best years," for by simple deduction if I'm in the best years then they are not. Second, I would like them to tell me why they think I'm in my best years to see if they really know why. The fact that these are my best years does not make me feel that someone who says I am necessarily understands why. The issue is one of authenticity. Like Jamie Lee Curtis, my peers and I value authenticity far more than when we were in the Summer of our lives. Also, we have gotten much better at sniffing out insincerity.

The fact that for many people the later years are the best years was celebrated by Robert Browning in his famous poetic entreaty:

FIGURE 12.2 *Candidates for Peak Catered Experiences*

- Thrilling theater performance; emotionally rewarding film; great concert
- A weekend getaway from the kids
- A great meal at an expensive five-star restaurant
- Attending a championship game that your team wins
- The best massage you can ever remember
- Invitation to and experience of playing on an exclusive golf course
- Attending a party at a famous person's home
- An exotic vacation; cruise ship adventure; African safari
- Having an interior decorator present plans that knock your socks off
- Having a custom-made dress (combining possession experience aspirations with catered experience aspirations)
- Throwing a highly successful catered party
- Having unexpected pleasure in a buying experience
- Having someone take a big challenge off your hands

Grow old along with me!
The best is yet to be,
The last of life, for which the first was made . . .

His words suggest that destiny has stitched into the fabric of our humanness the promise of something very good and very special in the later years of life. Robert Browning was not creating a *faux* romanticized picture of old age such as seen in advertising that depicts older couples in posed pictures with pasted on smiles. Rather he was invoking images of joy that transcend the materialistic self of the early adult years. Being experiences are transcendent experiences.

Years ago, after struggling to define being experiences in a way that satisfied me, I found inspiration in an article devoted to sex and love relationships among elderly people. The article quoted an 83-year-old man who had just fallen in love with an 80-year-old woman:

> "I can't believe how I feel. It's like I was 18 years old again. I have the same feelings. I get clammy hands, have had loss of appetite; I get this pit in my stomach; she even makes me kind of embarrassed sometimes when she looks at me a certain way. I guess that means I'm blushing." Then he went on to say, "I feel more connected to life because of her. And I feel a stronger sense of reality."

Falling in love is one of the greatest of being experiences that can be experienced in all ages throughout adulthood. Love between two people is a powerful metaphor for birth, growth, and productiveness. Nature was most generous when she gave us the capacity to feel what we feel when we are in love. This is both Nature's enticement and her reward for behavior that secures the continuity of species. Inspired by the old man's story of finding new love in the twilight of his life, I finalized the definition of being experiences:

Experiences that enhance one's sense of connectedness, sharpen one's sense of reality, and increase one's sense of appreciation for life; in their most emotionally rewarding occurrences, they involve actions benefiting others, or actions that contribute to inner personal growth.

Being experiences may involve possessions, but are essentially of nonmaterialistic origins. They are exalted feelings in the moment. They are not about tomorrow, but about the feelings one has in the present. They bring to mind Maslow's descriptions of what he called *peak experiences* in which the means become more important than the end. He connected this idea to the idea of older people returning to their second childhood. In fact, children are quite good at living in the moment and often focus more on the doing than on the results.

Being Experiences Can Arise in the Most Ordinary of Situations

Being experiences may also involve or be coupled with catered experiences and often involve the sharing of a catered experience, such as taking a grandchild on a trip. They can also be invoked by the aesthetics of a meal's presentation and the charming and giving manner of a waiter.

My first trip to Chico's to buy my wife a Christmas present was a being experience. An early-fiftysomething sales associate was sensitive to my ignorance of Linda's size. I know her size in conventional terms, but Chico's has its own sizing scale: Sizes 1, 2, and 3 are the core sizes—no sizes 10, 12, and 14 for women who no longer have the body of a 20-year-old.

The sales associate, Rose, suggested that I look around the store to see whether I saw anyone who looked like my wife's size. "There, that lady over there," I said, pointing to another sales associate standing about 20 feet away from us helping another customer.

Catching the other sales associate's eye, Rose asked, "What size are you?"

Before the other sales associate could respond, the customer she was helping answered, "Size 2 Regular."

"No, I meant Valerie."

The customer laughed.

That's how I found Chico's to be on my first visit. Everyone seemed comfortable with who they were, even customers. No airs. Just authentic selves. Rose helped me through the transaction which involved getting slacks and a complementary blouse, never making me feel inadequate because I was a man, awkwardly shopping for his wife. My father would never have bought his wife any clothes. He would send his secretary out to do the job.

My first Chico's experience turned me into a loyal customer who no longer goes to a department store when I shop for my wife or middle-aged daughters. I wonder how many middle-aged and older men there are who buy clothes as gifts for women, but who aren't on the radar screens of any retailer of women's clothes. It seems to me that it's a market to which few pay any attention.

Being experiences are about how a person internalizes an experience, not about what the experience is. One woman may see a child in her care as a responsibility, while a grandmother may see the same child as a wonder of life.

My daughter Stephanie's grandfather was watching over her one day when she was about 4. Suddenly, she spied a yardstick and began playing with it. In one moment she laid it against her right shoulder and marched around the living room like a soldier. In another moment she placed two books about two feet apart on the sofa and spanned them with the yardstick to make a bridge for little plastic creatures to cross. In another scenario, she turned the yardstick into a piano keyboard and began playing it. In all, she turned the yardstick into more than a dozen different imaginary incarnations. Her grandfather was so moved seeing his granddaughter play so magically that he wrote a poignant essay about her play that he might share his wondrous being experience with his granddaughter's parents.

In common parlance, being experiences are about "smelling the latte." They are about getting much from little. They are more internally spiritual than they are outwardly dramatic. They do not have a self-serving orientation, though they serve the self by increasing satisfaction with self and life.

Jack and Margo have restless stirrings about not only simplifying their lives but also about giving new meaning to their lives. Jack's parents, John and Mary, know what those stirrings mean: Catered experiences are beginning to lose some of their edge, much as happened earlier with possession experiences.

At the peak of his career at around age 50 or so, Jack's father had wondered, "What I am going to do next." He wasn't talking about career, though he dallied for a while with the idea of setting up his own business. He even bought some books, took some courses, and talked with a couple of friends about going into business together. But nothing clicked. These stirrings went on for a few years. In the meantime, John became more involved with his church and, for a while, did more fly fishing. But, still, nothing clicked. John Erskine retired at age 61, about the age most men have retired in recent years. During his first year of retirement, John and Mary spent a good bit of time planning their future, which included plans for extensive travel. They sold the old house and moved into their condo to free themselves up. They briefly thought about buying an RV, but decided it "wasn't them." The biggest market for RVs are people in the Catered Experience years, looking for new experiences, usually after their kids have flown the nest or soon will.

Toward the end of that first year of John's retirement, he got involved with RSVP, a volunteer group of retired people who help small businesses. The RSVP experience energized him. He wasn't making a dime doing what, for years, he was paid well for—exercising his management skills—but the job he retired from never consistently gave him the fulfillment that he was getting from his RSVP work which included helping minority start-up firms draw up business plans to secure financing.

Meanwhile, Mary was moving ahead on her master's in art history and continuing her participation in the community theater group that she had joined a few years back. Her life after John's retirement was more about continuing the things that she was already involved with, while John's life was more about redirection and taking up new interests, and, overall, was a different lifestyle than he had anticipated he would have before he retired.

Some men do not make the transition to retirement as easily as John did. Perhaps that is something that companies marketing to retiree markets might benefit from by helping men in the preretirement years and early years after retiring understand better how to have a successful life in retirement. Certainly, financial planning companies, banks with senior membership programs, travel services organizations, community developers, and healthcare providers are among the stand-out candidates for helping retirees achieve a more satisfying lifestyle in retirement.

Though each category of experiential aspirations influences behavior throughout adult life (see Figure 12.3), people like the elder Erskines have a corner on being experiences. The young seek out being experiences, but often through artificial means, including mind-altering drugs. However, what they experience are not real being experiences. While feelings may be similar in some degree, artificial being experiences promote disconnectedness, not connectedness; they provide a false reality, not an objective reality; they promote dissatisfaction, (often in the after-state of an artificial high), not a deep appreciation of all life. Artificial being experiences are self-oriented. The object of the experiencer is primarily to indulge one's self. True being experiences cannot be gotten from a puff of smoke or a whiff of white powder.

Being experiences are natural experiences. They are as fresh as the dew-kissed spring morn. They are not sensual equivalents of fast food service. They are without regard to time, therefore, there is no motive for getting them fast. They are experiences to be savored. They are beyond the wearing-down effects of the behavioral equivalent of the law of entropy, for unlike possession and catered experiences, being experiences get better, produce higher highs, the more they are experienced. They become addictive.

There is a decidedly strong spiritual quality about being experiences that derives from their timeless qualities, their frequently altruistic nature, and their hypnotic command of more, more, more, like a chant whose repetition raises one's level of inspiration, rather than induces loss of interest and the onset of boredom. Once a person has discovered the world of being experiences with their whole being, there is no going back to dominance by the more mundane kinds of aspirations. That would be regression, not growth.

When thinking about "big ticket" possession and catered experiences, catalysts of being experiences often seem quite modest. Even

FIGURE 12.3 *Candidates for Peak Being Experiences*

- Heading up a charity ball
- Watching a fantastic sunset, especially when sharing it with someone close
- Observing a precocious child
- Helping a young person master a problem
- Completing a carefully planned and executed task
- Painting a splendid picture
- Getting "goose bumps" from a piece of music
- Having an inspiring religious experience
- Learning an exciting new thing (or fact)
- Taking joy in someone else's good fortune
- Taking great pleasure at the beauty of a restaurant and the presentation of the food (combining catered experiences with being experiences)
- Falling in love
- Special moments with a spouse, a child, a friend, a spiritual leader, etc.
- A patriotic experience (hearing "America the Beautiful" at the opening of the Olympics)

though older people have more complex behaviors, their lifestyles tend to grow progressively simpler because it takes progressively less to make them happier (see Figure 12.4). For this reason, message themes, content, and images that work for people in the possession or catered experience years often are out of tune with people intent on increasing the being experience content of their lives by experiencing the ordinary in extraordinary ways.

THE MARKETER AS A HEALER

Alice Erskine has struggled for years to get her life on a smooth running course, along with 12 million other people, referred to in a J. Walter Thomson study as "mature singles," who are "insecure, disenchanted, frequently depressed middle-agers." The report said these mature singles were good candidates for the travel industry; however, "Marketers will face the toughest hurdles reaching this audience, but Club Med and other vacation spots could benefit from repositioning themselves towards this group" (cited in Chapter 11).

Maslow would not rate the chances of Alice and others like her, over 80 percent of whom have been separated or divorced ten years or more, as promising for reaching a full state of self-actualization. Years lived do not automatically take one into a self-actualizing state. Nevertheless, this

FIGURE 12.4 *Distribution of Experiential Aspirations throughout Adulthood*

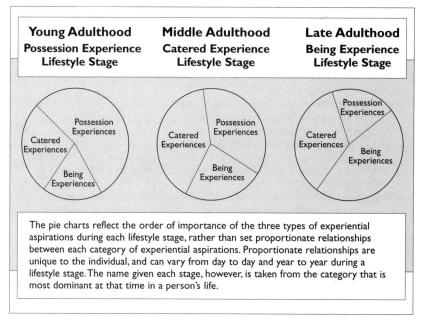

Young Adulthood
Possession Experience
Lifestyle Stage

Middle Adulthood
Catered Experience
Lifestyle Stage

Late Adulthood
Being Experience
Lifestyle Stage

The pie charts reflect the order of importance of the three types of experiential aspirations during each lifestyle stage, rather than set proportionate relationships between each category of experiential aspirations. Proportionate relationships are unique to the individual, and can vary from day to day and year to year during a lifestyle stage. The name given each stage, however, is taken from the category that is most dominant at that time in a person's life.

group of people is too large too ignore. They still want as much quality in their lifestyles as financial and emotional capabilities allow. Who knows, perhaps a healthy diet of being experiences might nudge Alice and others like her bit further along in the maturation process. Melinda Davis, CEO of the Next Group, might agree.

Davis launched the Human Desire Project in 1996 to figure out the major motivators of the 21st century. She says, "All of the most important consumer trends can be understood by looking at this state-of-mind calculus, where people make choices based on how it makes their heads feel . . . the possibility for *real* differentiation comes not in the product itself but in how you collaborate with the consumer's need to heal. . . . We are taking tentative steps into a new era: the era of state-of-mind marketing. This is the new imperative: The marketer must now be a healer."[2]

The marketer as *healer!* That might seem bit too new agey for some, but considering that Davis's clients include such mainstream corporations as AT&T, Merck, Procter & Gamble, Corning, and Viacom, her words bear serious thought, especially in light of the ebbing of materialistic values that have for so long determined the substance in favor of more experiential lifestyles. When people begin to realize in midlife that "things" do not cure one's feelings of spiritual emptiness, that "things" cannot heal painful feelings, that there must be more, why not approach customers as healers?

A friend once put me on a conference call with his brother who had complained that life had lost its spark for him. Mike—not his name to spare him embarrassment—was in his late 40s, a successful lawyer, reasonably satisfied with his marriage, with two lovely children, but felt that his life had gone flat. My friend suggested to Mike that he call me. Mike did, and began by telling me that for years, when he got into in a funk, he could always count on the Sharper Image to make him feel better, or at least it could take his mind off his troubles for awhile. "Last week, I was a bit down and went to the Sharper Image, and found nothing interested me. The more I tried to find something interesting, the more agitated I got. I began to wonder, 'What's going on with me? Why am I feeling so disconnected, so out of it?'"

Unbeknownst to the folks at the Sharper Image, one of its stores had long been a source of healing for Mike. People in the Summer of life may not as often feel that they are in need of healing because of the often audacious confidence of youth. However, many people in midlife, especially in the first decade of midlife, often feel a need for healing, but without knowing why they are in need of healing. Robert Snyder said how widespread this is in midlife came through loud and strong in the Values Portrait research conducted among people in the 45-to-64 age group.

Midlife is a time of passage that some people get through with little awareness that they have passed through anything, although sooner or later they realize that they are living in a consciousness that is much different than the consciousness they lived in during their 20s and 30s. However, a vast number of people do have a sense of changing consciousness, as Mike the Sharper Image fan experienced, and, like Mike, many of them are disturbed about what is going on in their psyches.

Stores like Chico's and Anthropologie, brands like New Balance and Harley-Davidson, and major airlines like Southwest and . . . and . . . well, like Southwest are healing brands. A lot of people who board airplanes are in instant need of healing. Southwest Airlines knows this, so its pilots and flight attendants do all they can to settle down the most tense air traveler using the universal medicine of humor. A friend told of the time he was on a Southwest plane that had landed and coming to a stop, a voice came from the pilot's cabin, "Whoa, big fella . . . WHOA!" One Southwest pilot announced during his welcome message: "We are pleased to have some of the best flight attendants in the industry. . . .

Unfortunately, none of them are on this flight!" A pilot on another flight said, "We've reached our cruising altitude now, and I'm turning off the seat belt sign. I'm switching to autopilot, too, so I can come back there and visit with all of you for the rest of the flight."

Mike Baumayr, one of the nation's leading advertising specialists in retiree markets—he has serviced Del Webb Sun City communities for a dozen years—tells a poignant story that exemplifies Southwest's commitment to doing what it can to help heal its customers. His wife Marsha called Southwest to get a ticket to journey from Phoenix to Florida to be with her gravely ill parents. Her mother was in her last days, and her father would soon follow her. The Southwest ticket agent got into Marsha's story with such empathetic feeling that she told Marsha that she was going to send her a coupon that she had earned in an employee recognition program.

Several days later, after receiving the coupon, Marsha called the ticket agent to say how much she appreciated the offer, but she didn't feel she could accept it. The ticket agent, knowing that Marsha faced challenging days and weeks ahead said, "I want you to take the coupon. You are going to need it. The only thing I ask is that you rent the Kevin Spacey movie *Pay It Forward* and, after you have seen it, please tell three people about it."

Pay It Forward is the story of a young boy challenged by his teacher (Kevin Spacey) to think how he could make the world a better place. The boy, Trevor McKinney, played by Haley Joel Osment, comes up with the "pay it forward" concept in which one person does a good deed for a stranger who then does good deeds for three other people he or she doesn't know, asking each person to also do good deeds for three other people and so on. Trevor shocks his mother by bringing home a homeless person as the first person for whom he will do a life-changing good deed. By simple arithmetic, Trevor figured that the "pay it forward" concept could transform the world.

The Southwest ticket agent had joined Trevor's mission and made Marsha Baumayr a subject of one of her good deeds on the premise that Marsha would tell three people about the movie who in turn might be inspired to join the "pay it forward" mission.

Viewing the idea of marketers as healers from the perspective of how Southwest Airlines makes air travelers feel better, Melinda Davis's idea makes great humanistic—and economic—sense.

The marketer as healer idea squares with the proposition in Chapter 11 that was inspired by the Trappist monk, Abbot Joseph, when he talked about how storytellers help us process our lives. That idea, as you will recall, led to the proposal that marketers should see themselves as helping customers process their lives. Now that is being truly customer-centric.

Being experiences have healing powers. They promote a sense of connectedness, sharpen one's sense of reality in pleasing ways, and heighten one's sense of appreciation for life.

Brands perceived as gateways to being experiences will be more attractive to people in second-half markets, including Alice and others like her. Though many like Alice may be poor customers for luxury items, household furnishings, new cars, and upscale service establishments, and tend to be price sensitive in what they buy, perhaps companies in those lines might find more sales and even better margins among Alice and her psychographic peers by heeding Davis's words about the marketer as healer.

Great Customer Experiences Generate Great Profit Margins

The elder Erskines are good prospects for quality service establishments, better quality grocery items, fine home furnishings, and upscale anything they want to buy. Most of their lifestyle spending is discretionary. In fact, the percentage of household income classifiable as "discretionary" is highest for their age group, 65-to-74-year olds, according to the Bureau of Labor Statistics. Generally speaking, people who have passed beyond the possession experience years, with materialistic desires substantially satisfied, tend to become less price sensitive about purchases they perceive as having high experiential value. This can be even truer with respect to purchases that customers perceive as serving as gateways to being experiences.

John and Mary Erskine, sometimes come close to being outrageous in what they pay for something. While John often does comparison shopping when he's in the market for something and Mary still watches sales and takes cents-off coupons to the grocers, he has budgeted over $10,000 for the trip he plans to surprise Mary with upon her graduation from graduate school that will take them to Russia to visit the world famous

Hermitage art museum in St. Petersburg. No bargain basement fares and lodgings on this trip. When they see something they want, and they perceive it as having high experiential value, they are willing to pay a greater difference between *generic* value and *perceived* value than when they are buying something they simply need, like replacing an appliance or buying a TV.

Obviously, how much a person is willing to pay beyond the generic value of something is highly subjective. But just as obvious, the more a person anticipates a product will lead to a highly coveted experience, like the Erskine's trip to Hermitage, the greater the spread between generic value and perceived value. However, this is not true just of retirees who have become more relaxed about life and spending.

Joseph Pine and James Gilmore, the deans of customer experience specialists and authors of *The Experience Economy,* say that whoever your market is, "The experience is the marketing." If you get the experience right, you've done all the marketing you need to do. Well, not quite, as they recognize. You still have to get the word out that you're around. But a great experiential environment, such as Anthropologie offers customers, or the American Girl Place in Chicago (a favorite of Pine and Gilmore), will draw attention from media and generate buzz among customers. Readers who want to learn more about the American Girl Place, where customers in effect pay for the right to shop, and others that have successfully made the customer experience the centerpiece of marketing can find satisfaction at Pine and Gilmore's Strategic Horizons Web site.[3] They have graciously provided links to a large number of sources of information about the customer experience.

In the wheels business—two-wheeled or four-wheeled—Harley-Davidson stands out for its success in capitalizing on customers' experiential appetites. The average customer of a Harley is 46, makes $78,000, and rides a $16,000 machine.[4] He or she loves the Harley experience so much, that the company is able to price its products with a wide enough margin to net more than seven times the net that General Motors realizes per unit sold. Harley nets $1,922 on each unit sold, as measured by the results of the Spring quarter of 2001, in comparison with $292 per unit netted by General Motors in the same quarter.[5] For most people, a car is a car, but for everyone who buys a Harley, a Harley is an experience—often, a being experience—whatever the age of the Harley owner.

PREPARING LANDING SITES FOR MARKETING MESSAGES

Communication is information exchange. A television commercial may be transmitted but is not a communication—that is, no information exchange takes place—if a customer does not hear it. It's like how a tree falling in the forest makes no sound if no one hears it because sound is defined as vibrations between 20 and 20,000 hertz that activate a human auditory system.

To have a successful exchange of information between marketer and customer there must be a landing site in the customer's brain to receive the information. The brain won't issue a building permit for a landing site unless the information that's trying to land is relevant to the customer's interests.

Landing sites for marketers' messages are constructed from building materials taken from customers' dreams, needs, and desires. But marketers can catalyze or accelerate the construction of landing sites for their information by communicating with the brain using symbols that already have meaning and relevance to the brain's owner. Also, to be cleared for landing, a marketer's information must be perceived as credible.

Believability is not a function of reasoning to the extent many believe. Nothing does more to establish believability with customers than for them to feel that a marketer empathetically understands them. People are their own favorite subject. When another person shows empathetic interest in them—that is, identifies with and understands their circumstances, emotions, feelings, and motives,—they likely perceive the empathizing person as engaging and believable. "Someone showed interest in me and they understand me!"

The final part of this book deals with building information landing sites in customers' brains and making connections with landing sites already in place.

13

SYMBOLS

When a Rose Is Not a Rose

With due respect to Gertrude Stein, a rose is not always a rose. When the word *rose* refers to something other than a flower—as when Rose is a person's name or a past-tense verb—it is *not* a rose. But even when referring to the flower, that which we call a rose can be far more than a biological specimen of the plant world. A gift of roses can indicate, "I'm sorry," or "You are special," or "Congratulations!" Thus, even the meaning of the flower *rose* is not fixed, but rather depends on context. In some Arab countries, a gift of roses to a woman would be received with horror because the rose is a symbol of death.

These observations are grist for thought mills that grind away in a field called *semiotics.*

Linguists and semanticists study language, but semioticians go beyond language to mull over contextual influences on the meanings of words, symbols, and images. What a word or symbol stands for in a person's mind is subject to an infinite range of influences including the time and place it is invoked, the mood of the perceiver, and the circumstances in which the symbol appears. "My Country 'Tis of Thee," heard often in the days following the 9/11 tragedies, brought tears of sadness to millions of eyes, yet when played at a Fourth of July fireworks show, it fills many of the same eyes with tears of joy.

The central focus in this chapter is the art of choosing and using words, symbols, and imagery in marketing messages that have enough emotional surcharge to break through the brain's formidable information triage screens. Remember, marketing messages will only get into customers' conscious minds by earning a thumb's up in the unconscious reaches of the brain.

SAM 1990 quoted a researcher from a global ad agency who cogently observed that combining pictures and music in advertising tends to cause people to make judgments in a different way than they would if they were just reading.[1] Words—abstract symbols of things—are primarily processed in the left brain; music (for all but trained musicians, interestingly) is processed primarily in the right brain. Myers expresses a semiotician's view that words alone have different meanings than words heard to the accompaniment of music. So maybe there's something after all in teens' claim that they study better with the radio blaring.[2]

FIVE BRAIN FACTS TO KEEP IN MIND WHEN CREATING MARKETING MESSAGES

Previous chapters discussed several facts about the operation of the brain's hemispheres that bear on a marketing message's chances of escaping the recycling bins of information triage:

1. The right brain works in sensual imagery, not in words.
2. Right brain images are analogs (direct reflections) of reality as gauged by the senses, not abstract symbols of reality, such as the words on this page.
3. The right brain plays the lead role in determining the relevance of incoming information.
4. The right brain, which looks for patterns or relationships, forms more complete or holistic images than the left brain, which focuses more on details.
5. The right brain is inclusionary and detects relationships; the left brain is exclusionary and detects categories.

The right brain, in a sense, is the gatekeeper to the left brain. If the right brain fails to sense a relationship between the interests of the person it works for and the contents of a product message, the product message has little chance of surviving information triage with enough strength to engage the person's sustained attention. Despite all the attention devoted to novelty of presentation, more often it is information relevance that catalyzes *intentional* attention to the contents of a product message. This is more so among second-half customers who are less intrigued by fantastical, whimsical, outlandish, eye-popping, mind-exploding novelty than younger minds.

Consider the reaction of my wife to a Saturn commercial that ran during the 2002 Olympics. It showed a Saturn weaving over hill and vale in a desert landscape filled with German shepherd–sized ants fanning out across the barren stretch. Technically impressive, the commercial was substantively empty. Even silly. My wife turned to me after the commercial ended and said, "What was *that* about?"

The commercial was probably tested in focus groups, but focus groups are often as far removed from reality as the computer-drawn ants. It was a clean disconnect from Saturn's original right brain–rooted, customer-oriented brand persona which portrayed warm, empathetic relationships through its stories, first about its workers, then about its customers. The humanistic aura projected by the brand inspired Saturn owners to swarm to Spring Hill, the Tennessee town where Saturns were built, for hot dogs, hamburgers, and potato salad, and to meet and share with each other Saturn stories and other tales, much as Harley-Davidson owners do. The tagline, "A different kind of company. A different kind of car." symbolized the original humanistic bent of the Saturn brand, which included its policy of no price haggling.

Saturn's first ads, which appeared before it arrived in showrooms, pictured workers in their family and community lives, not in their jobs on factory floors putting pieces of cars together. After Saturn was on the road, following its "tradition" of promoting Saturn through the stories of people instead of pushing automotive technology, ads told stories of Saturn owners. Hal Riney Partners, Saturn's original agency, convincingly showed in its ads that *people*—workers and customers alike—were the driving influence on management. This gave Saturn a right brain, *first-impression edge* because competing brands were all defined around product features, functional benefits, and deals of the week. The emotional right brain cares more about relationships than it does about horsepower and 2.2-liter, DOHC, 16-valve, 4-cylinder engines which is grist for the *quantitatively* minded left brain. The left brain will get into analyzing a product message's contents once the right brain has determined that message contents are relevant to its owner's interests.

The folks at Hal Riney might not have known the brain science wisdom behind their strategy, but they were spot on. However, things have changed quite a lot since General Motors brought Saturn into its centralized management and marketing operations. Saturn's original customer-centric, right brain bias is no longer prominent. Marketing messages have a product-centric, left brain tilt. Marketing is now mostly about the product. Features, benefits, and deal of the week have replaced the human relationships and the brand as the primary marketing focus. This has cost Saturn its former first-impression edge. Now, Saturn ads must work harder to break through ad clutter. Also, there's less inspiration now for folks to get on the road to Spring Hill for Cokes, hot dogs, potato salad, and sharing stories about their Saturn experiences.

Connecting with customers is about doing the right things to get their attention and generate positive first impressions. First impressions are mainly a product of right brain mental processes. This makes getting the most favorable first impressions a bit more crucial in second-half markets because middle-aged and older people's first impressions can be harder to reverse than those of first-half customers, especially when first impressions are negative.[3] It's often one strike and you're out!

Asking focus group panelists to talk aloud about first impressions is not productive because of group dynamics influence. Instead, ask panelists to write down their first impressions.

Product messages work best when first impressions are pleasing. Despite this, "fear ads" are often used under the misbegotten belief that scaring the hell out of customers is a good strategy. It works with some people, but it can damage a brand's image in the eyes of the larger market. A few years ago a Prudential Securities ad ran with the headline "Will you outlive your assets?" Below the headline was a man diving into an empty swimming pool. The ad had a short run. The right brain–generated image of a man crushing his skull on a dry pool floor to symbolize "out of money, out of luck" was a ghastly picture that turned people off. Ads that disturb people are generally not good ads for second-half markets. Older customers would rather be pleased than shocked.

THE DYNAMICS OF FIRST IMPRESSIONS

Many years of experience make older customers more comfortable going with their gut feelings. Their first *perceptions* tend to be more complete than those of younger customers. The young parse reality with greater attention to detail and are likelier to miss the big picture. Older people's perceptions are likelier to capture the forest rather than a few trees. Developmental psychologist Cynthia Adams of the University of Oregon has conducted research indicating that middle-aged and older people comprehend the gist of a matter more quickly and completely than younger minds do.[4] Another intriguing finding is that when younger and older people are asked to recall a story they have read, the younger people tend to recall the sequential actions in the story while older people tend to recall the meanings of the story. So, once again, we see the left brain bias dealing with details in younger people's perceptions in contrast to older people's right brain bias in perceiving the larger context of meaning.

The quickness of second-half customers to make decisions based on first impressions gives rise to the belief that older customers are more opinionated and less likely to switch brands. However, that long-held belief in marketing has been shattered by a Roper ASW study conducted in 2002. AARP, which underwrote the study, posted a summary of key findings on its Web site <www.aarp.org> (keyword: Roper), in which the study made these observations:

- Before making a purchase, most Americans (62 percent) typically research different brands. *This behavior peaks among 45-to-55 year-olds (68 percent).* (Italics added.)
- Seven in ten Americans age 45-plus will try (but not necessarily switch to) a new brand if a person they trust recommends it.
- About half of Americans age 45-plus are "always looking for better products," indicating their brand loyalty is often tenuous. Americans 45-plus, contrary to conventional wisdom, are no more brand loyal than younger people in most categories. For instance, they are as likely as those under 45 to agree with the statement "in today's marketplace, it doesn't pay to be loyal to one brand" (55 percent of those age 45-plus, 58 percent of those younger).

The Roper ASW study, which found product category to be a better predictor of brand loyalty than age, also found price to be a stronger motivator for switching brands among younger people, while older people are more willing to switch to higher-priced brands to get better quality.

HOW CONTEXT SHAPES THE MEANING OF SYMBOLS

Had Saturn's tagline "A different kind of company. A different kind of car." been introduced in advertising that pushed features, functional benefits, and economic value, the meaning of the tagline would have been different than it was originally. However, by first appearing in people-oriented advertising, the tagline took on a customer-centric meaning. In other words, context determined the core meaning of the tagline—*not the words that formed it.*

Symbols and images have both *objective* and *subjective* meanings. Objective meanings are determined by consensus—shared views among a number of people about what something means. Subjective meanings are what individuals infer something means, independent of social consensus. People in first-half markets generally depend more on consensus-based objective meanings because they cue more of their behavior on what others think. People in second-half markets tend to depend more on subjective meanings (e.g., gut feelings).

Some symbols have meanings that are particular to given peer, socioeconomic, and ethnic groups. Other meanings are somewhat, if not wholly, universal—archetypal meanings that people the world over see in a symbol.

Some symbols have meanings that are uniquely shared among people in particular developmental stages, including the lifestyle stages of adulthood we examined in the last chapter. For example, meanings inferred from an ad promoting a racy sports car may be quite different between people in their possession experience years and people in their being experience years. The former are more likely see the car as a symbol of social status, while the latter perceive it as a symbol of coveted experiences.

Mood is another contextual influence on meanings. Deborah Tannen has a deep understanding of that. Tannen is a sociolinguist who teaches and writes books about the subtle unconscious influences in what and how people say what they want to say, and on how people often respond to what another person says as though that person were speaking a different language. This often happens when a person says something that isn't literally what he or she means, but is rather an indirect reference to what is meant, and the other person interprets the statement according to its literal meaning. We often express ourselves indirectly instead of directly because we've learned that seeking collaboration in forming a decision often works better than directly indicating what we would like to do.

Tannen tells a story in her book, *You Just Don't Understand,* that shows how conflicts can arise when a person indirectly indicates a course of action she wants to take only to have the other person interpret her words literally. In Tannen's example, a wife becomes miffed with her husband after she asks him if *he* would like to stop for coffee and he answers her in the negative. The wife was the one who really wanted to stop for coffee after a long day on the road, perhaps seeking an affectionate moment with her husband before getting back into the real world.

The husband might have been in a tired mood and thinking only of getting home, so he inferred from his wife's question, "Would you like to stop for a coffee?" that she was asking about what *he would like,* not making a statement in the form of a question about *what she would like.* The take-away from this: Don't automatically assume that what you think is the meaning of what you say in an ad is the same meaning customers will see in it. As was true of the husband in Tannen's story, customers are more interested in the meanings they *infer* from an ad than in the meanings you imply in an ad.

CAN MARKETING MESSAGES THAT ARE DIRECTED AT EVERYONE BE EFFECTIVE?

Given the differences that can exist between older and younger customers in the meanings they draw from marketing messages, how realistic is it to develop messages for multiple age groups? This is a pertinent question given that ageless marketing is about marketing to multiple age groups.

It is widely believed, of course, that showing older people in ads tends to alienate younger people. But that is too simplistic a view. In fact, *it is easier to target older people and pick up younger buyers than the other way around.* The successes of brands like New Balance and Harley-Davidson across a wide age range support that. The trick is to project values and use presentation techniques that speak across generational divides. New Balance invokes values that have cross-generational appeals while Harley-Davidson uses conditional positioning that allows people of all ages to picture themselves on a Harley. A few years ago, Wachovia Bank used children in an enormously successful campaign to dissolve the issue of age.

Wachovia posed a sizeable challenge to Interpublic agency, Long Haymes Carr, now Mullen LHC in Charlotte, North Carolina. The agency drew on the tenets of ageless marketing to solve the challenge. Wachovia Bank had some unknown number of unsettled customers stemming from a wave of mergers and acquisitions, a condition that commonly occurs in banking. Long Haymes Carr's challenge was framed by Wachovia's desire for a single campaign that would resonate positively throughout its entire customer base, from heads of major corporations and small businesses to young people starting careers and families to empty nesters and retirees.

The campaign theme was Wachovia as a ready partner helping customers meet their needs. That was implicit in the theme line, "We are there." To put legs on the theme, a new action-oriented tagline was scripted: "Let's get started." The tagline was not about the bank brand, but about relationships with customers. At face value, neither the campaign theme nor tagline may seem to be prize-winning. But the context in which they were used gave the theme and tagline distinctive meanings. They were contextually grounded in the lives and minds of children.

A more conventional approach might have used different commercials and print ads for each customer type. That could have been more costly, and as measured by the campaign's stunning success, less effective. To give you a feel for the campaign, the most successful at the time in Wachovia's history, as measured by ROI analysis, here is the storyline of one of the commercials:

> A nerdy, plump nine-year-old sits plaintively on the sidelines at a dance while his peers are having a great time on the dance floor. A winsome young lady of about the same age, but a few

inches taller, approaches him and asks him for a dance. Suddenly, the room is electrified as the other boys cast their eyes on the newly formed couple, wondering how the chubby nerd did it. The underlying message of the commercial, which caused eyes to glisten, is that with the right partner, your prospects can be dramatically improved.

Wachovia said in its next two annual shareholder reports that the campaign had played a significant role in its continuing growth. It also influenced internal operations. Wachovia CEO Bud Baker, Jr. initiated efforts to ensure that values reflected in the campaign were reflected inside the company. By so doing, he revealed his belief that a company must live the brand if it is to build strong, enduring relationships with customers. The take-away from the Wachovia story: By projecting values and images that have cross-generational and even cross-cultural meanings and appeal, you can often bypass the more exclusionary practice of segmenting customers and approaching each segment separately and differently.

Hallmark Cards has long distinguished itself with advertising that crosses generational divides by invoking family values and themes. Many of its ads and commercials give proof that it is easier to transcend age with right brain–oriented messages and imagery than with left brain–oriented messages. Hallmark has never sold features and benefits. It sells relationships.

McDonald's used to draw quite effectively on right brain humanistic themes. It established empathetic connections with people of all races, cultures, age, and personal circumstances. Some years back it ran a poignant commercial featuring a young man with Down's syndrome. In the late 1980s and early 1990s, several commercials featured older people to the acclaim of all ages. One commercial, showing an elderly gentleman eyeing an elderly woman he is obviously interested in as he looks for a place to sit, evoked pleasure among people of all ages because it projected that universal opiate, romance. McDonald's may have not fared so well in the marketplace in recent years, at least in part, because it abandoned its right brain perspective on marketing to be drawn into Burger King's left brain promotion of economic value. McDonald's stopped projecting human values in favor of projecting alleged product values.

ADVERTISING ETHICS SOMETIMES BECOME MURKY WHEN INVOKING PRINCIPLES OF SEMIOTICS

Semiotics has special significance in generating nonverbal communications, for often what can be morally implied through visual stimuli cannot be morally stated in words, as indicated by the story of how extras-large taillights came to be standard.

In the 1980s, Mercedes-Benz and several other overseas automakers, highly regarded for engineering excellence, were the first to install extra-large taillights on their cars. They did it for safety purposes. U.S. car manufacturers soon followed suit, persuaded that Euro-styled taillights on a car would suggest high-tech performance to car buyers, irrespective of the actual attributes of the vehicle in front of the taillights.[5] Imagery would thus transcend reality in a positive way without a vehicle's marketers having to say what might not be true.

Writing on semiotics in *Advertising Age,* Jay C. Houghton raised an interesting point when he said: "While we are legislated to truthfully depict a product's performance or substantiate our claims, no legislation governs the depiction of what it stands for or is symbolic of. How often do we see products positioned as symbols of success or achievement or sexual prowess when, in fact, they can contribute nothing to those ends?"[6]

Houghton's point has special relevance in second-half markets. If marketers *explicitly* project an unrealistic relationship between a product and the experiences it might provide, older customers who place the utmost value on honesty and authenticity are more likely to be repelled. However, *implying* that customers will have positive experiences as a result of buying a product is a different matter. In fact, that is essentially what successful conditional positioning is about. Is this manipulation? That is not the question. A better question is: Is this *unfair* manipulation? It depends. If what is implied is not possible, then it's unfair manipulation. If what is implied helps customers see themselves in an enjoyable relationship with a brand, that's fair, whether you call it manipulation or just damn good marketing. Marketers would do well to think in terms of Google's benchmark for maintaining its integrity: "Do no evil." Persuasion techniques are evil only when they lead to promises embodied in legal and emotional contracts being broken.

HOW A PLAIN, UNMARKED DELIVERY TRUCK MADE EGGS TASTE BAD

Houghton, who was marketing manager for Audi of America at the time I first cited him in *SAM* 1990, used the term *transformation process* to describe how people infer attributes and benefits from a product's design (e.g., big taillights on a Chevy mean good engineering because Mercedes has big taillights) without regard to objective reality. Perhaps a more descriptive term than transformation process would be meaning transference, referring to the transfer of values from one object to another object without respect for objective reality. Its acronym, "MT," carries an appropriate irony about it, when pronounced out loud.

A client once told me a story that illustrates how people infer meanings from symbols that lead to perceptions that reality does not support.

The client, a developer of extended services retirement communities, sometimes stayed overnight in his communities to learn firsthand about residents' feelings about their community and its management. On one visit, residents complained, "The eggs don't taste as good as they used to before you started buying them from that low-cost outfit."

My client checked with kitchen staff. No one had changed egg suppliers. Instead, the egg supplier had changed trucks. Eggs were previously delivered in trucks marked with, let's say, "Farm Fresh Eggs from Farmer Brown." For some reason, Farmer Brown switched to delivering his eggs in a plain, unmarked truck. Residents associated the symbol of an unmarked truck with cheaper, inferior products. This inference translated into poorer-tasting eggs.

Obviously, there's no relationship between taillights and engineering excellence or between how good eggs taste and what the truck delivering them looks like. Yet, people can and often do draw such irrational conclusions, thereby trumping logic.

Richard Nixon gave us one of the most celebrated examples of meaning transference as a candidate for vice president in 1952 when he suddenly faced calls to step aside because of charges that he had accepted money from a secret political slush fund.

Toward the end of his speech, with cameras moving in on a cocker spaniel at his side, Nixon said:

"A man down in Texas heard Pat on the radio mention that our two youngsters would like to have a dog, and, believe it or not, the day we left before this campaign trip we got a message from Union Station in Baltimore, saying they had a package for us. We went down to get it. You know what it was?

It was a little cocker spaniel dog, in a crate that he had sent all the way from Texas, black and white, spotted, and our little girl Tricia, the 6-year-old, named it Checkers.

And you know, the kids, like all kids, loved the dog, and I just want to say this, right now, that regardless of what they say about it, we are going to keep it."

What Nixon was *really* saying was "regardless of what *they* say about *it*, we are going to keep *Richard Nixon.*"

Nixon's creative employment of meaning transference was amazingly successful. Over the next 24 hours, more than a million Americans generated an avalanche of phone calls, telegrams, and letters to register their support for Nixon. If any of those people viewed the matter rationally, they would have seen that the fate of the dog was unrelated to the fate of Richard Nixon. Nixon proved masterful in moving the issue from one invoking left brain logical responses to one invoking right brain emotional responses. It was a case of pure left brain bypass in what has since come to be famously known as Nixon's "Checkers speech."

As the Checker's speech demonstrates, marketing messages that stimulate meaning transference can be more powerful than messages designed to invoke rational responses because they produce emotionally charged responses that provide less of a target at which a person's left brain cynicism or prejudices can take pot shots.

PACKAGING AS A SYMBOL OF THE PRODUCT INSIDE

A phenomenon similar to meaning transference is what Davis Masten, of California-based Chesken & Masten, a firm specializing in image consulting, calls *sensation transference.* He describes it as a process by which consumers transfer feelings from advertising and packaging to the product itself.[7]

Apple Computer's early success has been attributed in part to the trendy, forward-looking design of boxes containing the high-tech electronics inside. It was a positive and powerful contrast with Big Blue's cool, utilitarian product design. Steve Job's designs resonated with values reflected in the symbols vocabulary of people who would become Apple's most dedicated users: people in creative design professions, especially advertising. Big Blue's products were for a stodgier crowd. After being booted out of Apple for awhile, then coming back to try and save what many thought was a dying company, Job's again drew on his own artistic soul and produced the sensational, multicolor iMac line, once again proving that people often do judge books by their covers, independent of what lies within. Enough people wanted a colorful new iMac that Jobs successfully reversed the company's fading fortunes. Cosmetics alone did not save Apple, but they did do much to put new life into a fading brand.

TWO MINDS IN ONE

Both sides of the brain are involved in processing symbols, but each plays a different role. It will serve well to go a bit deeper into the topic of *lateralization,* the term that brain scientists use in referring to the discrete specialties of the brain's hemispheres.

That there are two minds in one—the right brain mind and the left brain mind—has been subject to speculation for centuries. Neuroscientist Joseph E. Bogen, who shared a Nobel prize with Roger Sperry for studies of right and left brain specialization, quotes an 18th century speculator on the subject, "I hope you will believe Pythagoras and Plato, the wisest of the ancient philosophers, who, according to Cicero, divided the mind into two parts, one partaking of reason and the other devoid of it."[8]

Bogen once summarized the differences in specialties of the two hemispheres: "The left hemisphere of the cortex, which subtends language and mathematics, seems to process information primarily in sequential manner, appropriate to its specialties. The right side of the cortex processes its input more as a 'patterned whole,' that is, in a more simultaneous manner than does the left."[9]

Neuroscientist, Richard M. Restak, MD (author of the book *The Brain,* upon which the award-winning PBS series of the same name was based), addressed the right brain's role in emotions thusly: "Subjects have been shown to strongly favor the right hemisphere for the memory storage of emotionally charged material."[10]

"Emotionally charged material"—isn't that what marketers have always tried to get into their messages? That fact that emotionally charged material is processed first in the right hemisphere is more than just a matter of academic interest to marketers. As said several times before, to get a message securely into a customer's conscious mind, the right brain must gauge the message's relevance, which it does by its measure of the emotional responses to the message.

Because each hemisphere processes information differently, reaching each requires different approaches. Sometimes marketing messages are nearly pure right brain; beer ads are generally more right brain–oriented than left brain–oriented. Sometimes ads are nearly pure left brain; ads strongly promoting features, functional benefits, and price are left brain ads. Car ads, especially models in the middle and lower price ranges, tend more often to be more left brain–oriented than right brain–oriented

Marketing communications can be made more effective by taking into account the fact that though the two hemispheres operate somewhat independently, they tend to cooperate in determining a final course of action on a matter. A well-balanced ad speaks to both hemispheres.

Scientific validation of the "two minds in one" premise grew from research begun in 1961 by Bogen and Sperry at the California Institute of Technology when Bogen severed the cortex of 16 epileptic patients suffering from life-threatening seizures. Thus separated, each hemisphere could be independently studied. The most startling discovery was that "instead of the normally unified stream of consciousness, these patients behave in many ways as if they have two independent streams of conscious awareness, one in each hemisphere, each of which is cut off from and out of contact with the mental experiences of the other. In other words, each hemisphere seems to have *its own separate and private sensations, its own perceptions, its own impulses to act . . .*"[11] (Italics added.)

THE HEMISPHERE PRINCIPLE OF MARKETING COMMUNICATIONS

Perhaps no point in this book has more importance than the following confirmed fact:

Absent emotional response to a stimulus, a person cannot substantively relate the object of the stimulus to his or her personal interests.

From this fact flows the *hemisphere principle* of marketing communications:

Lead with the right; Follow with the left.

One might challenge the claim that emotional arousal is essential to engaging customers' attentions by arguing that price circulars, which only name products and list their sales prices, are devoid of emotional stimuli. However, you only need to recall an instance when you found a favorite wine, an item of wearing apparel, or some component for your computer assembly at a rare, deep discount to see otherwise. The urgency you suddenly felt to go shopping for the item is a signal of emotional arousal. So, even those television ads shouting 0 percent interest rates and $2,000 rebates on cars must trigger emotional responses in customers to be effective.

While emotional arousal is precedent to rational processing, what induces emotional arousal is subject to season-of-life factors. One 18-year-old watching another 18-year-old wearing an Old Navy sweat suit, careening down a hill on a skateboard in a television commercial, can usually be more deeply (emotionally) drawn into the ad than a 48-year-old watching the same commercial. On the other hand, a 48-year-old is far likelier to be drawn into a Princess Cruise Line commercial than an 18-year-old. It is not simply a matter of difference in affluence, but season-of-life differences in lifestyle or experiential aspirations.

In principle, targeting brain hemispheres is easy. Headlines and body copy that deal with facts and reasons may involve more left brain processing unless some attention-getting fact like "50% to 70% off sale" grabs the right brain to signal "This is important; I've been wanting a new fall coat, and now's my chance to get one and save a lot of money." However, a sense of the need for a fall coat may have to be present before the announcement of a deep-discount sale grabs a person's attention. Because I don't play computer games, an ad announcing steep discounts for games won't get my serious attention. On the other hand, a PlayStation 2 television commercial showing a grandpa and his grandson zapping alien spaceships might get my attention because I have six grandsons, all of whom are into computer games. This is not an inconsequential thought because, as noted in an earlier chapter, the grand-parent market is exploding. Companies that think their primary market is kids, are missing an opportunity if they ignore grandparents who buy a lot of stuff for grandkids.

Applying the Hemisphere Principle to Direct Response Marketing

Fund-raising organizations regularly employ the hemisphere principle with some skill because experience has taught them that they must stir people's emotions to get their attention and move them toward making a donation. Recall solicitations from organizations like Save the Children. The first thing that grabs your attention is the face of a distressed child or sometimes the face of a child so angelic looking that an involuntary smile might crease your face. After the solicitation piece has your attention, it presents grist for the left brain mills of reason—numbers of children needing help, how many die each year for lack of help, what little amount of money it takes to save a child, and so on. Save the Child mailers speak first to the right brain, then to the left brain, and generally close with an integration of left and right brain–oriented stimuli.

Some time ago, I was engaged by Alexander Hamilton Life Insurance to write two prospecting letters for 45-to-65-year-olds. In a 60,000-unit mail drop, my letters, which had right brain leads, were mailed with two standard letters that had left brain leads and had previously delivered satisfactory results. The best-performing left brain letter read:

Dear _____

Imagine the perfect vacation. Would it be traveling to some exotic new resort? Or reading a stack of mysteries at home? Would it be mastering a new golf course? Or visiting your grandchildren?

Now consider a relevant fact: retirement for many people lasts 20 years or more. Can you imagine 20 vacations?

My point is that it will take a little bit of planning to accomplish all you want in retirement. That's why many of my clients are reviewing their retirement plans now. After all, one's retirement should be meaningful, fulfilling, and free from financial worry. Through careful planning now, you can do everything—travel, sports, theater, community work—that makes for a highly rewarding retirement.

My right brain letter read:

Dear _____

I was walking through the woods behind my house awhile back and saw a sixtysomething couple with what appeared to be a grandchild, a little girl of about 7. It was one of those scenes in life you sometimes unsuspectingly come across that stirs something in you deeply.

The grandmother was sitting on a tree stump, eating a bright red apple while writing something on a pad. Granddad was on his knees, holding up a rock, pointing out to his granddaughter tiny creatures that were clinging to the rock and scurrying about on the moist musky ground he had uncovered. Curiously, a crow perched high in a nearby tree was frantically squawking as though letting me know he was enjoying the scene as much as I was. That must have been so because crows usually don't like people around.

That scene has replayed itself in my mind many times since that day. I have been wondering about the joys I will seek in my retirement and wondering about all those I have helped in planning life in retirement.

At first blush, the first letter might seem to have a right brain lead. However, the series of questions it asks require cognitive processes in the left brain to analyze and appraise preferences. The letter goes on to state an alleged fact (the left brain loves facts), and then *lectures* the reader about how to have a rewarding retirement through wise planning.

The second letter is friendly from the start. It asks nothing of the reader but to enjoy what is being read. The opening paragraphs create a word picture. The right brain doesn't care much about words—it can't even process them without the help of the left brain—but it loves word pictures. The first paragraph sets the mood—a standard practice of good storytellers. The second paragraph was designed to invoke responses in all five senses. (Remember, the right brain works in sensory images.)

There was a good reason for stimulating neuronal activity in all five senses in the right brain letter. Many of the same sensory neurons that fire when you bite into an apple may fire when you see the picture of a person biting into an apple or read about someone eating an apple. If big red juicy apples appeal to you, reading about someone else eating one may incline you to lower your defenses against the messages in the letter. Also, if you are in the target age group for that letter and have a granddaughter, the idyllic scene may especially appeal to you.

Before learning about the response rates to the two letters, consider the kind of response the letter sometimes provokes in other marketers.

"I don't like the mushy letter about walking in the woods at all," said a creative director in a prominent New York independent agency. Given that she appeared to be in her later 40s, I was surprised.

"When I get something in the mail from someone who's trying to sell me something, I want them to get right to the point," she lectured me.

Remember the New Balance ad that said, "The shortest distance between two points is not the point," to reflect a runner's motivation to enjoy his outing rather than have it be a test of efficiency and endurance? The creative director was allegedly into efficiency, and preferred the shortest distance possible between the letter's opening and its call for action at the end. However, many recipients obviously felt differently. It drew nearly a 14 percent response in contrast with just about 1.5 percent response for the standard letter—same mail drop, same list.

Perhaps had the creative director seen the right brain letter at home instead of in a professional venue she might have liked it better. Seeing it on the job caused her to trot out the old line that consumers don't like to read a lot of copy. I wondered why she wasn't interested in turning the encounter with the letter into a learning experience ("David, I'm surprised. I like the other letter better. But why do you think your letter pulled the biggest response?"). The trouble was, as my friend George the engineer complained at the beginning of Chapter 4, "Marketers are too defensive, too close to the chest. They're not open. They get pissed off when you challenge them. Engineers are much more open to challenge."

Right Brain Ads Can Bypass Customer Skepticism

Effective right brain–oriented communications tend to be more subtle than left brain–oriented communications. Stuart Agres, executive

VP/director of strategic planning for Lowe Marshalk at the time I wrote *SAM* 1990, said, "A subtle approach works better because it has a chance to get past the consumer's barrier of skepticism."[12] A subtle approach also frees up customers' imaginations to define the product or service in terms of their own values, needs, and desires—again, the essence of conditional positioning.

Agres's firm conducted studies of rational (left brain) ads versus ads combining rational and emotional (right brain) messages and found the latter to score significantly higher in both recall and persuasion. By combining elements that appeal to *both* sides of the brain, the marketer presents a *cognitively holistic* message that will be more effective with older consumers. An ad that appeals to only one side of the brain, especially the left side, invites buyer skepticism and resistance because of uncertainty about the total nature of a product.

Stories trigger responses in both hemispheres, while didactically delivered claims about a brand are likely to trigger lopsided processing in the left brain. I use a Nestlé's Classic Coffee commercial in workshops to demonstrate the power of storytelling because it is a *whole brain* approach to communicating with customers. In the commercial, "First Date . . . Again," a middle-aged cowboy is gussying up for what is presumably his first date in years. His young daughter, appearing just on the cusp of adolescence, watches with loving amusement as her father nervously prepares for his "first date . . . again." She boils a kettle of water to make her father a cup of coffee. No words are exchanged, nor are any spoken by a narrator. The only sounds are a whistling tea kettle and Fats Domino singing "I'm in Love Again" The story ends as the cowboy meets his date standing on a street outside a rather plain-looking restaurant where she either works or they will dine together. You never quite know.

The commercial triggered hundreds of letters from viewers, mostly older women. Many told of how "First Date . . . Again" made them cry. Some called the station running the commercial in their area to find out when it would next air so they could record it. Many said the commercial was a topic of conversation among their friends. One woman said she bought a jar of Nestlé even though she didn't drink coffee. Others said the commercial, which had no spoken urgings, motivated them to change brands.

As Abbot Joseph said, "Storytellers help us process our lives." In fact, one woman wrote in telling Nestlé that years ago she was "a first date . . . again" (the commercial opened with those words, as the cowboy was coming in from the range). She said the story of the cowboy on his first date in years deeply touched her because of a similar experience 25 years earlier. Now all she had was memories, because her "a first date . . . again" passed on five years ago. Seeing the cowboy story brought it all back, and though it made her cry, they were tears of fond remembrance of a wonderful life experience.

Beware of Negative Symbols

One day while talking to a client about how negative symbols often repel prospects for senior housing communities, I told him of one I had visited whose designers really blew it on this score. It was a single building community with a "Y" footprint like many nursing homes have. I was there at the request of its owner to diagnose why sales were poor despite upscale ambience.

At the end of my daylong visit, a company VP escorted me down a *very* long hallway to an elevator on the way to the apartment I was to stay in for the night. The elevator door opened to reveal a cavernous space large enough to hold a small party. It looked like the elevators found in nursing homes and hospitals that transport gurneys. I commented on the size of the elevator and the VP smiled with obvious pride and said, "Yes, they're great. We wanted to use golf carts to transport residents from the lobby to their apartments so we made these elevators large enough to accommodate golf carts."

It never occurred to the community's designers or its developer that the golf cart service emphasized the long nursing home–type corridors and that the gurney-sized elevator made a grim statement about prospects for those who lived there. Show that elevator to a 25-year-old and he will say, "Great! Finally, an elevator big enough to hold furniture!" But show the elevator to a 75-year-old and he might think, This is where they carry the bodies out.

The client to whom I was telling this story responded, "I know what you're saying. We had Otis install the elevators we need for gurneys sideways and put in a small love seat. That makes our elevators look like pleasant oversized elevators rather than nursing home elevators."

My client and I had been discussing the semiotics of architecture. French semiologist Roland Barthes reminds us that the discipline of semiotics includes "any system of signs, whatever their substance and limits; images, gestures, musical sounds, objects, and the complex associations of all these . . ."[13] Every detail of the retirement community that looked like a nursing home was subject to approval or disapproval by every visitor because every detail projects a message. The same is true of every detail of every ad, and every detail of every design element of every product, and of every detail—body language, dress, voice, and all—of every person who has direct contact with customers. It might be a good idea if companies had a CSO—chief semiotics officer—to be in charge of evaluating the meaning of everything customers might experience.

Anti-Being Experience Symbols

Unwittingly, the architect of the nursing home look-alike community had created a design replete with strong symbols of *anti-being experience,* which are:

Experiences that discomfort a person, or tend to threaten or actually thwart a person from being what he or she wants to be.

When a product's design or a service program conveys symbols of conditions that repel a person, it conveys anti–being experience messages.

Everyone experiences anti–being experiences. We suffer countless incidents throughout our lives that threaten or thwart us from being what or who we want to be. Most of the time it is people we know who unwittingly or otherwise inflict us with anti–being experiences. A boss who fails to acknowledge a dedicated and productive worker subjects the worker to an anti–being experience. A spouse who seeks to control his or her partner does the same. Anti–being experiences can be so devastating that people quit their jobs over them or divorce their spouses, or they can be so mild that they do little more than irritate a person. Essentially, anti–being experiences interfere with a person's safe, comfortable, and pleasurable being.

An advertising executive told me once how he unwittingly subjected an elderly woman to an anti–being experience. Headed for church one Sunday, he encountered a neighbor in her 80s who reached the church steps at the same time he did. He reached for her arm, which she immediately withdrew with the instruction: "Don't take my arm. If I want help, *I'll take yours.*" She put him on notice that he was inflicting her with an anti–being experience. He was not letting her be what she wanted to be, or was assuming her to be other than she was.

Anti–being experience messages trigger identity values–originated self-preservation imperatives. They are the antithesis of a principle of marketing generally attributed to David Ogilvy: *People tend to buy products and services that reflect images of who they want to be.* No one wants to be ill or dependent. No one wants to be surrounded by cues that are reminders of what he or she does not want to be. Regardless of their ages, people don't like messages that group them with a class of people who are being what they would rather not be.

When marketers exalt the virtues of youth in advertising, thereby conveying the idea that young is good and older is bad, they unwittingly subject middle-aged and older people to anti–being experiences. Older is not bad. It's just different. How about doing a bit of idealization in product messages of the virtues of being middle age and older? More temperate, wiser, more caring, less judgmental, and indeed more interesting because they have more of a story to tell—all of which are attributes of people on the self-actualization track. Who knows what the payoff from the New Customer Majority would be for your company. Remember, the New Customer Majority is already 45 percent larger than the under-40 adult crowd, will be 60 percent larger in 2010, and will be, moneywise, a trillion dollar larger market.

Given the currently irreplaceable importance of the New Customer Majority—meaning many companies cannot grow their sales without it—it makes sense to "snake-check" every ad, every direct mail package, every word, and every picture of every marketing communication for anti–being experience symbols.

The imperturbable Alexander Haig, secretary of state under President Nixon, imposed a protocol at the State Department that called for "snake-checking" documents before they left the State Department. He appropriated the term from his military experience. When soldiers on bivouac return long after sundown to their sleeping areas, they check their sleeping bags for any snakes that may have slithered in during the heat of the day. Haig brought the colorful term to the State Department to encourage staff to double-check documents for "hidden snakes" that could create untoward results.

Marketing communications directed at older markets—and the older they are, the more important this is—should be carefully snake-checked for untoward readings of symbols, perhaps inadvertently created by less-experienced people who lack full sensitivity to the values of various symbols among older people.

CONCLUSION

It is not only important—obviously—to avoid anti–being experience symbols, but to draw on positive symbols to strengthen the mind-opening power of marketing communications. In this regard, using Figure 7.1 in Chapter 7, which reflects the primary developmental objective, survival focus, and life story theme of each season of life might be helpful. There is a panoply of symbols that stand for each of those dimensions of life seasons. To strongly connect with customers, project their values through symbols that stand for those values.

Consider, for example, Fall—the season of midlife. Its primary developmental objective is development of the inner self. This involves heightened focus on achieving balance between work and play, and between service to self and service to others. Symbols acknowledging the decline of materialistic and narcissistic influences can reflect a company's empathetic grasp of midlife. The midlife search for meaning, reflected in some New Balance ads, can be a strong plank in the empathetic bridge to midlife customers' minds. Also, think of the objective in Fall to *be someone* that contrasts the objective in Summer of *becoming someone*. The symbols standing for each are different. The primary symbols for Summer have a social orientation and cast a materialistic shadow. The primary symbols for Fall have an inner self-orientation and cast an experiential shadow. In Summer, the shortest distance between two points *is* the point, but in Fall (and more so in Winter), it is *not* the point.

To avoid confusion, recommending marketing communications based on particular seasons of life is not in conflict with the core tenets of ageless marketing. Be ageless when speaking to all, be season-of-life relevant when speaking to an age group. New Balance has shown that you can market to older people without turning off younger people. Remember, it has had 25 percent annual growth in a category with no growth since the mid-1990s by appealing to both aging boomers and young people. That says much for the power of ageless marketing. It says much for choosing symbols that position a product comfortably in the minds of people of all ages.

14

BUILDING
EMPATHETIC BRIDGES

No one more profoundly affected acting in the 20th century than Constantin Stanislavsky, the creator of *method acting*. Among his tradition-shattering theories of acting was his belief that an actor's main responsibility was to be believed—even over being recognized or understood.

To achieve belief in the minds of the audience, Stanislavsky held that actors must draw on their emotional memories. To express fear on stage, for instance, the actor would remember a personal terrifying experience, and then reincarnate that fear on stage. Stanislavsky knew that this would generate empathetic connections between the audience and the characters on stage to tighten the relationship between actor and playgoer. Having actors inject their personalities into a play was a major break from theater tradition. Before method acting, actors were supposed to leave their emotions behind and become the character they played as envisioned by the playwright.

Another title for this chapter could be *method marketing* because it's about building empathetic connections with customers.

Stanislavsky taught actors how to emotionally connect with audiences because he knew that people go to plays to be moved, not taught. Playgoers might value a play for its power to enlighten, but unless its intellectual content is emotionally arousing, the play will not succeed. Similarly, customers must have strong emotional connections with brands to stay loyal to them.

Building customer loyalty is one of the biggest issues in business today. Everyone knows by now that it costs more to get customers than to keep them, and that long-term customers are generally more profitable than short-term customers. Nevertheless, weak customer loyalty has become a national corporate plague. CRM was supposed to help cure this problem through computer-generated personalized offerings and messages enabled by sophisticated data mining software. However, as Harvard's Susan Fournier and her colleagues reported in a 1999 *Harvard Business Review* article, the proliferation of mass-produced automated communications alienates many customers.[1] Beyond some threshold, automated personalization trivializes personal relationships. If customers don't feel special, they don't feel loyal.

Richard Forsythe, chief CRM guru at CRM-forum.com, reported in one of his weekly epistles that a Proctor & Gamble product manager sang the blues at a September 2002 CRM conference in Paris. He summarized the product manager's woeful tale as follows:[2]

1. Internet-branding doesn't work for us anymore because generic goods are gaining market share.
2. Advertising doesn't work for us anymore because there are no mass channels of communication left.
3. Product innovation doesn't work anymore because competitors can copy and roll-out successful innovations within three months of launch.
4. We've tried CRM, but we don't seem to be able to get it to work for FMCG (fast-moving consumer goods).
5. Could somebody please help? We don't know what to do.

To get a better insight into the marketing manager's plaint, let's revisit Stanislavsky's idea that achieving believability with the audience is more important than achieving recognition or understanding of what transpires in an actor's role. When an actor fails to act believably, he fails to engage his audience no matter the brilliance of the play. Similarly, a brand will not engage customers no matter its merits if it lacks believability—which makes it no more desirable than a cheaper generic product (as in complaint 1).

Saying that advertising is not working any more because there are no mass channels of communications left (complaint 2) disregards advertising's increasing irrelevance to customers because—let's face it— marketers are less in touch with customers, their needs, and what motivates them than ever before. If that weren't true, then marketing would be working.

The complaint that product innovation doesn't work anymore because competitors can copy and roll out successful innovations within three months of launch (complaint 3) is a product-centric perspective in a era when a customer-centric perspective works better in solving marketing problems.

The fact that CRM has not served P&G as well as it hoped in fast-moving consumer goods (complaint 4) is not unique. CRM hasn't worked for hundreds of companies across a wide range of categories. CRM initiatives have consistently overpromised and underdelivered because they have ignored the "soft side" or subjective dimensions of customer behavior.

"Could somebody please help? We don't know what to do." This is a cry that thousands of companies are issuing today.

DEFICITS IN EMOTIONALITY AND BELIEVABILITY UNDERLIE THE P&G PRODUCT MANAGER'S PLAINT

The P&G marketing manager might do well to look at his issues from a method marketing perspective. In an era of unprecedented poverty of public trust in institutions and organizations, the believability of a brand is prerequisite to emotional investment by customers. Some people may still argue that customers don't usually get emotionally involved with brands, but Antonio Damasio's studies of Mr. Spock–like brain patients have made it clear that lacking the ability to experience emotional arousal, a person cannot cognitively determine whether something is personally relevant to him or her. In other words:

A marketing message or brand *must* generate emotional arousal for customers to be able to experience the message or brand as having personal relevance to them.

That is *not* theory. It is *empirically proven fact.*

Messages and brands that don't arouse emotions won't survive information triage with enough force to be engaging and compelling. Consider what a recent study of how brains process brands found:

- "Brand names engage the 'emotional' right-hand side of the brain more than other words."
- "A brand's power is that it conjures up a whole range of associations and ideas, which are primarily emotional."
- "(This research) supports our instinctive belief that brands are a special class of word—they are like a poem all in one word in their ability to evoke and express ideas."[3]

Consider the matter settled: Brand loyalty starts in the *emotional* right brain. Customers don't attach themselves to brands for left brain rational reasons. They become bonded with a brand when it generates pleasure that customers want to sustain.

The idea that a brand is like a poem all in one word in its ability to evoke and express ideas, is consistent with the right brain's ability to present an image, complete and instantaneous, in contrast with the left brain's more plodding way of sequentially stitching the pieces of an image together. Even when the left brain completes a picture, it is an incomplete picture because the left brain works by exclusion. It bypasses details of least importance. The right brain works by inclusion. It "conjures up a whole range of associations and ideas, which are primarily emotional," to form a more complete picture than the left brain does.

This information begins to make it clearer why CRM widely fails promises made in its name by software vendors and CRM consultants. Customers' actions, their demographic profiles, and their rational responses as recorded in surveys, can be reduced to the bits and bytes of databases and manipulated by exclusionary left brain Boolean logic in data mining programs. But what emerges is an incomplete picture, not the much-promised and much-coveted *360-degree* picture of customers. What's missing is input from the emotional right brain, which plays the largest role in generating desire and the motivations to satisfy them, and gauging degree of satisfaction. You cannot pull people into a brand via the rational left brain. You cannot argue customers into buying a product. Only by stimulating their emotions can you entice them into buying a product—provided they have a need or desire for it.

One good reason why branding isn't working, nor advertising, nor product innovation, nor CRM—the P&G marketing manager's four complaints—is that a lot of marketing today does a poor job of engaging customers' emotions. Marketers invite customers into their theaters, give short shrift to the issue of believability, and fail to entice customers to make an emotional investment in the marketing play. As a result, marketers' plays are closing right and left in the theatrical realms of marketing.

Challenges to creating believability with customers have reached epochal proportions because of the tsunami of corporate misdeeds that broke into the open in the wake of the dot-com crash. Public distrust was driven further down by the complicity of the independent accounting firm of Arthur Andersen, that proved not to be very independent in the giant Enron collapse. The pandemic of purposely distorted stock analyses on Wall Street cost ordinary people trillions in loses in retirement funds, forcing many to delay retirement and others to retire from retirement. Throw in the Catholic church's egregious protection of pedophile priests and one is left wondering who can be trusted anymore. Customers' minds don't work in a vacuum. Never have so many trusted so few. Marketing is not only victim of its own mistakes, but it must cope with the side effects of the trust-withering misbehavior that haunts every sector of society today. Melinda Davis is quite right when she says that the times call for marketers to become healers. But the healer's power depends on believability.

Argument Advertising versus Drama Advertising

We believe people when we *feel* they are believable. We *think* people are believable only after they make us *feel* they are believable. For a long time, marketers widely argued for giving customers reasons to buy products by describing product features and benefits. In this era of pandemic unbelievability, selling features and benefits is not working so well anymore. A few years ago, a team of researchers decided to test left brain–oriented advertising based on reasons to buy versus right brain advertising based on evoking feelings, or in the researchers' terms, *argument* advertising versus *drama* advertising.[4]

The researchers found that argument advertising elicits counterarguments in customers' minds *before* believability is established if it ever does get established. On the other hand, provided that drama advertising drama engages them pleasurably, customers go directly to belief. While "drama draws the viewer into the action it portrays . . . argument holds the viewer at arm's length."[5] That is another way of saying that argument advertising invites defensive responses whereas drama advertising lowers defenses.

The study offers valuable insight into why customers connect more readily with drama advertising (provided it is well executed) than argument advertising (even when it is well executed): "Drama's subjunctive mood gives up the ability to make explicit claims in exchange for *the power of empathy*."[6] (Italics added.) A product message that empathetically connects with a customer immediately gets his or her attention. When customers experience this empathetic connection, they *feel* the sponsor of the connection is believable.

Observing that argument advertising "is plotless, characterless, and narrated [while] drama has plot and character but no narrator,"[7] the researchers found that argument advertising tends to be slower in generating attention and harder to cognitively follow than drama. This squares with developmental psychologist Cynthia Adams's finding that "with both younger and older subjects, recall for narrative text has been shown to be more reconstructive than is recall for expository text. . . . [In expository text] most of the critical meaning is explicitly represented."[8] By "reconstructive recall" Adams means that readers, young and old, subjectively contribute something of themselves into the story, whereas in recalling expository text (such as used in argument advertising), only the literal content is recalled.

From a marketing perspective, this means that customers can more easily identify with a brand and become emotionally involved with it when the brand appears as a character in a story than when it is the object of an argument or tutorial. Though this is true for all ages, it has particular relevance in second-half markets for reasons already discussed. So it would seem that marketers need to do more and better storytelling to increase marketing productivity. As Rolf Jensen says in *The Dream Society*, "Storytelling has become an important part of market strategy; whoever tells the best story, and whoever tells it best will win."

BELIEVABILITY IS MULTIDIMENSIONAL

Initial believability is less a derivative of rational proof than of feelings. That is why Stanislavsky put emotionally grounded believability ahead of a play's rationally grounded logic. Consider how many things we believe that cannot be proven. Many believe in God, though His existence cannot be objectively proven. On the other hand, people also find things believable that have objectively been proven wrong. The Flat Earth Society, which brags on its Web site, "Deprogramming the masses since 1547," offers strenuous arguments on why the Earth is flat and how scientists, governments, and businesses promote the fiction of a round Earth circling the sun for their own selfish purposes. In the end, believability is a function of feelings, which themselves are a function of emotions. Reason plays but a supporting role in what we believe. The lead character is emotion.

The doctrine of *one-to-one marketing*, as promoted by Don Peppers and Martha Rogers who coined the term, stresses the importance of dialogues with customers on the premise that ongoing dialogues will reveal important insights about customers and help in forming a so-called 360-degree view of customers. I have argued that simply talking with customers and tracking their actions cannot produce a 360-degree view of customers. One most go deep into the bottomless pit of the unconscious mind to dig out information that customers cannot tell anyone and that cannot be directly observed. Still, the idea of conducting dialogues with customers is a good one. However, how does one develop dialogues with customers that provide useful guidance? At the heart of the answer lie the social rules for creating believability.

Asking a customer what he or she wants and how he or she wants it delivered is not a dialogue. It's an information request. I have the impression that when most people praise the idea of having dialogues with customers, they are talking about ratcheting up information request activity.

In sponsoring dialogues with customers, a marketer's first task is the same as the first task Stanislavsky imposed on his actors: *accepting responsibility for creating believability.* Unlike directors before him, Stanislavsky did not depend on the content of the play to carry the performance. He wanted actors to be more than animated mannequins mouthing the words of the playwright. His actors were challenged to blur the boundaries between the make-believe on stage and the real worlds of people in the audience by bringing the play's lines to life through the personality of the actor.

Turning back to marketing, most marketing performances take place in the same kind of existential milieu in which theatrical plays took place before Stanislavsky transformed acting. Between marketers and customers lies a boundary as impermeable as the one that once divided actors and audiences. That boundary separates the marketer's imaginary world, which is populated by statistical customers and defined by hopes of bending customers to the marketer's will, from the real worlds of customers.

Stanislavsky's ideas, adapted to marketing, could help solve the P&G marketing manager's problems. Tear down that wall, marketer, now! That wall keeps you from connecting with your customers. Give life to your role as a helpmate in customers' efforts to process their lives. Humanize yourself as a method actor does and project that self into your audience. Make yourself believable, and you just may see amazing results. Take your product messaging out of the lecture hall into the theater as Virgin Atlantic's Richard Branson and Joe Boxer's Nick Graham have done.

Graham, self-designated as Chief Underwear Officer, turned one of the most boring items of apparel—men's underwear—into a fun product, or as Graham says, "the brand is the amusement park; the product is the souvenir." Graham and Branson have teamed up several times in one of the zaniest corporate alliances ever. In one cross-marketing venture, Graham and Branson once concocted an offer, "Buy Five and See London in Your Underpants," whereby people who bought five pairs of Joe Boxer underwear qualified for a $99 companion ticket on Virgin Airlines to London. On one Virgin Atlantic flight, Graham and Branson dressed up as stewardesses and announced, "U.S. Customs requires that all passengers change their underwear."

Each company must determine its own personality, but the personality should be human—and fun in some respect. If Nick Graham can make men's underwear an interesting experience, then certainly almost any product can be made more interesting than it probably is. Think of this in terms of the last time you were at a cocktail party, trapped in a conversation by a very boring person. Customers don't want to have dialogues with very boring companies. So the first social rule to honor in establishing dialogues with customers is *be interesting!*

The Three Dimensions of Dialogues with Customers That Lead to Believability

Once a customer perceives a company as interesting, the first step toward believability has been accomplished. Believable, sustainable, and *enjoyable* dialogues depend less on content, as in a Stanislavsky-directed play, than on style in the opening stages of dialogue. Ultimately, of course, substance is needed to give parties to a dialogue the feeling that what transpires is worth one's time.

Productive, believable, enjoyable dialogues with customers depend on the operating presence of three attributes: *conversational reciprocity, reciprocal empathy,* and *reciprocal vulnerability.*

Conversational reciprocity. This attribute is in place and fully operating when both sides in a dialogue exhibit evidence of listening to and being influenced by the other. It's not enough to invite consumers' input. Surveying customers for their feelings about a company or brand is not a dialogue. A company needs to show in palpable fashion how consumers' input influences the company. Running ads that say, "We listen to our customers" doesn't believably do it. Harley-Davidson's execution of conversational reciprocity helped bring it back from near extinction.

Two years after Vaughn Beals and his fellow executives bought Harley-Davidson from AMF, which pushed the company to the edge of bankruptcy, Beals and his executive colleagues founded the Harley Owners Group—the famous Harley HOGS. The HOGS provided Harley-Davidson with a neutral meeting ground for conducting two-way conversations between itself and customers. This gave the company subtle insights into customers that conventional customer research would overlook. It also gave Harley-Davidson a credible platform for showing customers how it allowed itself to be influenced by what its biker customers told them. Word spread that Harley loved its customers, and because everyone likes being loved, the brand was able to extend its reach across multiple generational divides. The average age of a new Harley owner is 46, but young bikers buy Harley-Davidson products, too, especially the Buell, with its flashier styling and signature throaty sound that announces the rider's macho presence from afar.

During the early days of Harley-Davidson's recovery, it suffered serious quality problems. However, by maintaining conversational reciprocity with its dealers as well as with its end customers, it was able to weather its product quality problems. Putting it another way, though Harley-Davidson was having problems keeping up with its legal contract, its delivery on its emotional contract held its dealer and customer relationships together until it got on course with its legal contract.

For another example of conversational reciprocity at work, check out "Don't Just Listen: Connect," by Paul Judge, in the August 2001 issue of *Fast Company,* accessible at <www.fastcompany.com> (keyword: Icenhower). Notwithstanding the earlier story of the depressed P&G product manager at a Parisian conference in 2002, P&G is doing something about sponsoring conversational reciprocity by using the Internet as a platform for two-way conversations between itself and customers. Building trust, not selling products, is the more important objective. Testifying to this, Bob Gilbreath, assistant product manager for Tide, was quoted in the article: "We tell you that you may have to scrub, or that there are some stains that no product (including Tide) will ever get out." Greg Icenhower, who manages Web-based conversational reciprocity for P&G, closed the *Fast Company* article stating, "So far, the biggest value of getting all this feedback has been letting consumers know we're listening."

Reciprocal empathy. Everyone talks about the value of connecting empathetically with consumers. However, it's not very often that one hears about the importance of making it possible for customers to connect empathetically with companies and brands. The customer-company/brand empathetic connection should be a two-way bridge. Mutual empathy will not only benefit sales, it can be a powerful antidote for an adverse event that threatens a brand. The makers of Tylenol learned this in spades in the early 1980s when someone laced Tylenol bottles on store shelves in the Chicago area with cyanide. A rash of sudden initially mysterious deaths ensued.

Tylenol faced overnight death as a brand. Famed ad man Jerry Della Femina proclaimed in *The New York Times,* "There may be an advertising person who thinks he can solve this and if they find him, I want to hire him, because then I want him to turn our watercooler into a wine cooler."[9]

It's not known whether Della Femina ever approached James Burke to transform his watercooler, but Burke did solve the problem. As chairman of Johnson & Johnson, owner of McNeil Consumer Products who made Tylenol, Burke ordered a total nationwide recall even though deaths had occurred only in the Chicago area. He stopped all advertising. In dealings with the media, he resisted any temptation to disavow responsibility for the poisonings. He advised everyone in the nation to not consume Tylenol, regardless of when it was bought.

Burke ordered company spokespeople to cooperate with the media, telling them that it was crucial in the interest of public safety to have the media as collaborators in getting information to the public rather than as antagonists playing to latent public contempt for greedy corporations. He invited *60 Minutes* pundit Mike Wallace in to observe him and his team working through the crisis. Media briefings were largely unformatted and scheduled for coverage on primetime news broadcasts. As a result of this openness, consumers empathetically related to Tylenol and its maker as victims along with those people who sadly had died from the poisonings, the first of whom was a bright, perky 13-year-old girl.

With public support, Burke saved the brand, which, after being returned to shelves in tamper-proof containers, saw its market share increase over what it had been before the poisonings. Compare those results with what Audi experienced after blaming drivers for injuries and deaths allegedly caused by the Audi 5000 suddenly accelerating from a standstill without warning. U.S. sales plummeted from nearly 75,000 to barely 12,000 cars. A little known fact is that Audi was vindicated. The National Highway Traffic Safety Administration ruled that driver error caused the unintended acceleration.[10] But it took Audi more than a dozen years to get back to its original sales levels.

For many years, it has been widely argued that basing brand communication strategies on the chance of consumers becoming emotionally involved is ludicrous. Give them reasons why they should buy the brand, *then they will feel good*. Resistance to the idea that emotions ultimately determine brand loyalty owes much to the left brain fiction of "the rational man" on which classical economics was founded. However, that notion has been retired by contemporary brain research, fortified by significant contributions from cognitive science. It seems that we automatically, though often unconsciously, think of nonhuman things in human terms and relate to them as though they were human. We *love* our cars and our homes, but may *hate* our computers when they crash, while being indifferent about the brand of detergent we use or the brand of washer and dryer in which we wash clothes. Love, hate, and indifference are emotional responses generated by the inanimate as well as the animate. Stanford University communications professors Byron Reeves and Clifford Nass have discovered some rather interesting things about this.

Reeves and Nass asked sophisticated computer users if they had any emotional connections with their computers. They all said no. Nevertheless, during Reeves and Nass's research, computer sophisticates demonstrated an unconscious bent for being polite to a computer when it asked how well it was doing in carrying out a task for the computer user. But when computer users were sent to another computer to be asked by it how well the first computer was doing its job, the computer users were less polite.[11] They criticized the first computer. In spite of what our rational minds tell us, we regard everything in terms of human qualities and interact with the inanimate as well as the animate accordingly.

Reeves and Nass ingeniously adapted studies of people's interaction with each other to their studies of people's interaction with media. They found, "It is possible to take a psychological research paper about how people respond to other people, replace the word *human* with the word *computer* and get the same results."[12]

Suspecting that people infer human personality affect from electronic media, Reeves and Nass wrote software that endowed computers with certain affects. Although these affects did not change a computer's performance, experienced computer users thought better of their machines, their work, *and themselves.*[13] Does this not suggest how a brand can contribute to healing? After all, Reeves and Nass remind us, "Virtually all interfaces have a personality. This literally applies to anything that presents words to a user, from toaster ovens and televisions to word processors and workstations."[14] I would also add brands, for they project images that customers convert to words. Thusly can creators of marketing communications endow a brand with human qualities that elicit desired responses from customers, especially—in the context of the present discussion—eliciting empathetic feelings for the brand.

I believe *brand empathy* played a role in consumers' rejection of New Coke by making them feel remorse over the demise of the original Coke that they had learned to love and cherish. This is not too far out for me, especially when I think about a stepdaughter who sometimes apologizes to vegetables that she rejects in the produce section of a grocery store. StarKist Tuna has long played to this human propensity to feel remorseful on behalf of the rejected. It has been drawing customers into its messages for years by rejecting Charlie the Tuna: "Sorry Charlie—only the best tuna go to StarKist." StarKist satisfies customers empathy for Charlie by making him StarKist's primary brand spokes . . . uh, spokesfish. He has played that role for over three decades. Tourists visiting Pago Pago, Charlie's official home, love having their picture taken in front of the Charlie the Tuna statue. StarKist has used a corny, Rodney Dangerfield–like fish caricature to humanize the brand so that customers can develop an emotional attachment to it—an enduring example of the idea that a brand's persona should say more about how it makes people feel than about its functional attributes.

Don't get me wrong. I am not saying anyone gets warm and gushy when they come to the tuna stacks at the grocers and see a can of StarKist. But anyone amused by Charlie's antics is likelier to pass on a can of Bumble Bee tuna and pull a can of StarKist off the shelf. After all, some people have such an empathetic affection for Charlie that they buy Charlie the Tuna statuettes.

Reciprocal vulnerability. Vulnerability and empathy are close cousins. A person becomes more vulnerable when he or she expresses empathy because something of the private inner self is revealed by the projection of empathy.

Marketers want consumers to make themselves vulnerable, to let down their defenses and not resist product messages. However, like empathy, vulnerability should flow in both directions. When you meet someone for the first time, you tend to be guarded. You each take baby steps toward more intimacy. As the other person lets his or her defenses down a notch, you lower yours a notch. Vulnerability humanizes both sides in a relationship.

Companies, encouraged by their legal counsel, often resist expressing vulnerability, sometimes at great expense. When the Bridgestone-Firestone tire problem involving Ford Explorers surfaced in 2000, Bridgestone-Firestone blamed drivers for not keeping tires properly inflated and Ford for not properly informing drivers. Ford was quieter, saying nothing about drivers' possible role, nor did it try to pin the blame on Bridgestone-Firestone. Meanwhile, Ford launched an ad campaign acknowledging that it had further to go to make vehicles what they should be, citing the need for better fuel consumption, less air pollution, and *greater safety*. There should be no surprise as to which company best survived the calamity.

Two years before the Tylenol poisonings, I was personally involved in a situation in which a client's willingness to make his company vulnerable helped solve a serious problem that threatened life and limb of his customers. The management company I owned managed a 1,683-unit rental community in Alexandria, Virginia, that had been renovated and converted into a condominium community. As part of the renovation, wall-mounted heaters were installed in bathrooms, just below the bathroom window. One night, a heater malfunctioned and started a fire, igniting the bathroom's window curtains. A week later, another bathroom fire broke out, then a few days later, yet another fire flared up. Clearly we had a serious, life-threatening product malfunction on our hands. Understandably, we also had an aroused and anxious community to deal with. People were afraid to go to sleep at night. The situation was tailor-made for a class action lawyer.

However, working with the developer, we brought the condominium's resident leadership into discussions about how best to deal with the crisis. Residents were involved in meetings with fire officials, representatives of the manufacturer, and the mayor and other politicians in Alexandria. We also had resident leaders join in on meetings with reporters. We hid nothing. Helping the developer's believability in this worrisome situation was the fact that he did not, as Bridgestone-Firestone did years later, slough off the crisis as the responsibility of someone else.

The problem was quickly solved with not even the hint of a lawsuit because the developer made himself vulnerable by making resident leaders full partners in solving the problem.

Over the 15 years that I was in the community management business, I learned about the critical importance of reciprocal vulnerability in building tight, collaborative relationships between customers and companies. When I founded Community Management Corporation in 1969, I adopted what then seemed a gutsy idea by organizing residents long before the developer had to turn the owners' association over to residents. Some client attorneys thought the idea was crazy because, "you're organizing the opposition." However, I learned from personal experience the value of reciprocal vulnerability in building loyal relationships with customers. *It reduces chances of lawsuits.*

In over 400 communities, representing more than 600,000 homes, no developer client was ever sued. We maintained continuing dialogues with residents, with a spirit of reciprocal vulnerability, according to what we called the four Cs—communicate constantly with candor and control.

Southwest's Herb Kelleher understands the power of reciprocal vulnerability. He has made it work handsomely for customers and shareholders alike. In an essay he wrote for the Peter F. Drucker Foundation in 1997, he summarized Southwest's marketing strategy thusly: "We market ourselves based on the personality and spirit of ourselves. That sounds like an easy claim but, in fact, it is a supremely dangerous position to stake out because if you're wrong, customers will let you know— with a vengeance. Customers are like a force of nature: You can't fool them, and you ignore them at your own peril."[15]

A 360-DEGREE VIEW OF CUSTOMERS IS A HOLISTIC VIEW

Empathy is not the same as *intellectually* understanding what another person is experiencing. Intellectual understanding results from different processes than those that lead to emotionally *identifying* with another person's circumstances, emotions, feelings, and motives. Damasio's patients can intellectually understand another person's situation because they have normal powers of reasoning, but they are incapable of empathetically identifying with other people. The power of reasoning is insufficient to produce a holistic 360-degree understanding of customers.

In a holistic understanding of another person, no attribute is seen alone—a truism that is commonly violated in consumer research by putting almost exclusive focus on getting information that relates to a brand and customers' perceptions of it. A holistic understanding of customers is indicated when a financial services company views its customers as more than just people with money to manage; a travel agent perceives its clients as more than just people who want to take a trip; a retailer thinks of customers as more than a means to move products; a health care provider sees customers as more than sick people. People in the second half of life generally have more holistic perceptions than people in the first half of life. To get in sync with members of the New Customer Majority, companies must work harder than most are doing now to see customers holistically.

We know from contemporary brain research that holistic perceptions are a specialty of the right brain. Given the apparent migration of mental activities toward the right brain in the second half of life, it may be that the strong desires of older people to "give back" is related in part to an increased ability to see things holistically—what happens to one of us happens to all of us—and perhaps even to the richer capacity for empathy that is implicit in the Fourth Face of the New Senior, *compassion for others and concern for the world about them.*

Young people are prone to feeling sympathy for people whose bodies have grown frail with age, are beset by painful chronic conditions, such as arthritis, and are facing the loss of aging spouses and friends. But sympathy is not the same thing as empathy, even though they share a common mother in emotion. Sympathy involves feeling *for* someone; empathy involves feeling *as* someone. One can have a capacity for sympathy without a comparable capacity for empathy.

Older people frequently complain about being patronized by younger people. Patronizing is an affect based on sympathy, not empathy. Most of us, regardless of our age, tend to be repelled by people feeling sorry for us. "I want your understanding, not your sympathy," is a common response to signs of sympathy. Marketers of pharmaceutical products, medical services, and extended services senior housing need to be especially on guard for unwitting symbols of sympathy or other undesirable affects.

One day while visiting my mother, who was in her mid-80s, she complained to me about how my oldest brother, Harry, had been after her to sign up for a medical alert system.

"He thinks I'm going to be out in the greenhouse one day and pass out and not be discovered for days. Well, just to get him off my back I agreed to see this man who was selling those things. You won't believe it. He wanted $2,500 and $40.00 a month! I can't afford that. Besides, I feel like someone is trying to take my freedom by signing up for one of those things. So I called your brother, Tony, and asked him to get me one of those portable memory phones. I can push 9-1-1 as I fall down in my greenhouse. And, hell," she concluded (she liked introducing bold ideas with "hell"), "where else would I like to go from?"

Mother saw a product commonly promoted as protecting freedom and independence as doing just the opposite. Being tethered to a medical alert call system wasn't freedom to her. Never mind that her 911 solution tied her to AT&T. By the way, the woman was really smart. The same medical alert system company was later shut down by the California attorney general's office because *its calls were being put through to 911.*

I later shared this story with two friends, one who had tried to get a ninetysomething aunt into a medical alert system, and another who tried to get his mother in her late-80s to buy the idea. Both men said their elderly relatives complained of people trying to take away their independence.

As a final comment on this story about my mother—to demonstrate the context sensitivity of people in the second half of life—she said she couldn't afford the medical alert system. Let me tell you what she could afford. While telling me her story about medical alert system, a crew was finishing up a Williamsburg picket fence around three sides of her acre-and-a-half yard. She was fencing the yard for, Beau, her 12-year-old Lhasa apso. "It's getting harder for me to walk Beau, so I want to give him his independence." So she spent $28,000 of my inheritance fencing in a middle-aged dog, but couldn't afford a medical alert system that might help keep her with this dog a bit longer.

The moral of the story about my mother's encounter with the medical alert system rep, is to not assume that the symbolic meaning that you see in a product is the same symbolic meaning seen by a person removed from you in age by a generation or more.

UNDERSTANDING PHYSIOLOGICAL CHANGES IN THE SECOND HALF OF LIFE

Assuming that most marketers under 40 are generally unfamiliar with how age-associated physical changes can influence customer behavior, and given that this chapter is about building empathetic bridges to customers' minds, it is fitting to close this chapter with a brief discussion of age-related physical changes that have marketing significance. Anyone committed to getting a 360-degree view of customers in their 50s and older need to be aware of these changes because they can influence product design, marketing, sales, point-of-sale environments, and post-sale servicing. By taking physiological and psychological changes associated with aging into account, you begin the processes of conveying empathy and establishing believability.

Age-related changes involve all five sensory systems as well as the muskuloskeletal system. Changes also take place in mental operations, some of which I have already addressed. The ensuing discussion briefly describes some of the more important of those changes, starting with changes to the visual sensory system.

Sight

Interestingly, visual acuity begins to reflect the effects of aging at the age of 8. Not 80, but *8!* At that age, the human eye reaches its optimum ability to maintain a crisp, clear image in constant fashion regardless of the vergence of light. At 50, that ability is virtually zero. The clarity of an image is altered by the differing angles of light. This produces discomfiting glare, especially in such a scenario as a woman trying to find the right cosmetic shades for her skin, or finding color-coordinated ensembles under the sterile essence of flourescent lighting.

Changes in visual acuity call for special consideration in choosing font and font size, paper finish, color of paper, and inks. Reverse type (white type on a dark background), which is commonly used ostensibly to get attention, is especially problematic. A brochure or ad may win an award for creative excellence but fail in its primary purpose if type size, ink choices, and production of glare thrown off by a high-gloss finish discourages a person from reading the brochure or ad.

Changes to the visual system in the second half of life should also be taken into account in designing ambient light in public accommodation areas from retail environments to restaurants. Product designers whose work includes design of instrumentation should likewise take these visual changes into account in designing gauges, thermostats, range and oven controls, etc. As a person well into the second half of life, after dark, I couldn't read the trip odometer on a Buick Park Avenue I had until recently. It was not only irritating, it was a matter of convenience and even safety when traveling at night in unfamiliar territory, trying to follow written directions that separated turning points by mileage.

While distance factors in visual acuity can often be corrected with glasses, no prosthetics can compensate for deficits in responding to illumination-related stimuli. For instance, slower response to light warrants special attention to ambient lighting, both directed and back-lighting of displays, and modulation of lighting in movies and television projections. Rapid contrast in scene changes, for example, creates problems like those experienced in adapting to the sudden appearance of oncoming headlights in night driving.

Important to remember is that the slowing down of information processing in the central nervous system reduces the capacity for distinguishing between colors and light intensities. Subtle gradations in color will not be detected by most people who are in their 60s and older. Visual responsiveness to pastels and combination of colors at the green-blue-violet end of the spectrum also declines. Experts in age-related visual acuities should be called in to evaluate retail and other public accommodation settings. Most certainly, architects, interior designers, and others who design visual environments in senior adult housing and health care facilities know about visual challenges created by aging optical systems. Those who prepare print and broadcast advertising should be educated about changing visual acuities.

Because of several conditions, including altered responses to light and changes in the curvature of the lens of the eye, depth perception decreases with age. This increases the importance of giving special attention to stairway lighting and to the use of color breaks to mark changes of elevation in public areas.

Accommodating the visual acuity changes that I am talking about doesn't just apply to the over-60 or over-70 crowd. All of these changes are underway by the early- to-mid 40s. These changes have never been a major issue before in marketing because youth and young adults dominated markets. Now, however, companies that want to succeed in New Customer Majority markets would do well to understand changes in visual acuity in the second half of life and how to accommodate them. Consider, for example, the effect of this fact on sales in retail environments: Distractions that glare produces can affect balance, orientation, attention span, and even short-term memory, all of which should concern marketers.[16]

Hearing

Hearing loss, beginning in midlife, is virtually inevitable in noisy societies. Some attributes of hearing deficits are not correctable, such as loss of responsiveness to high and low frequencies. Men tend to sustain more hearing deficits than women, and do so at earlier ages, and hearing decline is usually more rapid in the right ear—maybe because that is the telephone ear for most people.

Loss of sensitivity to tones in the higher ranges results in a fusion of sounds. Amplification of sound in such instances only amplifies the resulting confusion. Poor acoustics in restaurants and other public accommodation spaces can increase both physiological and psychological stress to the point that a discomfited customer will never return.

I once had a meeting with a woman at a conference who was accompanied by her husband. Both Peggy and Joe appeared to be their late 50s, maybe early 60s. I suggested we meet in the hotel cocktail lounge. Peggy thought that was fine, being the end of the day as it were, but Joe said he would just sit in the lobby and read. As we waited for our drink order, I jokingly asked Peggy, "Doesn't Joe know that the sun is over the yardarm?"

"Yes, but he usually only has a drink at home. We don't go out much anymore. We have even forsaken our favorite restaurant we've gone to for years. Joe says the service has gotten lousier. Says he likes the service at home better."

"Peggy, has Joe shown any signs of hearing problems lately?" I asked.

Her eyes lit up with wonder, "Yes, but what made you ask that?"

I explained that as people begin experiencing hearing loss, it is not uncommon to see changes in behavior. Decreased sensitivity to frequencies at both ends of the sound spectrum reduces the acoustical equivalent of visual depth perception. It gets harder for the brain to sort out sources of sound. This agitates the brain because its primary mission is to protect its owner from harm. When it can't clearly locate the source of a sound, it senses potential for danger. So the brain starts gearing up for possible imminent threat. It revs up the heartbeat, triggers the flow of adrenaline and other hormones, tightens the muscles, and generates other changes that might be required for fight-or-flight responses.

"Meanwhile," I said after explaining this to Peggy, "when Joe is trying to have a conversation in a noisy environment, he will have trouble fully concentrating because his brain has taken control of much of his body's resources that would be needed in some jeopardizing emergency. Joe doesn't know what his brain is doing, but he does know that he's getting irritated, which starts building on itself. Believe it or not, research shows that when people with hearing loss enter a noisy environment, they may show symptoms of mild paranoia. So, Peggy, your favorite restaurant probably makes Joe feel a little paranoid and he responds by staying home to have his drink."

Peggy was astonished. "I've noticed that Joe often gets a little bit edgy when we go out, but I never associated it with his hearing loss. I sometimes joke with him when he asks me several times to repeat something that I'm going to get him a hearing aid. I guess I should get more serious about that."

Loud restaurants and booming movie soundtracks may be to young people's liking, but it turns away older people, especially men. This is one way in which aging boomers will be different from previous generations of older people. Boomers were the first generation of youth to grow up thinking no music could ever be too loud. Numerous studies have shown that excessively loud music accelerates the onset of hearing problems. "At least 15 percent of American teenagers have permanently lost some hearing. That's about the same percentage you would find among people between 45 and 65."[17]

Given that many restaurants, watering holes, and movie venues cannot expect any real sales growth among 25-to-44-year-olds in this decade because their numbers are falling, their operators would do well to try and figure out how they can lower sound in their establishments without turning away young people. Can these industries afford to ignore the fact that many aging boomers—currently the biggest hope for sales growth in many categories—will be avoiding loud places like my friend Peggy's husband Joe does?

Another problem marketers face in aging markets concerns the practice of presenting television and radio commercials in time-compressed formats. The slowing central nervous system cannot process the sound itself, much less the meanings conveyed by the sound, as fast as younger central nervous systems can. Both sensory and cognitive processes slow down with age. Another problem is that the aging mind may experience difficulty following the message in commercials in which the voice-over competes with background sounds or parallel messages. Finally, as with visual acuity, quick cuts in sound messages can result in generating confusion rather than getting a customer's interested attention to a commercial.

Taste

Taste buds are designed to respond to four categories of stimuli: salty, sweet, sour, and bitter. In later life, the sensitivity to each of these categories decreases. Exacerbating the problem is a decrease in saliva. However, food tastes are also affected by subjective responses to color, temperature, and tactile responses, that is, to the texture of food as experienced in the mouth. Also, most of us are aware of the role that smell plays in food appreciation. It may account for as much as 80 percent of overall taste sensation, so restaurateurs should take this into account because declining sensitivity to smells compromises taste experiences.

Food is socially and personally such an integral part of a satisfying life for most people, that any organization marketing food products for retail outlets or directly serving prepared food to older people that does not recognize the need to accommodate the changes in the sensory system of taste as a result of aging, is inviting unnecessary criticism. Hospitals and nursing homes are customary objects of criticism in these regards. But what about restaurants, airlines, bowling alleys, and other businesses that sell and/or serve food? If you want the older consumer to return to buy again, accommodate them in nonobtrusive ways for decrements in their physiological systems.

Smell

Our sense of smell becomes compromised by the loss of olfactory cell population as early as age 30. Marketers of products ranging from deodorants, perfumes, toothpastes, and other personal products to foods, flowers, and certain household products need to give changes to the olfactory system serious attention as the second-half population grows larger. Some food preparation firms are now chemically enhancing the aroma of foods to increase their attractiveness. While purists may object to one more chemical being added to food, it may not be such a bad idea to make eating a bit more enjoyable for residents of a nursing home, for example, by compensating for declines in the sense of smell through artificial means in order to increase the appeal of food.

The sense of smell has been shown to be more effective at inducing nostalgia than any other sense. A word or a picture harkening back to the times of childhood may not do as much for pleasant reverie as the smell of a home-baked apple pie. Think of what this might do for a prospect in a senior adult community as he or she tours the dining room or kitchen. One of the first things I noticed on my first visit to an Anthropologie store was that it was not aromatically neutral. Rather, with shocks of eucalyptus leaves and candles, I found the olfactory environment quite pleasant.

Touch

The skin, source of most of our tactile sensations, declines in sensitivity with age the same as other sensory receptors. Yet, at the same time, older people are subject to less tolerance of extremes in temperature. Stores and other public places in which older people will be a significant part of the user population should maintain ambient temperature and humidity conditions that recognize the differences between young and old in terms of tactile responses to environmental conditions. Also, textures in floor treatments can be modulated for both tactile pleasures as well as safety. Newer subway systems use changes in floor textures to help blind riders orient themselves. So far, I have not seen any retail environments that have followed suit. Also, because depth perception declines as well as sensitivity to light even for sighted older people, it is not a bad idea to announce the beginning of steps with changes in floor texture.

Other Physiological Changes

During the first decade of midlife, measurable loss in various muscle systems becomes noticeable, though not severe. However, strength reduction begins to accelerate in the 60s, with severe reductions commonly occurring in the 70s and beyond. As of yet, however, there are very few products marketed that take these facts into account. From bags of peanuts you get on a plane to tamper-proof medicine bottles, the older person is waging a continuous battle against muscle discrimination. A walk through any grocery store will reveal a vast array of packages that are hard to open, not just by people in their 70s, 80s, and older, but for people in their 40s and 50s who have developed symptoms of arthritis earlier in life than most people. Companies invest great sums in package design, but few seem to be giving much serious thought to how people can more easily get their packages open.

DESIGNS FOR AGE OR DESIGNS FOR ALL?

It is not within the scope of this book to enter into a detailed discussion of all the major physiological and psychological changes that may be correlated with aging. However, anyone who is seriously interested in second-half markets will be well served by consulting expert sources of knowledge about these changes. This means being willing to let no currently held idea go unchallenged. For example, in the psychological changes department, the use of incomplete sentences is a staple in marketing messages on the premise that it helps hold attention. But, among older customers, incomplete sentences can turn the ad creator's creativity into an exercise in futility. Single words, phrases, or nonsequential images may be perceived as valueless (meaningless) because of fractured or nonexisting contexts. They can, in other words, severely inhibit attention, cognition, and comprehension.

The good news is that many, if not most, changes in the design of products, packaging, marketing messages, and service delivery suggested by this discussion of age-related physical and mental changes would be embraced by customers of all ages. For example, Whirlpool designed a washer/dryer unit with oversized dials and controls that were also backlit for the specific purpose of selling more units to older women. To its surprise, it found that these design changes appealed to young homemakers as well. Additionally, how often have any of us tried first to read the microscopic directions on a bottle of medicine, and then had to endure the indignity of wrestling the cap open. You don't have to be old, frail, myopic, and arthritic to have experienced such problems.

Fortunately, there is a growing view that products and services styled for older people need not be stigmatized as being for older people, for what's good for older people generally will be good for younger people.

15

THE *TRULY* AGELESS MARKET

Everybody wants to live long, but no one wants to grow old. Yet, once they get old, many people find it quite different than they imagined. Third-century BC Chinese philosopher Mencius averred, "The wise man retains his childhood habit of mind," to remind us that the insatiable curiosity, capacity for awe, inventiveness, nonjudgmental nature, and quick recovery from assaults to our composure that we have as children will stand us in as good stead at 80 as at 8. Because those virtues of childhood also happen to be virtues of the self-actualizing mind, it seems that a return to second childhood is in service of growth. To that point, anthropologist Ashley Montagu observed, "In a certain sense, aging is but another name for growth."[1] The late Stephen Jay Gould described the idea of aging as a growth process to be "the most important, neglected theme of human life and evolution."[2]

Continued resistance by Corporate America to the aggressive pursuit of second-half markets betrays the depth of antagonism throughout our society to the idea of aging. However, with second-half markets projected to be 60 percent larger than adult markets under age 40 and to be spending $1 trillion more than those markets by 2010, there is no rational defense to the entrenched corporate preference for younger adult markets. Being rationally indefensible, by simple deduction, the problem must be emotionally grounded. Personal enmity toward aging has to be influencing corporate decisions about markets. Not that this is done consciously. Rather, hostility for aging operates in the background of our psyches like music in a film. Consciously, we are reacting to the unfolding story, but unconsciously how we react is influenced by the music. So it is with negative attitudes toward aging.

My objective in this chapter is to change the background music to the story of aging, to present it as those for whom it is a growth experience—those who make up the *truly ageless* market.

Aging is the arrow of time that enables us to be more today than we were yesterday, and more tomorrow than we are today. Whether that is true for any of us is up to our grit, will, and wisdom. The picture drawn is not one in which aging is portrayed as something to be denied, or to run away from, or to mask with potions and surgery; nor does the picture of aging drawn in this chapter present successful aging as a function of youthful behaviors. Successful aging is about what goes on in the mind and the soul, not the body.

I fervently believe that people who harbor strong negative attitudes about their own aging betray a deep misunderstanding of aging that bars them from understanding people who are aging. If building empathetic connections to customers' minds is a worthy objective in marketing, how can one who hates one's own aging identify with and understand an aging customer's circumstances, emotions, feelings, and motives? Without an understanding of aging and aging customers, how can a marketer be successful in marketing to the New Customer Majority?

"A BEAUTIFUL, WISE, AND TENDER EXPRESSION OF THE ESSENCE OF OLD AGE"

In several sonnets and in his three final plays, Shakespeare celebrated the sunset of life in ways that that moved literary scholar Helen Luke to shine her critic's spotlight on King Lear's words to his daughter Cordelia on old age and intone, "Surely in all the poetry of the world there could be no more profoundly beautiful, wise, and tender expression of the essence of old age, of the kind of life to which one may come in the last years if one has, like Lear, lived through and accepted all the passion and suffering, the darkness and light, the beauty and horror of one's experience of the world and of oneself."[3]

Luke goes on to reflect on "those two wonderful lines, 'When thou dost ask me blessing, I'll kneel down and ask of thee forgiveness.' If an old person does not feel his need to be forgiven by the young, he or she certainly has not grown into age, but merely fallen into it, and his or her 'blessing' would be worth nothing." Luke, in her early 80s as she wrote them, captured in those words the essence of the self-actualizing person: proud yet humble, self-possessed yet egoless, sharpened by unalloyed realism yet tempered by awareness of paradox and irony in every moment, in every thought, as in "ask me blessing, I'll kneel down and ask of thee forgiveness."

All our lives we strive for an ambient sense of completeness and fulfillment. For most of us, this remains an elusive quest for many decades and, sadly, too many of us never achieve that sense. But, as Helen Luke

Lear's Gentle Counsel to His Daughter Cordelia

CORDELIA: For thee, oppressed king, am I cast down;
Myself could else out-frown false fortune's crown.—
Shall we not see these daughters and these sisters?

LEAR: No, no, no! Come, let's away to prison:
We two alone will sing like birds I' the cage:
When thou dost ask me blessing, I'll kneel down
And ask of thee forgiveness: so we'll live,
And pray, and sing, and tell old tales, and laugh
At gilded butterflies, and hear poor rogues
Talk of court news; and we'll talk with them too,—
Who loses and who wins; who's in, who's out;—
And take upon's the mystery of things,
As if we were God's spies; and we'll wear out,
In a wall'd prison, packs and sects of great ones,
That ebb and flow by th' moon.

hints, our natural destiny is to experience the glory promised in Robert Browning's famous entreaty to his beloved in which he spoke of "The last of life for which the first was made."

One of the soothing delights that awaits us in old age, provided we make the right choices during the earlier years of our lives, especially during the middle years, is glowing feelings of satisfaction with life that are beyond the conception of the young mind seized by narcissistic and materialistic preoccupation.

It is symbolic of Luke's own splendid aging that she titled the book in which she invokes King Lear's wisdom on age simply *Old Age*. No subtitle, just *Old Age*. No euphemisms, just *Old Age*—plain, simple and forthright.

Luke is quintessentially *ageless,* having passed that liberating moment when age loses temporal significance—when euphemistic references to age become small-minded contrivances, when denial of aging becomes a hollow response to the inevitable that empties the last of life of meaning. She wisely teaches that if you enter old age despising it, you will be hurt by it for failing to "accept all the passion and suffering, the darkness and light, the beauty and horror of one's experience of the world and of oneself." Luke preaches the gospel of the *truly ageless*.

To underscore a repetitive theme in this book as we near its end, gaining an understanding of customers beyond what database technology can capture requires empathetic connections with their minds. Only then will you be able to consistently speak to them in words and images that resonate with their inner voices—those voices that never speak to researchers, yet silently guide them into and through their customer experiences and, indeed, through every aspect of their lives. This chapter will take you deeper into the minds of the *truly ageless* that you may speak to them in a voice that blends in sweet harmony with their voices.

WHEN YOU KNOW YOU HAVE REACHED THE SUMMITS OF MATURITY

Browning's words, "The last of life for which the first was made," poetically acknowledge the influences of *teleological* forces on us throughout our lives. A teleological perspective holds that the developmental destiny anticipated in our genes has a molding influence on our present-day behavior. The future, in other words, influences us in the present.

In this sense, we are pulled through stages of personal growth by the attracting force of our final developmental destination. Those who reach that destination are greeted by a sense of completeness and timelessness that puts them emotionally beyond harm's way.

When does one know when the summits of personal growth have been reached? Perhaps when slights don't hurt any more; and each morning is greeted with the enthusiasm of a child eager to step forth into a new day of wonder and discovery, despite slower movement and aches and pains. The person who reaches the summits of maturity—the summits of full humanness, in Maslow's words—takes deep delight in the smallest of things that never seemed important in the years of most feverish ambition. Those at the top see life through a poetic lens, much as my friend James is now doing. James biked across the country several years ago with 25 other people, most of whom were 60 and older. The oldest was 74. James, formerly a vice president for maturity market programs for a major life insurance company, was 55.

For James, the trip was not a Nike "Just do it" sort of thing to prove his physical competency, which had benefited from months of training. Instead, it was a sustained period of meditations. With James's permission, I share two of those mediations with you.

James said that from time to time across the country a dog would spot him and his companions, charge after them, yapping and barking and snapping at frantically pumping feet. Sometimes several dogs would appear all at once to make the man-beast encounters more frightening.

One day, while trying to outpace yet another of those threatening interlopers, James had an epiphany. The dog was not the interloper, *he was!* The big, woofing, hard-charging cousin of the wolf had at least as much right to the road as he did, and was only doing what dogs are supposed to do when strangers enter their territory. Thereafter, James's reaction to each new canine encounter was delightfully wondrous—even as he peddled like hell to keep his ankles from the clutches of eager teeth. This transformation of feelings in James's attitudes about attacking dogs brings home the fact that we each create our own reality by the meanings we assign to our experiences. Those who are fortunate to realize that—and it takes many decades for most of us to do so—no longer feel the need to blame others for life's disappointing moments.

On another occasion, the soft touch of a pleasant cooling wind on his face reminded James of a less benign wind several days earlier that had pushed hard against his chest as he pedaled up a steep incline. Suddenly, as he basked in the pleasure of a more comforting wind, a lifting thought came over him. This is how I recall him telling me about it:

> The wind is not just *the* wind. It is Nature's breath that takes many forms. There are winds that cool and winds that chill; there are winds that push you from behind to help you, and winds that push against your breast to hinder you; some winds blow away putrefied air while other winds bring noxious fumes into your nostrils. Then there are winds that bring to you the sweet fragrance of honeysuckle or the bracing aroma of salty sea air.

Such were the reveries of James as he made his nearly 2,500-mile coast-to-coast trek across the country. Those musings speak to the mature mind's bent to extract pleasure from the most mundane of the mundane, to pleasurably experience what might seem odd to others, such as taking pleasure from a confrontation with an itinerant canine bent on sinking its teeth into your ankles. Doing as James did, is to connect with eternity, much as Danny Glover's character in the movie *Grand Canyon* said happened to him when he stood at the edge of that great primordial abyss. In such moments, time ceases to exist.

THE *TRULY AGELESS* LIVE IN A ZONE OF RELATIVE TIMELESSNESS

In preparing for a talk on thoughts about marketing to older people before a Japanese audience in Tokyo, my translator and I were going over key words to determine their closest equivalents in Japanese. My translator, Shigenobu Ueoka, was struggling with the term *ageless market,* saying that he was finding it difficult to come up with the right word. Suddenly, Ueoka said, "*Timeless*—that's it! The Japanese word for *timeless* is the best word to use in the translation."

Timeless market will do just as well in English because it well conveys what I mean by the *truly ageless* market. At the pinnacles of maturity, time loses much of its importance. Without time, there is no aging.

The term *ageless market* is not a poetic or romantic substitution for *senior market* or *elderly market*. Even people who by no one's definition are neither "senior citizens" nor "elderly" can be members of the ageless market, for the term refers to people to whom age *per se* has no significant influence on their behavior. At age 43, Jamie Lee Curtis began taking her first steps as an ageless spirit.

It does so happen, though, that members of the *truly ageless market* are usually in their 50s and older. To reiterate a key point, it is not a matter that people deny their age after reaching the half-century mark. In her fierce indictment of society's indifference toward old people, Simone de Beauvoir wrote in *Coming of Age:* "Great numbers of people (worldwide), particularly old people, told me kindly or angrily but always at great length and again and again that old age simply did not exist!"[4] It did not exist because their worldviews, values, and behavior were not defined by their ages.

The ageless spirit has graced frequent episodes marked by a sense of timelessness, when "a day is a minute, a minute is a day," as Maslow described it. This subjective alteration of time diminishes concerns about the travails that might arise in the future. This benign experience of timelessness is accessible mainly by young children who play with no sense of time passing and older adults who have acquired an ageless spirit. Almost everyone else is governed by time as they fill their appointment books, make lists of things to do, and block out their calendars with a relentless stream of time-sensitive events they cannot avoid without adverse consequences.

THE YOUNG CONFRONT AGING; THE AGELESS INTEGRATE IT INTO THEIR BEINGNESS

Helen Luke's compelling words about the joys possible at great age validate the idea that wisdom is less a function of experience than of maturation. Two people can pass through life with similar experiences, with one falling into the pit of bitter regrets and depressing self-recrimination while the other soars above all that would be devastating earlier in life. The difference is a matter of personal growth.

Luke teaches us in *Old Age* that we have a choice between *getting* old and *growing* old.[5] Growing old means evolving into a personality that transcends chronological age and to some extent, the physical self that defined the preponderance of our needs earlier in life. Indeed, it is in the later years that the mind most easily and naturally takes its place over matter. But that only happens among those with the grace and skill to *grow* old.

For others, aging is a life event to be confronted. Skin creams, mud baths, massages, Botox treatments, cosmetic surgery, and other means are used copiously in hopes of reversing the sculpting hand of aging. Countless companies depend on people's battles against aging. But these companies need to deal with the twin problems of shrinking young adult populations and growth in age groups in which many become increasingly comfortable with their aging. As Gratiano says in *The Merchant of Venice,* "With mirth and laughter, let old wrinkles come, and let my liver rather heat with wine than my heart cool with mortifying groans."

None of this is to suggest that people stop caring about their appearance as they age. Instead, it's more a matter of many second-half customers being less preoccupied with "looking young" as they age. First-half customers' concern about appearance is generally stronger because of their greater need to make social statements in how they visually present themselves. A 60-year-old may enjoy her body massages and liberally treat her skin with anti-aging creams, but she is more likely to be doing it mostly for her own pleasure rather than to make social statements. After all, a good body massage is a being experience on an ethereal plane.

Recall Jamie Lee Curtis's words from Chapter 1: "I don't have great thighs. I have very big breasts and a soft fatty little tummy. Glam Jamie, the perfect Jamie . . . it's such a fraud . . . the more I like me, the less I want to be other people."

Notice that she did not say, "the less I want to be *like* other people." She said, "the less I want to *be* other people." The difference is subtle yet sweeping. Jamie wants to be herself, not someone masquerading as something she is not. She projects authenticity by her words—a virtue paid too little heed in the era of the New Customer Majority. Jamie has renounced the affectations of youth to become a more genuine person who has brought the *real* self out into the open.

Jamie Lee's blossoming regard for authenticity raises the bar for others around her. Simply put, her tolerance for BS has sharply receded. As a 25-year-old she might have thought she was genuine, didn't play games, told it like it was, and wanted the same from others. However, few

25-year-olds in Hollywood or elsewhere will get very far being as forth-rightly honest about themselves as Jamie Lee Curtis now is. For every-thing there is a season.

Jamie, at 43, exemplifies the Franciscan idea of courageously con-fronting what can be changed (she can change how she processes her life), serenely accepting what cannot be changed (she knows she cannot alter the fact of her aging), and having the wisdom to know the differ-ence (thus having balance). By integrating the unchangeable fact of her aging into her worldview and comfortably adjusting to the idea that the blush of her youth is fading, Jamie has clearly caught on to the idea that after youthhood comes a higher and more complex state that offers more.

Those who relentlessly confront aging rather than integrating it into their psychic fiber risk not reaching the advanced state of beingness that takes one beyond materialistic striving, beyond what might have been. Preoccupation with stemming signs of aging makes harder the develop-mental tasks of the Winter of life of discharging pettiness from one's life, dissolving disenchantments and regrets, and extinguishing the pain of second thoughts about one's life.

Revisiting the Idea of the Marketer as Healer

Think back to the words of Melinda Davis in Chapter 11: "We are taking tentative steps into a new era: the era of state-of-mind marketing. This is the new imperative: The marketer must now be a healer." She ad-vanced this thought as, "the possibility for *real* differentiation," which is not based on the product but "in how you collaborate with the con-sumer's need to heal."

The biggest winners in the era of the New Customer Majority will be companies that do the best job of healing. Marketing is no longer about pushing products out the door, but about helping customers process their lives. This makes establishing empathetic connections with cus-tomers not an option but a mandate.

Playing the role of healer in second-half markets does not mean showing 60-year-olds trying to act like 35-year-olds. An ad for a California HMO that ran a few years ago showed a 93-year-old on a surfboard. The ad positioned him as a model of aging. While his vigor is commendable, he is hardly typical. In fact, he represents less than a fully realistic picture of aging. Members of the *truly ageless* market don't like such ruses, as *Reader's Digest* learned.

When *Reader's Digest* took over *Fifty Plus*, which had been quite successful, it changed its name to *New Choices*, set a subscription target well beyond its then 500,000 subscriber base, and initiated a new look. *New Choices* began showing older people as slimmer, smoother of skin, absent of liver spots, and generally more colorful looking than the older people in the original *Fifty Plus*. I met the first managing editor of *New Choices* at a conference after she had resigned. She told me how mistaken they were in airbrushing, using selective photography, and showing a disproportionate number of "beautiful people." This angered many *Fifty Plus* subscribers who had appreciated its authentic depictions of aging. It seemed to them that the folks at *New Choices* viewed aging as negative, something to be denied, confronted, and overcome. The takeaway from the blunder of *New Choices* is *avoid transparent attempts to make aging what it isn't; represent it honestly in marketing communications.*

Incidentally, *New Choices*, once successful as *Fifty Plus*, folded in mid-2002 under *Reader's Digest*'s "enlightened" view of aging. Among the reasons cited by *Reader's Digest* was "the downward trend in circulations," a curious rationale given the explosive growth in its target 50-plus market.[6] Also folding in 2002 was AARP's *My Generation*, a magazine the venerable seniors advocacy group hoped would appeal to aging baby boomers. But it turned out to be another example of failing to connect with people in the more complex second-half markets.

Why Mature Adults Seem to Live for the Moment and Feel Time Goes Faster

How is it possible that as a person gets closer to his or her last dawn, life can be more beautiful and satisfying than ever, and concerns about future dire events seem to abate? The answer may involve the progressive migration of mental activity in the second half of life toward the right brain. Unlike the analytical left brain, the emotional right brain cannot quantify anything, including time itself. Regarding the present-centeredness that becomes more frequent in a state of self-actualization, psychologist Robert Ornstein suggests that we "regard these 'present-centered' moments as shifts towards a right brain dominance."[7]

Everyone experiences present-centeredness. How many times have you been enjoying yourself at a party when your companion gives you a tug and says, "It's time to go," and you respond, "My God, where did the time go?" People in the last quarter of life commonly say time passes more quickly as they have gotten older. But does time pass faster or is it more like a person having such a good time at a party that they are unaware of the passage of time?

Imagine that you are on your way to an important meeting when an accident brings traffic to a standstill. You look at your watch. It's 15 minutes before your meeting—just enough time to get there if the traffic were moving at a normal pace—but traffic shows no sign of moving. A wave of anxiety sweeps over you; your body becomes taut, your hands turn clammy, and your heart starts beating faster. The stalled traffic has not created your anxiety, but time—or rather your perception that not enough time remains to get you to your meeting on time—has created your anxiety.

Meanwhile, in the car behind you is a retired couple. By coincidence they are headed for the same building as you to have lunch at a restaurant they've wanted to try. You, of course, aren't aware that their destination is the same as yours, but you look in your rearview mirror and see them talking and laughing and muse, "I wish I could be so carefree and unconcerned." However, the real difference between you and the couple is perception of time. It has greater value to you; therefore, its depletion can be traumatic. For the couple, it is only a background phenomenon, a kind of ether in which things take place rather than being a driver of action.

Sense of time collapses or expands according to the nature of events experienced. In other words, time is relative. Einstein once joked, "When you sit with a nice girl for two hours, it seems like two minutes; when you sit on a hot oven for two minutes, it seems like two hours. That's relativity."

We can sense time as moving rapidly, slowly, or not at all. Ernst Poppel, in *Mindworks: Time and Conscious Experience,* says differences that occur in our subjective perceptions of time's passage are a function of mental content.[8] The less content there is in the mind, the longer an increment of time seems to be. Boredom slows time to a crawling pace.

Supporting the idea that decreased cognitive activity in the left brain alters a person's sense of time, Ornstein writes, "It has been found that left hemisphere damage interferes with the perception of sequence (time order of events), while right hemisphere damage does not. These 'timeless' experiences (present-centered moments) . . . overwhelm the linear construction (of the left hemisphere) and allow an infinite present to exist."[9]

A sense of timelessness protects the psyche. People in early midlife are usually more disturbed by the prospects of aging and dying than people in their 60s or older.

"Time Is of the Essence" Pitches Don't Work in the *Truly Ageless* Market

Marketers of extended services senior housing are often frustrated by how long it takes prospects to make a decision. Prospects often visit a community six to eight times over a period of many months or several years before they make a decision. Exhortations to sign up because "there are only two apartments like this available," seem to have little effect on most prospects.

Decreased sensitivity to time in older prospects' minds weakens the classic marketing strategy of creating a sense of urgency. The more the present seems ever-present, the less influence the future has. A sense of urgency is a sense of time running out. With the present always being, time can't run out because it doesn't exist to do so. Mature consumers (mature in terms of personal development, not age) rarely perceive a purchase as essential to their life satisfaction. They generally lack the "must have it" imperatives that young people have. If they miss one opportunity because of not buying in time, they know that other opportunities yielding equal levels of pleasure will soon arise.

A sense of timelessness curbs anxieties about the future. Marketing pitches telling older people they should buy something now to avoid unwanted consequences in the future generally get poor responses. Despite this, extended services retirement housing prospects are urged: "Move in now, while you are *still* independent. You may avoid going into a nursing home if you do." That pitch motivates few. Most decisions to move into an extended services retirement community are event driven, not planning-for-the-future driven. Health crises and spousal deaths are the most common drivers of the decision, not concerns about what the future might hold.

Mature people do not like to be reminded of what could be in their future. "We're not children," one woman said in a focus group, "even though whoever created *that* ad thinks so." The ad had a litany of things that can go wrong to older people who don't wear a medical alert system device. Many older people intensely disliked the commercial that ran in the 1990s showing an older woman falling down stairs and crying out, "Help! I've fallen and can't get up." The stronger sense of autonomy that older people usually develop makes them more resistant to marketing messages that tell them what is in their best interests. Don't take any chances. It's a good idea to never preach to people over 40, and especially, never preach to people over 60.

THE PHENOMENON OF COGNITIVE AGE

It's gospel fact in marketing circles that older people see themselves as 10 to 15 years younger than their chronological age. Because of this, it is advised, ads should show people 10 to 15 years younger than the target market. This factoid can lead to marketing mistakes.

"If you didn't know how old you are, how old do you think you would be?" is a question I often ask audiences. The majority of responses yield answers that range between 70 to 85 percent of people's chronological age—whether they are 25, 35, 45, or older. In other words, it is rare that anyone feels as old as he or she is, even in childhood.

Baruch College marketing professor Leon Schiffman has found close ties between degrees of life satisfaction and cognitive age in his research: The stronger one's sense of life satisfaction, the younger one feels. He developed a more complex picture of cognitive age by defining it as a composite of several perceptions of one's age:

- *Feel-age.* The age one feels independent of physiological conditions.
- *Look-age.* The age one believes they physically appear to be.
- *Do-age.* The age that corresponds to associations of certain activities with certain age groups.
- *Interest-age.* The age that corresponds to associations of certain interests with certain age groups.[10]

Schiffman arrives at cognitive age by averaging the midpoints of each decade a respondent has identified as being his or her perceived age for each category. For example, if 69-year-old Mary Erskine says she feels in her 30s, looks in her early 60s, participates in activities that are typical for people in their 40s, and has interests that are generally perceived as characteristic of those in their child-free late 40s, then her cognitive age would be 47.5 (35+65+45+45 divided by 4)—In any event, there is too much emphasis on having the right age models in marketing communications targeting older people. A key rule of marketing in second-half markets is *Commit no deception.* Be honest about age as *Fifty Plus* was before *Reader's Digest* took it over and renamed it *New Choices.*

THE TRANSCENDENCE OF TIME THROUGH BEING EXPERIENCES

We experience time in two modes: *event time,* in which our awareness of time passing is strong, and *being time,* in which awareness of time passing is weak or nonexistent. Event time is *materialistic* (left brain), while being time is *experiential* (right brain). Being time is experienced by people in all age groups, but most often by people in second-half markets because they more often pursue being experiences, which are right brain–mediated experiences.

Ornstein posits that we incorporate into our picture of reality, things that support and embellish that reality. That being so, symbols and icons that reflect "timeless" values can be highly effective in marketing communications intended for second-half markets, especially for people in the Winter season of their lives. Examples of timeless symbols often associated with or acting as catalysts of being experiences include houses of worship, parents with children, grandparents, children playing together, hearth and home, friends, pets, the American flag, civic buildings, and heroes.

The camera eye or artist's brush aimed at such symbols and icons should be soft and gentle, and seek expression with a child's wonder, rather than try to amaze and startle the senses. It is unnecessary to shock the right brain to get its attention. In second-half markets, sensitivity and good taste will more often outweigh the circus barker's command to come and experience the extraordinary. For people living life in the summits of maturity, everything is extraordinary. They don't need someone to advertise the extraordinariness of a product or service in outsized images and claims.

Vignettes for Projecting Being Experiences in Advertising

Ageless marketing is experiential because it focuses less on the physical product thing than on metaphysical values that cut across generations. A recent Michelin tire commercial is a worthy example of this. It showed the angelic Michelin baby under rainy skies floating downstream in a tire filled with stuffed animals resembling Noah's ark. Because cooing smiling infants melt nearly everyone's heart, the commercial had a better chance of surviving information triage across a wider age range of people than a more materialistic commercial discussing product features likely would. Not only does the universal appeal of a smiling infant create message relevance across multiple age groups, the commercial connects with the universal desire to protect the very young: Michelin provides safety in weather, fair and foul.

Most of us have caught ourselves being distracted from a serious conversation in a restaurant or from shopping in a grocery store by an infant with a smile that could melt a stone. For a brief moment, we forget the important business we are transacting as we uncontrollably smile back, wanting to make some contact with the little cherub, even if only through our own smile. It's a being experience, albeit, not likely a major one. For an instant, it makes everything else secondary. Michelin's commercials and ads that feature a smiling infant connect with people's being experience aspirations.

Figure 15.1 lists activities, a number of which have particularly high being experience potential, hence high appeal to the right brain. Certain activities have been asterisked to indicate those that involve significant contributions by both hemispheres of the brain. The nonasterisked items are primarily right brain–oriented.

Also, note that the activities in Figure 15-1 align rather closely with the Four Faces of the New Senior that were described in Chapter 10:

1. *First Face.* Creativity and intellectual involvement
2. *Second Face.* Wisdom, experience, and the desire to share them
3. *Third Face.* Productivity and vitality
4. *Fourth Face.* Compassion for others and concern for the world about them

FIGURE 15.1 *Being Experience–Oriented Activities for the* Truly Ageless *Market*

Sharing Products of Skills with Others	Sharing Wisdom with Others	Entertaining Others	Caring for Others
1	2	3	4
assisting	acting*	collaborating*	composing
caring	arranging*	consulting*	creating
catering	demonstrating*	cooperating*	decorating
counseling	hosting*	educating*	designing*
curing*	joking*	influencing*	drawing
encouraging*	performing	proposing	fixing
helping*	public speaking*	teaching*	painting
humoring	singing	training*	writing*
nurturing	staging		
petting	story telling*		
supporting			
tending			

*Activities involving significant contributions from both hemispheres of the brain. The other items involve primarily right brain functions.

SOURCE: Adapted from Jacquelyn Wonder & Priscilla Donovan, *Whole Brain Thinking*, Ballantine Books, New York, 1984, p. 268.

Column 1 is primarily Fourth Face–oriented, while column 2 is biased toward the Third Face, column 3 to the Second Face, and column 4 to the First Face. Rather than seeking the right age models to use in advertising and other marketing collaterals, it is better to project universal values associated with the symbols and icons and with the activities listed in Figure 15.1. Age is a side issue—when it is not altogether irrelevant—when marketing to people 60 and older, because generally speaking, the relevance of age to marketing success in second-half markets declines the older the target market is. Recall the successful Wachovia Bank campaign described in the Chapter 13. All the main actors were children.

The Power of Intergenerational Vignettes in Marketing Communications

A number of activities listed in Figure 15.1 can be projected in intergenerational scenes. Many older people have an aversion to age segregation and symbols of age segregation. Age-qualified prospects for retirement communities often say, "I wouldn't move into a seniors community. I couldn't stand being with nobody but people my own age or older." This is a bit strange given that for most of us, throughout our lives, people near us in age form the majority of our friendships. I have argued that much of the antipathy older people have toward age stigmatized products is because they want to avoid symbols of aging that mark them as physically and mentally inferior to younger society. One way to blur the issue of age in marketing communications is to present marketing messages in intergenerational settings, such as illustrated in Figure 15.2.

The ad in Figure 15.2 for a high-end watch is a masterpiece of ageless advertising. It reflects a timeless moment—ironic since the ad is for a timepiece—and addresses a strong motivating force in older people's lives—*concern about their legacy*. Starting with "Begin your own tradition" and concluding with, "Any woman who owns one will treasure it, enhancing its value for the one who wears it next," the ad acknowledges the ultimate subjective nature of value. To the nonmaterialistic mind, the value of a Patek Philippe watch is not gauged by an objective appraisal of its precious metals and jewels, but by what it subjectively means to the person who owns and wears it: *enhancing its value for the one who will wear it next*. For contrast, think about typical Rolex ads. They project values of the materialistic social self, which likes to "show off." The Patek Phillipe ad projects the values of the experiential inner self that craves what Maslow termed *peak experiences* and are called being experiences in this book.

Most older people want to experience connections with people of all ages. Though they want to be regarded as individuals in their own right, they don't want to be seen as a separate species by virtue of their age. Remember, one of the key elements of being experiences is "a greater sense of connectedness." Scenes in advertising that emphasize "separateness" deny the importance of "connectedness."

People in the *truly ageless* market tend not to be comfortable with the idea of age-based separateness. They see things all of a piece. Maslow observed this when he said self-actualizing people "tend to de-differentiate figure and background, [and things that are] relatively important become unimportant; all aspects [are] equally important."[11]

The *truly ageless* are truly remarkable. Their outlook is often surprisingly like that of idealistic youth, only tempered with a sharper sense of reality. Maslow characterized the fully mature person as more democratic, less judgmental, and more forgiving. He would have liked the Patek

FIGURE 15.2 *Patek Phillipe Ad*

Begin your own tradition

Every Patek Phillipe watch is crafted by hand
So each one is subtly different from the next
This is what makes it uniquely personal to its owner
The ladies Golden Ellipse has 160 of the
finest diamonds set in 18 karat gold.
Any woman who owns one
will treasure it, enhancing its
value for the one who wears it next

PATEK PHILIPPE
GENEVE

Phillipe ad because he also said this of the mature: they see the "world and self as amusing, playful, comic, funny, absurd, laughable."[12] They not only aren't as easily bent out of shape as others often are, but they take life with several grains of salt and a lot of hearty laughter. The strings of laughter, you should know, are pulled by the mirthful, child-like right brain who wouldn't know how to use a Patek Phillipe timepiece for anything but having fun and feeling good.

FINIS

We've been together through a long journey that began as journeys that are the most successful usually do—by identifying at the outset the challenges and opportunities that should be considered to reach an intended destination. The first major challenge identified in this journey is the extraordinary population shrinkage taking place in the historically most important age group in the consumer economy—adults from 25 to 44. The grim outcome of this is a total absence of sales growth in this age group throughout this decade.

The first major opportunity identified is the extraordinary population growth of the New Customer Majority, particularly among adults between the ages of 45 to 65—mostly aging baby boomers. However, with that opportunity comes another challenge: adapting to changes in the rules of marketplace engagement, many of which have been brought about by the "middle aging" of the marketplace. Most of the 126-million-member New Customer Majority think, shop, buy, and consume differently than members of the 86 million adults who are under the age of 40.

The new rules have either seriously compromised or altogether canceled out many old rules of marketing, starting with the presumption that customers are the best source of information about what motivates them. Through the miracle of neuroimaging, brain researchers have determined that motivations originate in the silent reaches of the brain, outside the realms of consciousness. Another change in rules concerns what it takes to create marketing executions that succeed: The customer experience has replaced product features and benefits as the most important factor in achieving a competitive difference that highly motivates customers.

No old rule has been more deeply compromised than the long-standing practice of basing marketing primarily on statistical analysis of customers' needs, motivations, and behaviors. This is evident in the declining accuracy of consumer research and weakening of responses to product messaging—ironically so in an era unprecedented for the amount of customer information available and the speed in which it can be analyzed. The values, needs, and behavior of the typically more individuated, introspective, and autonomous members of the New Customer Majority cannot be reduced to mere numbers. Mathematics is a proper foundation for engineers, but not for marketers. The foundation of marketing should be assembled from tenets of behavior.

Early in this journey, I proposed that the lack of a common foundation in marketing—virtually without parallel in any other field—is the greatest challenge to overcome in adapting to the new rules of marketplace engagement. Without a common foundation from which everyone in consumer research and marketing practice works—one based on tenets of behavior—the 360-degree view that many say CRM affords, is not achievable because neither CRM nor any dimension of traditional marketing takes into account the drivers of human behavior that operate in the bottomless pit of the unconscious.

Among the most prominent unconscious drivers of human behavior are the developmental objectives, life focuses, and life story themes anticipated in human DNA. However, even more basic than those drivers are the five systems of primary core values that underlie all behavior, whatever the season of life.

My objective in writing this book was to was to serve up to readers for the first time in a business book, insights into human behavior derived from classical developmental psychology, enriched by extraordinary new discoveries coming to the surface in the fields of genetics and brain science. My hope is that this book will help foment an historic shift in consciousness that marketing desperately needs to regain the confidence of clients and customers alike.

But I have an even a broader hope for *Ageless Marketing*. I once saw a cartoon in which one person says to another, "How can we ever hope to understand each other when marketers can't figure us out?" I will be deeply gratified if readers reach the end of this book with a more profound understanding of themselves, those around them, and indeed of the Family of Man. That is the legacy that I hope flows from my having written *Ageless Marketing*.

RESEARCH METHODOLOGY

AMERICANS AGE 45 TO 61

The Seniors Research Groups at Market Strategies, Inc., conducted three phases of research among a nationally representative sample of Internet users age 45 to 61. Each phase built upon and informed subsequent phases of research.

Phase One: Development of Pilot Instrument (n=492)

The first phase of research focused on the development of a Value Portraits pilot to assess boomers' values. To begin, a comprehensive list of potentially significant values was culled from the academic research literature on values, including existing measurement and segmentation schemes. The measurement of values typically involves asking respondents to rate and/or rank the importance of several values. To circumvent the tendency of respondents to consider all values "important," we developed multiple *indicator statements* for each of the value constructs in our theoretical framework. Existing scales drawn from the literature were utilized whenever feasible. To assess the reliability and validity of the value indicator statements, a pretest was conducted using a Web sample of mature Americans demographically balanced to the U.S. Census. A total of 492 pretest interviews were completed. Following this data collection, a construct validity analysis was completed.

Phase Two: Web Survey of Internet Users (n=3,087)

The second phase of research focused on the collection and analysis of quantitative data, based on thirteen hypothesized values dimensions. The primary objective of this phase was to identify and profile unique segments within a representative sample of leading-edge boomer Internet users and to test the hypothesized dimension. In addition, a comprehensive questionnaire was developed to gather data on media use, lifestyle and behavior, and health and caregiving. A total of 3,087 interviews were conducted via Web survey of a nationally representative sample of Internet users age 45 to 61. Following the data collection, a cluster analysis was conducted. The result of this analysis was to identify nine leading-edge boomer segments and to describe how they varied across 14 overall values dimensions.

Phase Three: Cognitive Interviews (n=30)

Upon completion of the quantitative phase, Senior Research Group (SRG) conducted qualitative research in order to obtain rich, highly descriptive data regarding the cognitive and psychological "profile" of each of these values-based segments. In-depth telephone interviews were conducted with three or more members of each segment who have values that most closely reflect the core of each segment. The moderator probed the "cognitive structure" of participants' belief systems using a qualitative interviewing technique known as *laddering*. This technique was developed to gain an understanding of how consumers think about a product or service, while uncovering the hierarchical structure of attitudes and values that drive their preferences. The qualitative data collected in this phase of the study both validates and augments the quantitative phase, providing even greater insight into what truly motivates these diverse segments.

AMERICANS AGE 62 AND OLDER

The study design included three primary phases of research conducted among Americans age 62 or older. Each phase built upon and informed subsequent phases of research.

Phase One: Development and Pretest of Values Instrument

The first phase of research focused on the development of a measurement tool to assess seniors' values. To begin, a comprehensive list of potentially significant values was culled from the academic research literature on values, including existing measurement and segmentation schemes. The measurement of values typically involves asking respondents to rate and/or rank the importance of several values. To circumvent the tendency of respondents to consider all values "important," we developed multiple *indicator statements* for each of the value dimensions in our theoretical framework. Existing scales drawn from the literature were utilized whenever feasible. To assess the reliability and validity of the value indicator statements, a pretest was conducted via mail survey. A nationally representative sample of 600 Americans, 62 years and older, was drawn from the SRG's proprietary research panel. The Seniors Research Panel comprises a diverse group of nearly 20,000 mature adults who have agreed to participate in research studies. Participation in the Seniors Research Panel is voluntary and members are not compensated financially for joining. Although the panel does not represent a true probability sample, our sampling design matched panel members to the general population based on key demographic characteristics.

Phase Two: Industry-Specific Questionnaires

The second phase of research focused on the collection and analysis of quantitative data. The primary objective of this phase was to identify and profile unique segments within the mature market defined on the basis of similar belief systems. In addition, in order to assess the capacity of values as a predictor of consumer behaviors within specific business contexts, theoretical models were developed and tested within two key industries: health care and housing. For each of these industries, a comprehensive questionnaire was developed to gather data on personal values as well as domain-specific attitudes and behaviors. A total of 2,920 (response rate = 73%) Seniors Research Panel members completed the Social Values Survey (1,424 completed the Social Values Survey with Health Care Supplement, and an additional 1,496 panel members completed the Social Values Survey with Housing Supplement). Preliminary values-based segments were created using data derived from the Health Care Supplement survey, and validated with the Housing Supplement data. Each sample consistently produced eight distinct segments with similar value profiles.

Phase Three: Cognitive Interviews

Upon completion of the quantitative phase, SRG conducted qualitative research in order to obtain rich, highly descriptive data regarding the cognitive and psychological "profile" of each of these values-based segments. In-depth telephone interviews were conducted with six members of each segment who have values that most closely reflect the core of each segment. The moderator probed the "cognitive structure" of participants' values-system using a qualitative interviewing technique known as *laddering*. This technique was developed to gain an understanding of how consumers think about a product or service, while uncovering the hierarchical structure of attitudes and values that drive their preferences. The qualitative data collected in this phase of the study both validates and augments the quantitative phase, providing even greater insight into what truly motivates these diverse segments.

Chapter 1

1. Michael Tchong, "Truth Is, Marketing Is Facing a Crisis," retrieved March 3, 2003, from <www.iconocast.com/issue/9001,2,1101,13,1.html>.

2. Ibid.

3. Robert M. McMath and Thom Forbes, *What Were They Thinking, Marketing Lessons You Can Learn from Products That Flopped,* Three Rivers Press, New York, 1998, p. 4.

4. Michael Tchong, op. cit.

5. Roger Siddle and Darrell Rigby, "Which Management Tools Are Most Popular?" *European Business Forum,* 2001.

6. The Food Channel "Trend Wire," Noble Communications, June 18, 2001, retrieved from <www.foodchannel.com> around that date.

7. March 9, 2002, broadcast. *On the Media* is produced by WNYC in New York. <www.wnyc.org/onthemedia/transcripts_030902_myth.html>.

8. Hillary Chura, "Ripe Old Age," *Advertising Age,* May 5, 2002, p. 16.

9. Kevin J. Clancy and Robert S. Shulman, *The Marketing Revolution: A Radical Manifesto for Dominating the Marketplace,* Harper Business, 1991, p. 1.

10. David B. Wolfe, "What Your Customers Can't Say," *American Demographics,* February 1998.

11. Timothy D. Wilson, *Strangers to Ourselves,* The Belknap Press of Harvard University Press, 2002, p. 151.

12. Larry Wheeler, "Giving Till It Helps," <www.nccbi.org/mag12 .01execvoices.htm>, North Carolina Citizens for Business and Industry.

13. Amy Wallace, "True Thighs," *More,* September 2002, pp. 90–95.

14. The paper was delivered September 26, 2001, as a special presentation of the Yankelovich MONITOR LIVE Teleconference series. At the time of this writing, an MP3 audio file was available at <www .yankelovich.com>.

15. Abraham H. Maslow, *Toward a Psychology of Being*, Van Nostrand Reinhold Company, 1968, p. 26.

16. David B. Wolfe, *Serving the Ageless Market*, McGraw-Hill, New York, 1990, p. 12.

Chapter 2

1. Frederick F. Reichheld, *The Loyalty Effect, The Hidden Force behind Growth, Profits, and Lasting Value*, Harvard Business School Press, Boston, 1996, p. 10.

2. Suzy Welaufer, "The Business Case against Revolution," *Harvard Business Review*, February 2001, p. 115.

3. Scott Bedbury, *A New Brand World: 8 Principles for Achieving Brand Leadership in the 21st Century*, Viking/Penguin Group, New York, 2002, p. 41.

4. Ibid, p. 41.

5. Gayle Sato Stodder, "How to Build a Million Dollar Business," *Entrepreneur*, September 1997.

6. Kevin Clancy and Robert Shulman, *The Marketing Revolution: A Radical Manifesto for Dominating the Marketplace*, Harper Business, 1991, pp. 99, 85, and 62, respectively.

7. Richard Restak, MD, *The Modular Brain*, Charles Scribner's Sons, 1994, p. 71.

8. Bernard J. Baars, *In the Theater of Consciousness*, Oxford University Press, 1997, p. 122.

9. John Ellis, "Digital Matters," *Fast Company*, September 2001, p. 92.

10. Anthony Edwards, conversation with author, Fall 2002.

Chapter 3

1. Abigail Trafford interview with Becca Levy, "Second Opinion: Aging Stereotypes," *Washington Post Live on Line*, July 18, 2000, <www.discuss.washingtonpost.com>.

2. Carolyn Yoon, et al, "Cross-Cultural Differences in Memory: The Role of Culture-Based Stereotypes about Aging," *Psychology and Aging*, Vol. 15, No. 4, p. 694.

3. Scott Bedbury, *A New Brand World*, Viking Penguin, New York, 2002, p. 95.

4. Norihiko Shirouzu, "This Is Not Your Father's Toyota," *The Wall Street Journal*, March 26, 2002, p. B–1.

5. *J. D. Power and Associates Reports: Outstanding Vehicle Service Programs Emerge as Key Driver of Customer Satisfaction and Retention*, July 14, 1999.

6. Ralph L. Day, "Relationships between Life Satisfaction and Customer Satisfaction," in *Marketing and the Quality of Life Interface*, edited by A. Coskin Samli, Quorum Books, New York, 1987, p. 308.

7. Gail Sheehy, *The Pathfinders*, Bantam Books, New York, 1981, p. 236.

8. Art Weinstein, *Market Segmentation*, Probus Publishing Company, Chicago, 1987, p. 13.

9. Don Peppers and Martha Rogers, "The End of Mass Marketing," *Marketing Tools*, March/April 1995, p. 42.

10. Ibid, p. 46.

11. Polly LaBarre, "Sophisticated Sell," *Fast Company*, December 2002, p. 92.

12. Ellen Langer, *Mindfulness*, Addison-Wesley, Reading, MA, 1989, p. 120.

Chapter 4

1. Gerald Zaltman, *How Customers Think: Essential Insights into the Mind of the Market*, Harvard Business School Press, Boston, 2003, p. xi.

2. David Ogilvy, *Ogilvy on Advertising*, Vintage Books, 1983, p. 205.

3. "@Issue: PT Cruiser," *The Journal of Business and Design*, Vol. 7, Issue 1, 2001.

Chapter 5

1. Melinda Davis, *The New Culture of Desire*, The Free Press, New York, 2002, p. 2.

2. David B. Wolfe, *Serving the Ageless Market*, McGraw-Hill, New York, 1990, pp. 166–167.

3. David B. Wolfe, "The Psychological Center of Gravity," *American Demographics*, April 1998.

4. Lisa Miller, "Rebels with a Cause," *The Wall Street Journal*, December 18, 1998, p. W1.

5. Alf Nucifora, "Marketers Should Get to Know Gen Y," Bizjournals .com, November 19, 2001.

6. Michael S. Grollman, "Talking about the Y Generation: Part One —Who They Are and What They Believe In," <www.smartpros.com>, November 3, 2000.

7. Shelley Branch, "What's in a Name? Not Much According to Clothes Shoppers," *The Wall Street Journal*, July 16, 2002.

8. "Are Older People Getting Younger," aired on PBS's *Think Tank*, hosted by Ben Wattenburg, March 29, 1996. The transcript as of March 11, 2003, appears at <www.pbs.org/thinktank/show_301.html>.

Chapter 6

1. Robert Rieher, *Marketing to Today's "Expectant Brain,"* written for <www.zmarketing.com>.

2. Gregory L. White and Shirley Leung, "American Tastes Move Upscale, Forcing Manufacturers to Adjust," *The Wall Street Journal*, March 29, 2002, p. A1.

3. Abraham H. Maslow, *Toward a Psychology of Being*, Van Nostrand Reinhold Company, New York, 1968, p. 26.

4. Antonio Damasio, *Descartes' Error*, G. P. Putnam's Sons, 1994, p. 197.

5. Mark Cooper, telephone interview by author, March 14, 2003.

6. Tom's of Maine Web site, <www.tomsofmaine.com>, extracted December 2001.

Interlude

1. Daniel J. Levinson, *Seasons of a Man's Life*, First Ballantine Books edition, Ballantine Books division of Random House, New York, 1979, p. 27.

Chapter 10

1. James Lardner, "Building a Customer-Centric Company," *Business 2.0*, July 2001.

2. Ibid.

3. Conversation with David Wolfe c. 1989, as reported in *Serving the Ageless Market*, McGraw-Hill, New York, 1990, p. *ret*.

4. Kathy Keen, "Wisdom Tied to Life Satisfaction in Old Age, Says UF Researcher," <www.napa.ufl.edu/oldnews/wisdom.htm>, July 26, 1996, taken from Web site December 19, 2002.

5. As reported in D. B. Wolfe's *Maturity Markets Perspectives*, November–December 1988.

6. Extracted from BBC's Web site, <news.bbc.co.uk/1/hi/health/1541706.stm>, December 21, 2002.

7. I agree; she was Rose Wolfe, my mother, who remained remarkable until 1993, when she passed on at age 89.

8. *Marketing Communications*, March 1987.

9. Gail Sheehy, *The Pathfinders*, Bantam Books, 1981, p. 15.

10. Extracted from the Civic Venture's Web site, <www.experiencecorps.org>, December 9, 2002.

Chapter 11

1. Gene D. Cohen, *The Aging Brain*, Springer Publishing Company, New York, 1989, p. 32.

2. *Lifestyle Monitor Fall/Winter 2000*, Cotton Inc., <www.cottoninc.com/LsmFallWinter2002/homepage.cfm?Page=3010>.

3. Robert Ornstein and David Sobel, *Healthy Pleasures*, Addison-Wesley Publishing Company, Reading, MA, 1989, p. 229.

4. The Surgeon General's Call to Action to Prevent Suicide, 1999, *At a Glance: Suicide among the Elderly*, extracted from Web site January 1, 2003, <www.surgeongeneral.gov/library/calltoaction/fact2.htm>.

5. Data in this paragraph from research by AARP and Age Waves, Inc., as reported at <www.suddenlysenior.com/maturemarketstats2002.html>, January 5, 2003.

6. Dan DeLuca, "Rock of (Middle) Ages," *Philadelphia Enquirer,* April 23, 2002.

7. Gary Levin, "JWT Researches Stages, Not Ages," *Advertising Age,* June 26, 1989.

Chapter 12

1. Gary Levin, "JWT Researches Stages, Not Ages," *Advertising Age,* June 26, 1989, p. 30.

2. Bill Breen, "Connecting with What Customers Want," *Fast Company,* February 2003, pp. 86–89.

3. <www.customization.com/MarketingExperiencesWhitepaper31202.pdf>.

4. John Helyar, "Will Harley-Davidson Hit the Wall?" *Fortune,* July 22, 2002, extracted from <www.fortune.com>, March 20, 2003.

5. Geoffrey Colvin, "Wall Street's Easy Rider," Inside Business, *Fortune,* August 28, 2001, extracted from <www.fortune.com>, March 19, 2003.

Chapter 13

1. S. Stiansen, "Non-Verbal Messages in Ads Gain New Importance," *Adweek's Advertising Week,* January 4, 1988, p. 23.

2. Scientists researching neuromusicology discovered music trains the brain for higher levels of thinking, claiming that college students who listen to classical music while studying absorb, retain, and retrieve the information more easily than those studying in silence. Source: <www.lsureveille.com/vnews/display.v/ART/2002/12/05/3deef3ca2fa1b>, February 5, 2003.

3. Thomas M. Hess and Sharon M. Pullen, "Adult Age Differences in Impression Change Processes," *Psychology and Aging,* The American Psychological Association, Vol. 9, No. 2, June 1994, pp. 237–250.

4. Cynthia Adams, "Qualitative Age Differences in Memory for Text: A Life-Span Developmental Perspective," *Psychology and Aging,* September 1991, Vol. 6, pp. 323–336.

5. J. C. Houghton, "Semiotics on the Assembly Line," *Advertising Age*, March 16, 1987.

6. Ibid.

7. J. Motavalli, "Probing Consumers' Minds," *Adweek's Marketing Week*, December 7, 1997, p. F.K. 8.

8. Robert Ornstein, *The Psychology of Consciousness*, Penguin Books, New York, NY, 1986, p. 120.

9. Joseph E. Bogen, MD, "The Other Side of the Brain: An Appositional Mind," *Bulletin of the Los Angeles Neurological Societies*, Vol. 34, No. 3, July 1969.

10. Richard M. Restak, MD, *The Brain: The Last Frontier*, Warner Books, p. 201, 19.

11. Ibid, p. 196.

12. *Adweek's Marketing Week*, January 4, 1986, p. 38.

13. Curt Suplee, "In Search of More Perfect Persuasion," *The Washington Post*, January 18, 1987, p. C–3.

Chapter 14

1. Richard Forsyth, "Why Marketing Isn't Working Anymore," Part 2, <www.crm-forum.com>, March 3, 2003.

2. Richard Forsyth, "Why Marketing Isn't Working Anymore," <www.crm-forum.com>, February 17, 2003.

3. Hazel Muir, "Brand Names Bring Special Brain Buzz," *New Scientist Journal* report, Vol. 82, August 2002, p. 327.

4. John Deighton, Daniel Romer, and Josh McQueen, "Using Drama to Persuade," *Journal of Consumer Research*, Vol. 16, December 1989, pp. 335–343.

5. Ibid.

6. Ibid.

7. Ibid.

8. Cynthia Adams, "Qualitative Age Differences in Memory for Text: A Life-Span Developmental Perspective," *Psychology and Aging*, September 1991, Vol. 6, pp. 323–336.

9. Jerry Knight, "Tylenol's Maker Shows How to Respond to Crisis," *The Washington Post,* October 11, 1982.

10. John K. Teahen Jr., "Ford Should Change Explorer Name," *Automotive News,* July 23, 2001, extracted from <www.automotivenews.com> on March 3, 2002.

11. Byron Reeves and Clifford Nass, *The Media Equation, How People Treat Computers, Television, and New Media Like Real People and Places,* CSLI Publications, Stanford, CA, 1996 (paperback).

12. Ibid, p. 28.

13. Ibid, p. 97.

14. Ibid, p. 97.

15. Extracted from <www.creatingcustomerevangelists.com>, March 3, 2003, and from the book by Ben McConnell and Jackie Hubba, published by Dearborn Trade Publishing, Chicago, 2002.

16. Charles D. Schewe, "Marketing to Our Aging Population: Responding to Physiological Changes," an unpublished paper, School of Management, University of Massachusetts, 1987.

17. Bernard D. Sherman, in *Early Music America, 2000,* extracted from <homepages.kdsi.net/~sherman/hearingloss.htm> on March 4, 2003.

Chapter 15

1. Ashley Montague, *Growing Young,* Second Edition, Bergin & Garvey Publishers, New York, 1989, p. 99.

2. Ibid, endorsement on cover.

3. Helen M. Luke, *Old Age,* Parabola Books, 1987, p. 25.

4. Simone de Beauvoir, *Coming of Age,* Warner Paperback Library, New York, 1973, p. 8.

5. Luke, op cit, p. viii.

6. Jon Fine, "Reader's Digest Folds Baby Boomer Title," *Ad Age,* March 6, 2002.

7. Robert Ornstein, *The Psychology of Consciousness,* Penguin Books, 1986, p. 138.

8. Poppel, Ernst, *Mindworks: Time and Conscious Experience,* Harcourt, Brace, Jovanovich, 1988, p. 86.

9. Ornstein, op cit, p. 138.

10. Leon Schiffman and L. L. Kanuk, *Consumer Behavior,* Prentice-Hall, Englewood Cliffs, NJ, 1987, p. 531.

11. Abraham Maslow, *The Farthest Reaches of Human Nature,* Penguin Books, 1971, p. 249.

12. Ibid, p. 253.